A Hippopotamus at theTable

by
Anna Meryt

This is a memoir, a true story based on real events that happened to the author from 1975-1977 in South Africa. Some names have been changed to protect identities.

First published in June 2015
by Tambourine Press Ltd
5 Harringay Gdns, London, N8 0SE

Tambourine Press

ISBN 978-0-9576122-4-2

Front cover designed by Dee Edmonds, artist. ©
All photos from a collection owned by A. Meryt .

A Hippopotamus at the Table

by
Anna Meryt

Tambourine Press

Also by Anna Meryt
Two poetry collections
Heart Broke
Dolly Mix

Her blog: http://www.ameryt.com/

Dedication

This book is dedicated first to the two people who accompanied me on this journey and who have always supported my writing efforts with such enthusiasm – my former husband Dave and my daughter Pascale, it's their story too. It's also dedicated to my second daughter Tamlyn who was born after the events in this book, who read the manuscript, and gave me notes - they were all good.

The many writer's groups to which I've belonged have patiently listened, read and given feedback, most recently Greenacre Writers, Finish that Book group.

Students at London Metropolitan University and various tutors on MA Professional Writing course, 2010.

Finally Dee Edmonds, who designed the cover brilliantly.

Good friends have also cheered me along, in particular my dear friend Val Mulligan, who always encouraged me with such enthusiasm.

This book is dedicated to all of you.

The Prologue

Everyone always asks why, why did you go to South Africa in 1975? The answer is complex, not the simple one that people want to hear.

We both had African connections - I was born in what was then Southern Rhodesia, although we returned to the UK when I was a small child. My father was in the RAF and had been posted there. Dave had been brought up in Nigeria and Uganda, where his dad worked as a physics professor. We loved Africa and we wanted to go back there. It gets in your blood.

When we travelled there with our baby, Pascale, we were both 25 and full of optimism and naivety. Apartheid was the backdrop to the events of our lives and, in the end, because of apartheid and all the other things that went wrong, we left.

In 1975 before we left, we knew little about South Africa and, like most people in the West, had hardly heard of Nelson Mandela, then on Robben Island. In the UK, the government seemed to be on friendly terms with the Pretoria government.

We were part of a new idealistic generation, the post-war baby boomers, who were against war, listened to rock music and wanted peace and love across the world. We were young and full of hope for the future.

The previous two summers in London had been a washout – miserable, wet, rain-sodden summers and cold wet winters – grey, grey, grey. We wanted to go to Africa, a place where the sun shone every day.

Dave had graduated from the Royal Academy of Dramatic Art [RADA] in 1972. Afterwards, he had struggled to get his precious Equity card, without which he could not work in the UK as an actor. There was a series of small parts in plays and tours – nothing substantial. This was the guy who on his 21st birthday, [after lots of alcohol], I found weeping into his beer, saying, 'I'm a genius and no one knows it!'

As for me, I'd dropped out of university due to illness [and an operation] and had done a series of clerical and typing jobs in London, which I hated. I was quite happy to play a support role to Dave and be a mother to our 18 month old child. I had no burning career aspirations at that time, which is strange, as I was an ardent feminist even then.

What we both wanted was to do something different with our lives, something new. We wanted to travel, to see the world.

I did some library research into different countries in Africa. Most were unstable, Uganda had the murderous Idi Amin! Few African countries had English theatre companies which paid a living wage. Kenya, with a relatively well-established independent democracy, attracted us. Dave wrote to their one English-speaking theatre group, but they weren't recruiting at that time – maybe in 6 months' time? We couldn't wait that long. We wanted to go NOW!

South Africa was easy to get in to, had English-speaking theatres in all the big cities, particularly Johannesburg, Cape Town and Durban. It was Africa and perhaps, once we were there, we could use it as a springboard to somewhere else on the continent – maybe that post in Kenya would come up and we could move on fairly quickly.

We discussed the apartheid situation at length until finally, I pointed out,

'It's the only place we can get in to easily, we fulfil their main criteria.'

'You mean we're white? Dave raised an eyebrow. 'Well, OK, South Africa it is then. I'll try and get work in mixed-race casts. I'll take what I can to start with, but that's what I'll be looking for.'

I nodded, 'Perhaps we can live in mixed-race areas, avoid the whole apartheid machinery, somehow. We don't want Pas growing up in some segregated white neighbourhood.' I was nervous about how, but determined to give it a try.

'It'll be an adventure though, won't it?' Dave grinned. And it was, it most certainly was, in ways we could not have foreseen.

A Hippopotamus at the Table

Table of contents

Chapter 1: A journey

When I was a child, I had a telescope and sometimes I would up-end it, look through the larger end, at an object made tiny, distant. Looking back is like that now, to that time in June 1975, when we were on a long journey across South Africa.

Today, the road across the Karoo is a wide motorway with many lanes. At that time, it wasn't like that; the road was two-way, forward to Cape Town, back to Jo'burg. It meandered across the dry flat landscape of the Karoo and then up, up through dramatic mountain scenery and down, down to the grape valleys of Paarl, crossing the Cape flats to Table Mountain, whose long table top was often hidden by mist, clinging round the heights. Covered wagons had come along this route from Cape Town a hundred and fifty years before, bringing the Afrikaaners looking for new land, on a journey to escape from English rule.

From an eagle's viewpoint high above, the road from Jo'burg across the Karoo, would appear like a thin grey ribbon crossing this large flat expanse, this endless scrubland of grey stony ground and low dust-green bushes. Back then, the traffic on this road travelling towards the Cape was light. On one day in June that year, a small battered blue-grey VW Beetle was driving down this road. From way above it would have appeared like a distant moving blue dot, its occupants were crossing the Karoo on a great adventure, heading for a new life in Cape Town. They had sunk most of their cash into buying the car and now had only fifty rand left.

The driver of the old VW was a twenty-five year old male, tall, slim, blonde, 'six foot two and eyes of blue', as the song went. He had a big grin and a gap between his two front teeth - my husband, Dave. He was having his first real driving lesson, which had begun after leaving the chicken farm, with the nightmare criss-cross motorway system out of Johannesburg and then out on to the highway, enroute to the Cape a thousand miles away. Beside him, was his driving instructor, navigator, wife-of-5-years, also twenty-five, slim pixie-cut brown hair, cow-like brown eyes, small firm mouth, and determined chin - me.

On the back seat crawling around was an eighteen-month-old girl-child, same slant eyes as her Dad, straight blonde hair cut in a bob, already talking in short sentences, mostly beginning with 'what' or 'why'. She was wearing blue denim jeans and jacket, same as her parents, our daughter Pascale, who we usually called Pas.

In the boot, there was a suitcase, big as a trunk, containing all our possessions. And the portable cot – canvas, heavy floral print, aluminium rods that dismantled - every night since leaving England, this printed cocoon of safety and stability was ritually assembled – the one unchanging place of security for her in a new, ever-changing and frightening world.

Also on the seat next to Pas, was a large portable tape deck, with 'Bridge of Sighs' by Robin Trower (known as the successor to Jimi Hendrix), playing loudly, as we drove. Laughing and chatting, we were drinking coffee from a flask. We had driven away from the farm before dawn, with frost on the ground and a hazy mist on the road. The mist had gradually cleared to a bright sunny day.

'I was ace driving over that motorway, don't you think?' Dave handed his mug back to me for a fill up.

'Bloody hell, I was scared out of my wits'. I poured him half a cup from the flask, being careful not to spill it as I handed it back to him.

Dave took a swig, balancing the cup on the steering wheel. 'That road was a bit tricky, considering!'

'Yes, considering you're still a *learner*!'

'Hey, I can drive. I just never got around to passing my test. It's a long straight drive now. Shit, that was a BIG pot-hole!'

'Ow! Be careful, look what you did...' My cup had jerked, sploshing coffee all over my knees. I started dabbing them with some napkins.

'Sorry – it's this bloody road. What sort of sandwiches you got there?'

'I'll give you three guesses!'

'Chicken, chicken or chicken, right?'

'Right!'

'Once we get to Cape Town, I'm not eating fucking chicken for a very long time.'

'Yeh they were really kind, but you did get sick of it after a bit.' We both laughed.

The adventure we were on was exciting but scary too, like all good adventures. We'd planned this journey for six months, sold up in London, then jumped on a plane. After two weeks in Jo'burg, which we hated, we'd escaped from the city to a farm in a rural area outside Jo'burg.

The car chugged on through the endless flat landscape. This was not like Wales, with its hills and valleys where, in between spells living in England or abroad, we'd spent much of our childhoods.

'How far to go, now?'

I had the map spread out on my lap, 'It's nearly five hundred miles more of Karoo and then we go over the mountains and it's another four hundred to Cape Town.'

'Mummy, mummy! Wan joos! Wan joos! Wan joos!'

'OK baby, here you are.' Passing the baby bottle of juice back to Pas, I turned back to Dave. 'Good job she doesn't get car sick like I did when I was a kid – poor Mum and Dad, all of us puking. She's getting sleepy, though – here you are, here's your dummy.' I pulled a light blanket over her. Then I handed Dave another sandwich.

'Another chicken sandwich?' I handed it to him.

He took a bite dropping crumbs everywhere. 'To live by the sea again, it's going to be great!' He hit the wheel with the flat of his hand. I smiled. We couldn't wait to be near the sea, I'd spent a large part of my childhood by the sea, in Swansea and West Wales.

'What'll we do if you don't get the job? I'd been swept along by Dave's enthusiasm and confidence and now was beginning to feel anxious.

'Don't worry, I'll get it'. 'Yes but ....'

'Look, I have to get it, don't I?'

I sighed, trying to dispel my doubts. 'Yes, now you've torn up our return tickets... what did you have to do that for?'

5

'Because we're NOT going back, we're going to make it here.'

'Yes well, we have to now, don't we...?' I looked at my hands...Dave was always so full of optimism, ignoring practicalities completely. I was excited about the adventure we were on, but anxious also. Where would we live? How would we survive the next week, with so little money? What if Dave didn't get the audition? There was no manual labour here for whites, no social security or dole for out-of-work actors.

Dave began singing, 'We're going to the sea, the sea, the sea' and I laughed, his mood was always infectious. The subject changed.

'What're you going to do for your audition?'

'I thought I'd do that monologue from the Scottish play, you know 'Is this a dagger...?' and 'Oh that this too too solid flesh...'

'Isn't that a bit ...'

'Risky? Yeh!' He grinned and the gap between his front teeth always made the grin seem more mischievous. With his eyes flashing, he was daring me to say something. But I knew that look, there was no stopping him once he'd decided. Besides, I also knew that as long as he knew the words, he'd blow them out of their seats, whatever the piece. Dave had left RADA (The Royal Academy of Dramatic Art) three years before, he had a powerful stage presence and his memory was amazing. It was my job to test his lines and he would always be word perfect after two or three run-throughs of a script.

Dave's mind quickly switched to the next topic. He was not worrying about the audition as he had absolute confidence in his own acting ability.

'First, we find somewhere to stay. Then, wire the bank at home for more money. Let's hope it won't take long.'

'Yeh, fifty Rand's not going far.' I kept my hands busy, brushing away crumbs and throwing them out the window... 'Let's hope these cousins of Pieter's can put us up or we'll have to pay for hotels...I don't know how.....' I was the pragmatist who worried about reality, but as usual, Dave swept such mundanities aside.

'We'll manage somehow. We'll find a cheap hotel...'

'It'll have to be VERY cheap. The money might last a week, if we're lucky.'

'Don't worry petal, we'll be OK. I'll chat up the bank....did you say there were some ham sandwiches?'

'You'll be lucky, chicken or nothing...'

* * *

Towards sunset, the Karoo seemed to be coming to an end, as we neared the distant hazy mountain range. The sun was moving towards the horizon, the darkening sky turning to oranges and reds. We had already been advised by Pieter, the farmer, at the chicken farm, that the journey to Cape Town would take more than a day and we planned to stop for the night at a small town called Beaufort West. Would we make it before dark? We'd got about half an hour. Dave was getting tired from the long drive.

'Look,' I pointed up ahead. 'The ground's getting greener, the road's climbing up, too. Have you noticed? And there's a bend up ahead – looks a bit less flat too.' Suddenly, a sign appeared, 'Beaufort West 10 kilometres.' Gradually, the road swept round the long bend, in front of us a distant mountain crag appeared. We turned off the main road to the right and headed for the town, just as the sun was dropping below the horizon.

Beaufort West was what Afrikaners would call 'a dorp', a small insignificant town. Soon, we saw a bed and breakfast sign before a white-fronted house in typical Cape Dutch style. We got out of the car, stretched our stiff legs and knocked on the door. A buxom, pleasant-faced woman with a floral apron, who spoke only Afrikaans, came to the door. She ushered us in. The place inside was spotless, so we asked how much and held our breath...

'Ten rand for room? Ja, ja, kom, kom.' She beckoned and took us up to look at it - clean and bright with a cream counter-paned double bed. Ten rand out of our fifty! I nudged Dave.

A double bed at last! Since leaving London, we'd slept only on single beds, sometimes pushed together. Tonight, we could sleep close to each other for warmth and comfort.

The cost was a big chunk out of our money, but we were too tired to look for anything else.

The last rays of the sun, now blood orange against a deep black sky, were visible from our window lighting up the distant crags, as I pulled the curtains relieved that we'd found a place before darkness had fallen completely. The travel cot was unfolded ready for Pas and we went down to a neat dining area, where a simple meat and potato stew was in a pot, on a scrubbed wooden table. We were starving by then and the meal disappeared fast. The woman smiled at our enjoyment of her cooking and our Afrikaans 'Danke', when we had finished. Her shrewd eyes watched us curiously. 'Goodnight', we said, as she smiled and nodded and we went upstairs to the bedroom. Dave shut the door and lay Pas, whose eyes were already closing, into her cot and we both fell into bed, cuddled up close, exhausted and slept soundly until dawn, blissfully unaware of all that was to come.

Chapter 2: Jo'burg, a farm and a piglet

The bright early morning sunshine streaming in through a gap in the curtains woke me and I lay on my pillow, looking round the clean plain room, trying to adjust to where I was. Beaufort West... oh yes, we'd driven across the Karoo yesterday. I'd get up in a minute and look out the window. It'd been dark when we arrived. My mind turned over the events of the last few weeks and months.

On the first leg of our plane journey from London, we were to change at Frankfurt. The man in the business suit next to me was clearly a confirmed child-hater; he glared at Pascale as I sat down beside him. I smiled to myself, as she tried to snatch his pen, wriggled about, looked up in his face and directed her curiosity about him to me....,

'Mummy, wat dat man doing? Wat he draw?'

'No Pas leave the man alone; he wants to do his work...'

He disembarked at Frankfurt looking relieved.

From there, on the second leg of the journey to Johannesburg, we touched down at Kinshasa, Zaire for refuelling. I looked out through the plane windows at my first view of 'real' Africa – glaring heat, flat, featureless and dusty single-story shacks to the horizon. Would South Africa be anything like this?

Then, there we were, emerging from the arrivals lounge and standing, all together with our bags and stripy pushchair, in the busy airport at Johannesburg, wondering where to go next. We had our return tickets from England and our passports had just been stamped with three month holiday visas. This was the start of a new life. We'd sold everything to get here. We both came from families where travel abroad had been part of life. We were not daunted but excited by the new adventure. Right now, we needed a place to wash and sleep so we could begin to explore this new world.

We were directed to the taxi rank, where a friendly black taxi-driver gave a reasonable price for the journey to Jo'burg. The driver knew of a hotel in town, in an area called Hillbrow. On the drive there, we sat in silence looking out the windows, stunned by the skyscrapers and this cosmopolitan city. Was this truly Africa, this modern world? All around, black and white hustled for space, in a hurry to get on with the business of life. Dust and heat rose from hot pavements and shimmered as we looked out the windows, trying to take it all in.

Unknown to us, Hillbrow, where our hotel was situated, was one of the most densely populated areas in the world. The taxi driver dropped us outside an eight-storey building, bleak and impersonal in a square surrounded by more high-rise buildings. Waiting at the reception desk to check in, I saw the toilet signs for the first time, in both Afrikaans and English- Blanke Dames (White Ladies), Nie Blanke Vrou (Non-white Females), and was shocked. I nudged Dave and he looked over too, 'Bloody hell', he whispered and we looked at each other. The first time I had to go, I stood outside, hesitating, feeling that by choosing one, I was accepting their distinction.

Later, we walked down to a cafe, a short walk from the hotel, where we had our first lunch. The proprietor was a short, fat, bald Afrikaaner and after we had eaten our omelette and chips, I asked 'Can I use the toilet?'

'We don't hev.'

'No toilet?'

'Well, only for the blek girls.'

I started to walk towards the door I could see. 'It doesn't matter – I just want a toilet?'

'No! (firmly), thet one's for the blek girls? You cahn't go there!'

I looked over his shoulder at the two black women working at the sink behind him, one of them glanced sideways at me and turned away. The other kept her head down. They had jobs, did as they were told, for them it was the status quo.

The cafe owner's face was set and immovable and, muttering loudly, saying it was 'bloody ridiculous,' we left. We had to walk all the way back to the hotel, so I could use the toilet for 'Blanke Dames'.

After a week in the hotel, searching through newspapers, we found an advert for apartments. We rung up, they had one available. It was on the fourteenth floor, in the centre of Johannesburg. We paid for a month. That would give us some time to look around for work. I was looking forward to making our own food too.

'At least we'll be able to make tea and cook when we want to'.

But the height and the big glass windows made me nervous. When Dave and Pas went out onto the balcony, I was terrified.

'Pas come back, don't go too close, it's a big drop, Dave bring her in.'

'Stop fussing. It's quite safe, I'm holding her!'

'It makes me feel dizzy, come inside, please!'

'Ooh look Daddy, look - likl cars.' Pas was fearlessly pointing down through the railings to the tiny cars below. Dave turned and looked at my tense face.

'OK Pas let's go in. You can play with your dolly and have some juice, good girl.'

As he brought her in, I slid the glass-door closed and locked it, it was too dangerous out there. This was not a great apartment for a child.

For the next few days, Pas and I were stuck in our high rise apartment or I'd be pushing the pram around the smart glass-fronted shops far below. In the shops, black women were sales assistants, supervisors were white. Shoppers here were nearly all white people and I seemed to be part of that throng, although with our tight budget, I was not spending any money. Sometimes, I would stop someone to ask directions, usually asking a black man or woman.

'Yis medem, go left at the end of thet block and then ut's on your raht. Would medem have a few coins to spare for mah bus fare home?'

My smile was often met with a stony stare and some kind of demand for money. I knew people were poor and oppressed but still it was dispiriting and, gradually, I stopped approaching them. A year or so later, a black friend told me that it was universal in Jo'burg for black to hate white on principle, that most black people preferred dealing with an Afrikaner to a 'liberal' white. After encountering the sullen atmosphere in Jo'burg, I could believe him.

Meanwhile, Dave was out all day, job-hunting. He went around the centre of Jo'burg, on foot or by bus, visiting theatres or phoning directors he'd heard about, to try and get work. But they were saying things like, 'Well yes, in a few months, we're starting a new production, but nothing now.' It was frustrating.

A week later, I was feeling homesick and began looking through my address book. I was thinking about sending a few postcards home. Out fell a piece of paper - it was in my mother's hand-writing, on it a phone number and a name. I remembered that she had shoved it into my hands before I left.

'I know the mother, she's from Swansea, nice woman. They live in that big house near Reynoldston. I met the girl once I think, years ago, when she was a teenager. She married a gynaecologist and they went out to South Africa last year... Her mother was pressing me to give you her number. Anyway it's up to you.'

Nervously, I dialled the number, thinking that it would probably come to nothing, that they'd be distant, uninterested.

I explained who I was and how I'd got her number.

'Oh yes,' she said warmly. 'I had a letter, I remember meeting your Mum once at my parent's place, quite a character. It'll be lovely to meet someone from home. How about next weekend, come up on Saturday?' We live next to a chicken farm, it's very rural here, you can stay the night in our caravan if you like, have Sunday lunch?'

Over the next few days, I wondered what they'd be like. It would be so nice to get away from the apartment block and meet someone from home. This alien world was beginning to oppress me.

Helen gave directions and, a few days later, we were on our way. Their place was outside Pretoria, about thirty miles from Johannesburg, so we got a taxi from a bus station a few miles away. They lived in a bungalow on the grounds of a chicken farm. The taxi drove down rural roads and up a stony dirt-track stopping in front of a bungalow with chairs and a wooden table on the front stoep (veranda). The warm sun was high in the deep blue sky and there was scrub-covered bush, as far as the eye could see.

Jim came out to greet us, followed by Helen, carrying the baby. He worked as a gynaecologist in Baragwaneth Hospital, in the black township of Soweto and was slim, earnest looking, his brown hair messy. Helen had shoulder-length curly brown hair and was more rounded, warm and welcoming.

'Hello, hello lovely to meet at last. Come in, can I get you some juice?'

'Oh lovely, shall I hold the baby for you?'

'Great, thanks.' Helen handed him over with some relief.

'Look Pas, someone smaller than you.' I turned to Helen. 'She hasn't met another child since we've been here.'

'Wan baby, wan baby.' She was holding out her little arms.

'OK, sit down over there and you can help me hold her.' We chatted for a while about breast feeding, which I'd not managed for long – my slim boyish figure had not produced enough milk for a hungry baby. Helen clearly didn't have that problem. Pas sat up close to me and 'helped' hold the baby, until he started grizzling and Helen took him back. 'He wants feeding now,' she said lifting her top and attaching him to her breast. We chatted for a while about breast feeding. I noticed a box of slides on the glass-topped table beside me.

'Are these yours Jim, what are the slides of?' I said idly picking it up.

'They're all slides of women's vaginas. Have a look if you like!'

'Oh, really! Later perhaps.' I put the box back quickly. 'What a strange job, looking at women's fannies all day!'

He laughed, 'I guess it is,' adding enthusiastically, 'but it's interesting!' He told us a little about the hospital where he worked. Soweto was the main township for black South Africans on the outskirts of Johannesburg. Living in this sprawling shanty township were large numbers of dirt-poor people, with all the health problems associated with poverty. Many travelled on foot or by bus every day, to work for the whites in their big houses in the smart Jo'burg suburbs.

'The main problem for the kids is Kwashiorkor,' he was warming to his subject now. 'Swollen bellies, coz of malnutrition and many pregnant mothers only come to the hospital when things go wrong in labour. It's hard to save them by then. Poor nutrition makes it all worse.'

After a glass of wine she handed the baby to Jim and brought a stew over from the kitchen. 'Chicken! Ooh lovely', I said. She smiled. 'You wouldn't be saying that if you lived here all the time. We have SO much chicken.'

Dave made them laugh all through the lunch, telling stories of our arrival and some of the theatrical people he was meeting.

'So I rang up and got put straight through to the director - he said 'Drop by anytime!' So I did, next day! It'd never happen in London. You're lucky to speak to the secretary's assistant's assistant.'

After the meal I was chatting to Helen, who had the baby on her lap again. Dave and Jim were outside on the stoep smoking. She was lively, cheerful and matter-of-fact, it was great for me to have someone my own age to talk to, who was also a mother.

'Where was he born?' I asked

'In Jo'burg. Jim came and helped of course'.

'Oh not in Baragwaneth?'

She sighed, 'No, that's only for black people from Soweto,' she explained. 'Everything's segregated here don't forget. It's poorly funded too, Baragwaneth. Facilities are basic. Apartheid's everywhere here – you probably haven't had time to get used to it, it's a real shock when you first get here.'

'Yes', I told her about the incident with the cafe owner in Hillbrow. 'I was so angry, I'll never get used to it. How long've you been here?'

'Eighteen months. Another six months and we'll be gone.'

'You're going back to Wales?'

'No, we'll probably go somewhere like Botswana or Kenya – can't wait to get away from this country, although on the farm it's OK.'

Clearly she and Jim did not like apartheid either, I could see we were going to get on.

'Dave's hoping to get a job in Kenya too, but they're not recruiting at the theatre yet.'

'Maybe we'll bump into you there,' she laughed.

'We want to go to Cape Town until then, have you been there?'

'Oh yes. Jim had some leave and we went down there about four months ago – the scenery is stunning. Long drive though.'

'How long?'

'About a thousand miles,' she laughed at my shocked look. 'Distances are big here – you get used to it, eventually. We'll introduce you to the farmer and his wife later – Pieter and Marianne – lovely people – Afrikaaners.'

'Oh?' I said warily

'Oh, they're truly nice people, a lot of Afrikaaners don't support the Pretoria government's line on apartheid you know.'

Pas was playing just outside in her t-shirt and shorts – a couple of the farm-workers' kids were standing a little way off, calling out to her, I could hear her giggling. It was sunny and warm. I sighed,

'You're so lucky living out here, it's beautiful.'

'Maybe Jim could take you out for a walk around the farm in a while, but first I want you to meet someone...'

She lifted the catch on the back stable door which was open at the top letting in the bright sunlight. As she handed the baby to Jim, in ran a tiny pink pig running on tiptoes and squealing. I put out my hand and she came and rooted and nuzzled my fingers.

'Here give her this,' Helen handed me a couple of nuts. 'She'll be your friend for life now.' Piglet squealed with delight and leapt nimbly onto the couch next to me.

'No!' Helen's tone was firm and piglet jumped down again.

'She's well-trained.' I laughed.

Later, as Helen had suggested, Jim took us for a tour of the farm area while she put the baby to bed. Piglet came for a walk too, much to Pas's delight, following at our heels, rooting in the mud and dust of the pathways, running back and forth busily. Jim showed us the caravan on the way back - it had a double bed mattress, a tiny kitchen and a cubicle for the chemical toilet. It would do. Pas loved it and lay on the bed, her eyes closing. I held her hand, as she fell asleep.

Standing in the doorway looking out, I could hear hens clucking in the distance. The warm winter sun was low in the sky; there was no traffic, just the hum of cicadas and, in the distance, a dog barking. The air shimmered with a honey coloured heat haze and I sniffed the earthy farm smells – a change from car exhausts. I sighed, it was lovely to be here, if only for a weekend.

Helen came out onto the stoep, once the baby was settled in his cot. She brought out a bottle of wine and four glasses and put them on the table. We all sat there, drinking wine and watching the sun setting.

Then Helen leaned forward, 'Jim and I've had a chat - we're going away for a week's holiday, next weekend'.

'Off to Botswana actually, to see a friend of mine,' Jim was looking at Dave. 'You could stay here for that week and do us a favour, if you don't mind taking care of piglet?'

Dave and I looked at each other and then back at them. I was already dreading going back next day to the impersonal high-rise apartment, the traffic and the bustle of the city.

The sun was now close to the horizon, the sky turning many shades of pink and orange, casting long shadows on the red earth of the bush in front of the bungalow. Earlier, Pas had been playing hide and seek among the dusty green bushes nearby, with one of the farm kids. We'd heard the shrieks of laughter. It was still warm, a distant cock was crowing, a dog barking.

'We'd love to,' I said.

* * *

The following day, Helen took us down to meet Pieter and Marian on the farm. Jim stayed behind to work on his research and to keep an eye on the baby...

'Come in, come in? Want a drink?' They poured large glasses, a whisky for Dave and a glass of wine for me. We all sat on the stoep chatting, the air was warm and we looked over at the farm, smelt the rich farm smells and listened to the distant sounds, a cock crowing, chickens squawking, children playing. Helen told them the plan for us to stay in the caravan and Marianne said,

'Well Pieter can come and fetch you from Jo'burg in the car, he has to go up there on Friday for some supplies. You must eat here with us on your first night.'

Returning to our high rise apartment on Sunday evening was a wrench – but at least we could look forward to returning to the farm in a few days. Dave was carrying a sleeping Pas as I opened the door of our apartment. He laid her on our bed and quickly assembled the cot. I looked across at the tall buildings, bright lights and traffic below and sighed as I pictured Helen and Jim sitting on the stoep, watching the sunset.

On Friday, five days later we were back; Pieter had collected us, the travel cot and our suitcase. Helen and Jim were waiting for us, their car loaded ready for their trip - they were leaving the next morning. Jim unlocked the caravan and carried in the suitcase for us. I stood in the doorway looking out at the scene, the bright sunny afternoon and the quiet all around. It was rural, but unmistakably African, miles of bush, the hum of cicadas, a cock crowing. It seemed so peaceful after the traffic and hurry of Jo'burg.

We slept soundly in our caravan that night, Pas in her squeezed-in cot. Jim and Helen slipped away in the early hours of Saturday morning without waking us. Maybe it was the contrast, but over the next few days we felt so happy there. Although it was winter, the days were like a warm summer in England. Pascale ran around playing in light summer clothes, exploring the pathways to the coups where speckled hens pecked the dusty earth. Some of the farm workers' children were also about and Pas was clearly a novelty – their curiosity spilling into laughter and games. She loved having kids to play with again. I began to relax and smile for the first time since we'd arrived.

That evening, we strolled down to the farm for more chicken casserole and wine with Pieter and Marion. We sat on the stoep again looking out into the quiet darkness all around. The sky was crowded with stars. Marion brought me out a blanket as the temperature in the evening had cooled quite fast compared to the warmth of the day. Pas curled up in my lap and soon fell asleep. Far off we could hear laughter and chatter in the still night.

'That's the farm workers,' Marion sipped her wine. 'The women cook outside their huts on a brazier, while the men have a few beers.'

'Sometimes they drink too much beer,' Pieter leaned over and filled up my glass ...ken be problems.'

'Oh?' Dave lit a cigarette and blew a smoke ring.

'Ja! Mostly it's fine, but if they have too much they sometimes git unto a fight and then out come the pangas!'

'Is that like a machete?' I asked, remembering friends of my parents talking about tribal violence in Nigeria where they'd lived for a while and an occasion when they had hidden a man who was escaping from a different tribal group who were trying to kill him. They'd described how they called a doctor to sew up a machete wound on his leg.

'Same thing as a panga,' Pieter took a big swig from his whisky glass. 'They're used all over Africa for cutting back the bush. One slash from a panga could cut off your arm.'

I shuddered. Dave talked about what he'd seen in Uganda when Milton Obote was Prime Minister, the tribal violence – he'd lived with his father and step-mother there.

'A couple of times I saw bodies covered with banana leaves on trucks - when I was about 14.'

Many African countries had only recently achieved independence from colonial rule and tribal violence was common in some of these. But right now there were other things on my mind - our own situation! I explained that we were getting worried...

'If Dave doesn't find work soon, I don't know how we'll be able to stay in South Africa. And we need a car.' I frowned as I stroked the sleeping child in my lap and Helen smiled sympathetically.

'Yes,' Dave was saying, 'Here it's essential, it's a big country and we can't keep paying for taxis.'

Pieter interrupted, 'Well ah'll thunk about ut. Ah might know someone.' He gave Dave a wink. The conversation turned to the farm,

'There's a lot of chickens in your pens, how many do you have?'

'Too bluddy meny!' Pieter shrugged. 'About farv thousand right now.'

'And do you have to... kill them here?' I was very squeamish about anything to do with blood or killing.

Pieter laughed, 'Ya, one of mah men's job that one. Sometimes we hev to do it. Yew just rung their necks, lahk this,' he gestured twisting his two big hands. I shuddered again.

'Ah'll shew yew t'morrow Dave,' he winked again.

'OK.' Dave, unlike me, was not a bit squeamish.

Dave was drinking wine and telling funny stories, but I was tired after our busy day.

'Well, I think I'll take Pas back to the caravan and put her in the cot.' I looked at Dave, who was always reluctant to drag himself away from any social gathering, but he stood up. He was yawning too.

'OK give her to me, I'll carry her. Goodnight. And thanks for everything.'

'Come down on Monday in the morning.' Marion smiled at me. 'We'll have a coffee, between my chores and you can tell me what set you off on your adventure.'

Pieter shook hands with Dave, 'I'll show yew round the farm t'morrow? Not much to see 'cept a lot of chickens.'

* * *

On Monday, Pieter gave Dave a lift into Jo'burg, as he was going in on business. When Dave got back that evening, he walked down to the main house for a chat with Pieter, while I was settling Pas in her cot. Later, after he came back, he told me about his day and about his chat with Pieter. They'd sat on the stoep in the cool evening air and Pieter had poured them both a large whisky.

Dave had wanted to ask Pieter's advice as we were almost certainly going to have to go to Cape Town for him to find work. He'd explained that we might have to go very soon, due to our small reserves of money.

'We want to live by the sea anyway if we can.'

'Ja, the Cape's great al royt. Ah've been there once or twoice to visit mah cousin.'

Dave reminded Pieter that he'd said he might know where to buy a car and that we needed something cheap and reliable

'Thet's a long droive Dave, to the Cape – more than eighteen hundred kilometres, ah'd say'.

'Phew!' Dave said, 'That *is* a long drive. Do you know somewhere that sells cars?'

'We could troi thet little geridge down the road, Ah know the owner. He wudn't sell me some kek, hey?'

Dave's lack of a driving licence hadn't deterred him so far, he intended to drive in South Africa and see how he could get a licence later. The rules seemed to be fairly relaxed here, less likely to be enforced. Next day, Pieter drove him to the garage. It was two kilometres from the farm - a small place, an Afrikaans boss and a couple of black mechanics. I heard the whole story later – with Dave acting out the whole scene

'Wull, ah yev a customer who's sulling a VW, 'bout seven years old,' the owner had said, 'uts in good shaype and reloyble – I think he wunts four fufty for it though.'

When Dave came back, I was sitting outside the caravan, in my T-shirt, shorts and flip flops enjoying the warm sun and sipping a cold drink.

'This is the life,' the warm sun was on my face. 'And it's winter! This is what we came for ... to get away from British weather, grey skies.'

'Mmmm, yes ...the guy at the garage, he's got a second hand VW!' Dave seemed subdued.

'Oh great!' I was excited 'How much?' He looked at me steadily.

'The owner wants four fifty for it ... so I told him we'd think about it.'

'Four fifty, Oh no. That'd take a huge chunk of our money... two rand to the pound that's about two hundred and twenty pounds. God we can't afford that!'

'Don't worry,' Dave was smiling, 'Ah 'ave ze plan,' he twirled invisible moustaches and winked. 'What plan?' I frowned at him.

'We'll send to the bank at home for some more of our money!'

We'd left some money from selling our small property in our UK bank for when we returned.

'We can ask the bank here to get some transferred.'

'But how long will that take?'

'Oh not long.'Dave waved his hand dismissivley.

'You don't know that.'

'Look, just come with me to see it tomorrow. Then we'll decide.'

'It's too much.'

'Yeh I know.'

On Wednesday morning, Pieter drove us up the winding track leading from the farm and onto an old, tarmacked road to the small garage. The car was already out front. We took it for a test drive, a petrol-blue VW beetle. The bodywork wasn't too bad, a few small rust spots, but the engine seemed fine. The car was great, just right. I was sold. Never mind the dwindling money, I knew we had to take the opportunity and buy it.

'I'll give you R400,' Davespoke firmly. Pieter had told him to offer this the night before. The garage man was a stocky middle-aged Afrikaner – he looked at Dave shrewdly and then winked at Pieter.

'OK led, tell yew what – yew can hev ut for four twenty, ah'll make sure it goes well, mah boys will get ut into tuptop shape and yew can collect ut tomorrow evening, eh?'

Dave smiled and they shook hands. The mechanic, at the boss's instruction, took the car into the garage for a going over. We owned a car at last. It was small and slightly battered, but it went well, Pieter had looked it over too. We felt liberated. We would be able to get about now, without having to rely on lifts or cabs.

The following day, Pieter drove Dave to the garage and picked up the car, now in 'tip-top' shape. He parked outside the caravan with a flourish and we all got in and went for a drive. It felt great to know we now had our own vehicle to go where we chose.

Meanwhile, I had been adopted by the piglet. Before Helen and Jim went on their holiday, Helen had said,

'Er..., you said you'd look after piglet, yes? So, I'll show you what needs doing.'

She had demonstrated how to make up piglet's baby bottle with a big hole in the teat and we'd practised feeding it the night before they left, watching it guzzling, slurping and sucking. A lot messier than a human baby! Pascale loved it – a real live baby animal to look after.

'Mummy, Mummy, lek me give bokl, lek me,' tugging the bottle from my hand. But she soon got bored of piglet who sucked hard at the bottle, nearly dragging it from her small hands. She was not a bit cuddly, squealing if you picked her up and wriggling and squirming until she escaped. What piglet liked best was to follow me around everywhere, nose to my ankle like a puppy, dancing on her toes like a little pink ballerina. Each night we put her in a large cardboard box with food and straw and she squealed loudly every time, begging us to let her out and take her to bed with us.

Me, Pas, girl and piglet

Then I had to give her a good talking too. 'Now look piggy, you have to stay here (scratching her head with my hand in the box), but we'll see you in the morning, yes?'

'Squeal, squeal (take me with you, I'll be good).'

'No piggy, you HAVE to stay there, OK?'

'Squeal, squeal, squeal.'

Then I'd walk back to the caravan with Pas, leaving piggy in her box in the outhouse, next to the big house, and gradually her cries would stop. I never liked leaving her, but you can't exactly take a piglet in your bed can you?

Chapter 3: The Afrikaaner and the journey

The smell of toast drifting up the stairs and pots and pans clattering in the kitchen returned me to the present.

Dave was stirring beside me. Pas, in her cot would soon wake up and I began to think about getting up. The sun was moving across the floorboards towards her and I could already feel its warmth. I was tired after our long journey from the chicken farm the day before, but also excited. Today we would reach the sea. I got up, stretched and walked over to the window to see if any of the town was visible. On the right there were trees and green up to mountain crags, silhouetted against the blue sky. To the left were white buildings dotted along a wide road between trees and a distant tall white church spire.

I wondered how piglet was getting on without me. That chicken farm! I smiled to myself, remembering the little black girl called Prudence who came round to play with Pascale every day. She wore a thin faded blue frock and her eyes were bright and curious.

'Plees medem,' she was cupping her outstretched hands – I'd dropped in a boiled sweet, then 'Danke' with that shy smile. Say 'Thank you.' I'd smiled, seeing if I could teach her some English words. She'd repeated the words parrot fashion with exactly my accent –

'This is a cup, say cup – 'cup' and this is a chair – 'chair' - and this is a table ' 'table'.

She'd been shyly pleased with herself, her eyes sparkling, 'mmm, lekker,' she was sucking hard on the sweet.

Afrikaans was the main language of communication between white and black, but in her home Prudence would speak her family's tribal language – Xhosa or Tswana, depending which tribe her parents were from. There was no call for English here. If I'd been there longer, I knew that this bright child would pick English up fast.

Pieter and Marian had come to eat with us after Dave collected the car. We'd sat at the table on Helen's stoep, under the stars. I'd made a spaghetti Bolognese which they were pleased to have as an alternative to chicken. It was a small way of thanking them for all they'd one for us. They were great company and had made us feel very welcome. We dreaded the thought of returning to that fourteenth floor apartment when our week was over. It would be sad for Pascale to leave her new friends too.

Later that night, we'd been lying in bed in our little caravan talking quietly. I was getting a bit anxious.

'Look! We don't like Jo'burg. And there's no work here at the moment. I'm tired of big cities – can't you get an acting job in Cape Town? I want to live by the sea.'

Dave sighed, 'Yeh, that'd be great. Most of the best theatres are here though. Tell you what, I'll ring round tomorrow and find out who knows about theatres and directors in Cape Town.'

On Friday, Dave drove into Jo'burg and one of the directors he went to see told him that the Cape Town Performing Arts Board might be looking for actors, so he rang their number. Eventually he got hold of the director there, who said 'Can you get to Cape Town for an audition on Monday?

Dave thought fast 'How about next Friday, I could be there then,' (he was thinking 'Oh shit! We can drive, I suppose'). The director hummed and haa-d. 'Is that the earliest you can arrive? Well if we take you on, we start rehearsals the following Monday. Our next production'll be a Shakespeare, there'll be three weeks rehearsals, before it opens.'

Dave reported that he thought 'Whoopee! I'm going to get this one'. Dave was very determined when he set his mind on something.

As he was telling me, I got very excited – 'It's meant to happen. We're going to live by the sea.' We danced around the room hugging each other. We would have to leave on Monday at the latest – we'd have to find somewhere to stay in Cape Town. How long would it take to get there? It was such a distance. We decided to talk it over with Pieter and Marianne.

Later I was thinking about Jim and Helen's return the next day and the impending doom of our return to the bleak apartment, when Marianne dropped by and invited us to supper that evening. After the meal, we all sat on the stoep, drinking wine and chatting. Pieter looked over at Marianne and she nodded, he turned to us.

'Listen, we've been talking ...'

'Uh, oh.' Dave was smiling.

'No, we've decided, you can't go beck to thet apartment, you can't, ut's no playce for a child.'

'Oh I know' I sighed. 'We love it here so much and you've been so fab to us, we can't thank you enough.'

Pieter raised his hand to fend off any more thanks.

'Look, ut's all werked out – yew can stay in Jeck's room – we'll put Jeck un with Henny – they can double up for a few days, until you leave for the Cape. Go back to the apartment and collect your stuff.'

We protested (not too hard), but it was useless.

'We insist!'

I looked at their smiling faces with disbelief. They couldn't mean it – they barely knew us and were taking us in to their home.

'Are you sure that's OK, what about Jack, doesn't he mind?'

'No no no, don't yew worry about Jeck, he's fine, yew get your stuff and we'll move it all in t'morrow.'

Dave said, 'I'll help out on the farm, no honestly – anything I can do. Besides I love this work.'

'Yes you do, but not as much as acting... I smiled at him and he nodded.'

Dave drove over the next day and collected our stuff from the apartment. We moved in to the farmhouse putting our cases and the cot in to Jack's room. I was so happy that I didn't have to go back to that city high rise. Helen and Jim came back that afternoon, tired after their long journey.

'I'm so pleased for you,' said Helen, 'I didn't like to think of you going back there, I knew how much you hated it.'

* * *

That night, over the evening meal with Pieter and Marianne, I asked about the farm workers. In England, the impression one gained was that all black workers were cruelly treated by big, bad, oppressive bosses. Clearly, this was not the case on this farm. I asked Pieter about how things were managed here.

'Oh yus, our staff do all royt,' Pieter took a swig from his glass. 'Their families are supported; each family gets so many sacks of mealie a year, plenty of meat from the chickens, plus pay of course. Sometimes Ah yev t' sort out disputes – last year we even had a murder.'

'Oh no! How terrible.'What happened?'

'Oh I niver got to the total bottom of it – it was some troybal dispute between one family and another – two men got unto a fight, they'd both been drinking and out came the pangas.....anyway one men got his head chopped off...but these things are qoyte rare.'

I was taken aback by his matter of fact tone.

He continued: 'I loyke to keep mah staff heppy, some have bin with me for many years, we look after our workers here - sort out medical problems, schooling, they can feed their families. But ah hevn't always bin a farmer you know...'

'Really, what did you do before?'

'When I was a bit younger, I joined the Church of Scientology started by L Ron Hubbard – Ah don't suppose you've heard of it? Then ah sold real estate in America for a while. But in the end, ah hed to come home, it's in ma blood this land.'

We looked at him in amazement.

'Yes', Dave took a large swig of whisky and glanced at me. 'We've heard of them, the Scientologists. We've seen them in London – they stop you on Tottenham Court Road and try and get you to come in the shop. I always thought it was some kind of weird cult, but I like Ron Hubbard's sci-fi books, I've read them all.'

Pieter sighed and looked over at his wife,

'Ja, thet's what most people think, but I learnt a heck of a lot from them. You learn how to use the principles to get ahead, develop your hidden abilities. Ut's amazing stuff, yew know.'

There was silence for a moment as we considered this. But not knowing how to respond we changed the subject. Dave spoke first.

'We wanted to ask you about the drive to Cape Town?' The questions spilled out fast and I joined in...

'How long will it take, what's the road like, how do we get out from here?' Pieter held up his large hands to ward off more questions.

'OK, OK! One question at a tarm!' He confirmed that we could not attempt the drive in one day – we could stay for a night somewhere to break up the journey. He got out a map.

'Just here,' he planted a large finger on a spot along a long ribbon of road. 'There's a town called Beaufort West at the end of the Karoo – if you want to mek ut there by dark, you'll hev to leave here early men, by 6 am on Monday ah'd say....'

* * *

On the Monday morning, the farmer's children had looked out at the just-before-dawn grey light and shrieked with delight at the white hoar frost on the scrub grass - they thought it was snow which they had seen only in picture books. The rising sun quickly burned it away and rose into a clear blue sky. Our VW beetle had left by 6:30 am, out from the farm, across the countryside, swooping over the city on twisting dual carriageways, onto the long road ahead.

* * *

Now here we were on the last leg of our journey from Beaufort West – Cape Town was waiting for us. I slipped on my flip-flops. Pas who'd sat up and was rubbing her eyes, held out her little arms to be lifted from her cot. Pascale called out, 'Daddy, daddy, we go now, we go now.' Dave sat up yawning. 'We're going to Cape Town today' he was smiling broadly.

'I know.' I was pulling Pas's tiny jeans on and buckling her sandals, I started singing 'We're going to the sea, the sea, the sea ...' Pas clapped her little hands, getting excited.

Dave got up and started dismantling the cot. After we'd all brushed our teeth and washed, everything was packed and Dave carried it down to the lobby, ready for the journey.

We had a simple breakfast of fresh white bread, farm butter and honey and some boiled eggs. Then waving and calling 'Tot siens!' (Goodbye) to the smiling Afrikaaner woman, we got in the car and Pascale climbed onto the back seat. No baby seats and child seat-belts then, she crawled around freely in the back as we headed for the pass through the mountains. She was soon playing happily, chatting and cheerful, talking to 'Big Doll', who we'd bought for her in Jo'burg.

'We go see de sea today. You be good baby,. ...or me be cross wid you. Put dis on.' She was struggling to put a cardigan on the doll and getting frustrated. She handed it to me for help.

'Here you are, now see if you can rock the baby to sleep? Baby looks tired.' I laughed looking at Dave 'She loves bossing that doll around!'

As we drove on Dave frowned. 'How much money have we got left now exactly?'

'You know how much. After paying for the B&B it's worse – about R40. We have to send to the bank at home for more money as soon as we get there.'

'I'll go and speak to the bank tomorrow – we'll work something out,' Dave gripped the steering wheel firmly. 'I'm sure it won't take long. They'll telex for the info and get it back next day, won't they? We need to open an account too, so we can get cheques to pay for things.'

We forgot about such practical things for a while as the spectacular scenery unfolded before us. The mountain range before Cape Town is part of a chain that threads its way along the north side of Cape Province about 100 miles from the coast – it carries on for many miles. The Dutch settlers had originally settled in the Cape area c.1652, but chafing under British rule, which had been established around 1795, they had packed up and left in their ox-drawn wagons, crossing this mountain range and trekking into what had then been the wild African hinterland beyond.

As we approached Cape Province, we knew nothing of this history. We soon noticed that everything was getting greener - a soft green down covered the landscape and damp mist hung on the mountain slopes - a welcome relief to the eye after the dreary, brown Karoo. The mountains become more and more majestic as we climbed up and up in our laden, tiny beetle, the road winding to the top, through a narrow pass and out onto the other side. Then the long zigzag descent – the road twisting and turning down the mountains and gradually flattening out, as we approached the wine-growing valleys of Paarl and Stellenbosch, great fields of gnarled grape vines stretching into the distance.

Predominantly, as we came down into the valley, I remember the delicious cool green - the Englishness of the scenery - English trees were everywhere, oaks and chestnuts and sycamores and birches, interspersed with great trees like eucalyptus. These trees had been introduced by settlers in the previous centuries. And of course grass, great green swards of it were by the roadside, but other strange plants – cactus-like succulents, red lupin-shaped flowers and purple proteus with large artichoke-like, flower heads. For the first time, since leaving England, I began to feel that this foreign world might not be so shockingly different and alien for me.

In the distance now, we could see the unmistakeable outline of flat-topped Table Mountain, mist curling around the top. More and more it dominated the horizon. Gradually as we got closer, Table Mountain got bigger and bigger, until it towered high above the road.

As we drove into Cape Town, the wide road skirting the lower slopes, we had no idea where we were going. Being the map reader, I directed us along the road towards the sea. As we drove towards Sea Point, long before I saw it, I could smell and breathe the salty sea air deep into my lungs. It felt like we'd come home.

'Look Pas, look! What's that over there?'

'I see the sea! I see the sea!'

Chapter 4: Cape Town - nowhere to live

I was born in Africa, but brought up in Wales, by the sea - in Swansea. The smell, the sight of it calm, rough, in sunshine or in storm, were the constant background to my life all through my adolescence, and teenage years. I had been living in London for five years prior to arriving in South Africa, and had badly missed it there. Driving into Sea Point that day, and breathing in the ozone of the sea air was exhilarating.

Nothing mattered in that instant - no money, nowhere to live, just the smell and sight of the sea. Sea Point then, was a busy, bustling place rather like a majestic European port in places, with tall pastel coloured buildings and large street cafeterias on wide pavements - all overlooking the sea - or I should say ocean. The expanse of water here was immense, this was the Atlantic, stretching across to South America, and it was vast in scope.

We drove right through Cape Town, 'The sea, the sea the sea ' sang Pascale in the back. Tall, slim, blonde, bronzed girls in tight jeans sat in the cafes. Dave's eyes were wide.

'I think I'm going to like it here', I frowned at him.

'You just watch the road, mate. There's plenty of hunky guys around too you know'

The men wandering about were large-boned, tanned and muscular. It was difficult to take in everything, the people, the mountain, the beaches. Driving towards Cape Town we had seen Table Mountain outlined first, as always imagined, with its flat top. Then we'd driven past the docks on our right and come through the city area of Cape Town. Like any other modern European city it was full of wide streets, tall glass-fronted, sky-scrapers and smart shops underneath. After passing Table Mountain on the left, we could see a sort of horn-shaped hill up ahead – the road veered left, round the base of that. Here we were in Sea Point, the sun was shining, the sea was sparkling. It was already late in the afternoon however and the sun was low on the horizon.

'Ooh look over there,' a sign said 'Bottle Store', 'I think that's like an Off Licence.' Dave grinned, 'I'm going to stop and get a cold beer.'

'More important that we stop at a phone box and find a hotel for the night,' I said. 'Look there's one over there. We haven't got enough money for beer.'

Dave looked glum, but we pulled over on the wide boulevard. Inside we leafed through the equivalent of 'Yellow Pages' at 'Hotels and boarding houses'. A hotel room for the night could cost anything from 10-15 Rand upwards and we only had R40 left. We would have to see if we could get a bank here to contact our bank in England tomorrow for more money - we had left a small amount there. But how long would it take to arrive? After a while we found a hotel, which had a room and an address near Sea Point. We rang – yes they had a double room vacant, 15 Rand (£7.50). How many nights? Oh, just one.

Following our map, we eventually drove through some large wrought iron gates up a driveway, as dusk was falling, towards a Victorian Gothic mansion - Hammer Horror could definitely have used it in their films.

This impression became compacted as the evening wore on. There seemed to be hardly any guests. A gloomy staff member in dark uniform showed us to our double room, which was large, dark, oak-panelled and had high twin beds with black ornamental iron head boards. Dave and I put down our bags and looked around at the comfortless room. We looked at each other.

'I don't like these beds.'

'We could push them together, couldn't we?' Dave suggested.

After that was done, we set up the travel cot for Pascale, and felt a bit better. We went down to eat but as we were late for dinner, there wasn't much on - soup, sausage and chips. We were alone in the dining room and sat next to a vast Victorian stone fireplace with an empty grate. The wind howled down the chimney - and we began to giggle - it was too much out of a film set to take seriously. Every time the gloomy, laconic waiter walked in, we doubled up and spluttered behind our hands. And when he left the room, we exploded with laughter. Pascale joined in, without understanding what it was about, her baby chatter and constant curiosity about her surroundings cheered us.

'Mummy, what dat noise?'

'It's the wolves howling' Dave started howling like a wolf on the tundra, 'Owoo! Owooo!'

'Shut up! You'll scare her – it's just the wind darling, makes a funny noise coming down the chimney? Eat your soup.' I gave Dave a stern look.

'You've gotta laugh though haven't you?' said Dave

'Well the situation we're in, it's either that or join in the howling,' I shook my head.

'He should ask for his money back,' Dave had a big grin on his face.

'What? Who?'

'The waiter! What he paid the charm school for that course, he should demand a refund...'

We both started laughing again.

After the meal, we carried Pas to her cot and I rocked her to sleep, holding her hand. At about 11.00 pm I went down to see if I could make a cup of tea anywhere. The staff had all disappeared. The ground floor was completely deserted - empty, dark and echoing. I groped my way to the kitchens and found the light switch. Then my heart lurched to my mouth. Beneath the long wooden table was a tin waste bin and staring at me from the bin was the head of a springbok - eyes glazed, severed at the neck from its owner. I suppose they'd had springbok on the menu recently. But why its head was in the bin staring out I never discovered. I grabbed a breadboard and a plate and a knife as supplies for our new life and fled back to our room. Looking back I don't know why I took those silly objects - a sudden panic of insecurity? Who knows? But I took them and hid them in our suitcase and felt hot and guilty next morning when we walked out with suitcases to the car.

The next day, Tuesday, we all woke early and Dave went through our options, ever optimistic:

'We've now got about R30 left. I'm going to try the bank and I'm sure they'll give me an overdraft – I'll get the job and then I'll see if they can advance me some money from my salary!'

I was more sceptical, 'Well if not, at least you can get some money transferred from home. It should get here by the end of the week? We need free accommodation for a couple of days until it comes through. Hopefully that cousin of Pieter's might be able to put us up until then. We can find a place to rent once we have money. Until then we have to live on about R5-6 a day'

I was worried, knowing that this was going to be very, very difficult.

We had no cheque books, no credit cards, nothing. There were no cash points and no quick way to transfer money then.

We called to see our contact later that day— the cousin of Pieter's. She and her boyfriend and baby, living in a converted garage - one large room and basic facilities. They were sympathetic about our predicament but they obviously had no room.

'Well', she said looking round their small living space.... I suppose we might be able to borrow some sleeping bags and you can have some floor space for a night!'

We looked at them and decided this would be too much to impose. We were now beginning to feel desperate. She said she would make a phone call, but wasn't hopeful.

While Pas and I waited there, Dave went to see a bank manager at one of the large branches in Cape Town to open a South African account. He opened the account and was allowed a temporary cheque book, but we needed an overdraft – fast. He explained what happened later. He asked to see the manager...

'You see I have an audition on Friday for the Cape Town Performing Arts Board – if I get it I'll be starting work next week and by the end of the week should have my first salary cheque. Should be a contract for 3 months ...'

'What if you don't get it?'

'I wanted to ask you to wire my bank in the UK for 1000 Rand – that will keep us for a while. And there are other theatre companies here. I'll soon get a job. I've my wife and baby to support. Could you cover us until the money arrives?'

The manager looked sceptical and then delivered a long homily on the foolishness of youth, the carelessness of foreigners coming to South Africa without proper provision etc. etc. Dave ranted and raved, coaxed and wheedled - all to no avail.

'No, it's too risky. You got yourself into this situation. You'll have to wait and see if these 'funds' come through. It will take about two weeks.'

'Two weeks!' Dave shouted – he was wringing his hands, 'But what am I going to do – we have 25 rand left? We have to get milk and nappies for the baby. We have to pay for food and hotels?'

'That's not my problem is it young man? This is a bank – not a charity!'

'I've got the money in England – it's not as if there's no money! Please I'm desperate!'

The manager gave a thin smile... 'I've said all I'm going to say now.... Good afternoon.'

He rose and walked to the door, opened it and stood waiting politely for Dave to leave.

Dave had come back from the bank his face chalk white, stamping and cursing. The situation felt desperate and I didn't know what we were going to do, but before I had time to panic, the phone rang.

Pieter's cousin had phoned a friend of a friend called Tony. It was a long shot but it appeared this friend had an apartment which he was letting out - the new people were not moving in until the end of the month. She'd got through and he'd said 'OK' without enthusiasm. It was unfurnished but we could stay there - he could find a couple of mattresses and a primus. Tony took us round there - he looked gloomy.

'I just hope the new tenants don't find out.'

'Why should they ...?'

'They've got the key and they told me they want to get a few things ready... if there's any problem, they'll go mad.'

'...but you're the owner, right?'

'Yes, well....' his voice sounded uncertain, worried.

He went off in search of mattresses, leaving us there. Sometime later a key turned in the door - a well-built, hard-looking Afrikaner couple marched in, she had red hair tied tightly back in a pony-tail and a pasty complexion, he was bald and stocky –

'Who're yew and what are you doing in our flet?'

We explained that the landlord had given us permission to stay for a couple of days until we found our own place - they stamped out in a fury saying they 'would see about thet.'

We tried to contact Tony from a nearby phone booth but without success. He turned up eventually with mattresses and primus - we made a wood fire in the large grate, put Pascale's cot in one of the bedrooms. We explained what had happened, he looked unhappy and left to see if he could contact them. Just after I got her off to sleep, the Afrikaner couple appeared again and both stormed into the main room. They were angry, boy were they angry. The man marched over to Dave and started poking him in the shoulder, his face red with rage ...

'You peepl - squatters! Pinkies! Drop-outs! Drug-addicts! Hippies!'

'You've no royt, to be here, this is ar flet, men, an yew can jus get awt, now.'

The women started shrieking at me hysterically. I tried to calm her down,

'I've just got the baby to sleep, could you speak quietly?'

She shrieked even louder bearing down on me, her face was contorted.

'Don't yew tell me what I ken and karnt do in ma own flet, or I'll stick your focking hed in the foyre, men.' I backed away and Dave moved forward shouting. The conflict was escalating until I said to Dave quietly,

'Stop! ...look I think it's better if we don't' speak, don't say anything, don't reply, just be silent'. He was angry and reluctant, but I suggested, 'just try it for a while,' and he nodded 'OK.' We both sealed our mouths tightly shut. They ranted, raved, and hurled insults for a while longer but with nothing to react to, they ran out of steam and suddenly stormed out hurling threats over their shoulders.

'Don't think yew can stay, we'll be back when we speak to Tony. You'll be out tew-noit!'

We hugged each other, shaking with relief that they'd gone and that their screaming had not, by a miracle, woken Pascale. It was plain that we couldn't stay, they'd leave no stone unturned to get us out. Dave went out to the coin box to 'phone Tony. He came round - he seemed as scared of his new tenants as we were, even though their tenancy did not start for 2 weeks. He unveiled a possible solution.

'Look I can see you're in a difficult position, and you better not stay here now, but I'll phone this friend of mine.'

Apparently this friend had a big house and let out rooms. An occupant of one of the rooms was away until Saturday - it had a double bed - we could maybe stay there. We carried Pas and our belongings out of the flat with relief. He drove us to see this guy - a lecturer in politics at the University of Cape Town. Tony handed us over with great relief, we thanked him and he disappeared - we never saw him again.

'You can use the room, until Saturday - that's four nights though I don't know what Pete will say. It's his room. You'll have to be out Saturday morning. And you'll have to pay me three Rand a night. Don't touch Pete's things though, whatever you do.'

It was still cheaper than the hotel – although the room was basic and full of someone else's things, but it was warm, dry and safe, if only for a few days. What choice did we have anyway?

We moved our stuff in, returned sleeping Pascale to her travel cot and shut the door. What a relief! We were safe from the mad aggressive Afrikaner couple. The guy who owned the house, John, gave us a key.

'You'll have to pay in advance,' he waited. 'Can you give it to me now?'

Dave rooted around in his wallet. He handed R12 over, we now had less than R20 left.

John took no further interest in us that week. But in spite of his coolness, we were grateful for a bed and fell into a long deep sleep.

Chapter 5: Finding a home

The next day we were both exhausted - Dave went to try and raise money from another bank. I lay around all day, too emotionally drained to do much. I went out and brought a few papers and went through them looking for accommodation. There was nothing. It was Wednesday; we had until Friday to find something and no money if we did find anything. That day was pretty depressing, but it was also a recovery day. We could use the kitchen, so cooked ourselves a meal that night and went to bed early. John had gone out. The next day, Dave rose early and bought the papers again. We went through them. Nothing! Everything that looked interesting was gone when we phoned up.

One place looked vaguely right - a one-bedroom terraced cottage in Mowbray. But every time I phoned, it was engaged. We had lunch - things looked bad. It was now Thursday afternoon. Saturday morning we had to be out, time was slipping away fast. I went back to the paper and looked again at the place in Mowbray. I phoned again, still engaged. Then I happened to notice an agent's advertisement had the same telephone number next to it. I looked up the agent in the phone book - there was an address,

'Dave! Look! I know it's probably hopeless but ....'

'What have we got to lose?' he shrugged.

Right! Picking up Pascale, we hurried out and drove round to the agent's offices. A young clerk at the desk was offhand.

'Oh that place in Mowbray - I think it's gone.'

My heart sank. 'You *think* it's gone? Do you know for definite or not?'

He shrugged.

'Where's your boss? I want to see the boss.' Desperation made me determined. The clerk turned to the desk behind him. A young woman looked up from her typewriter, sighed loudly, stopped typing and got up to fetch someone. The guy that came out was about 28, skinny with dark spiky hair and a loosened kipper tie round a scrawny neck. I smiled and turned on the charm full volume...

'We were interested in your ad for the place in Mowbray - is it still available?'

'Oh that place…' I looked at him without hope. He frowned, thinking about it.

'Well, it might be…' My heart leaped, I could feel Dave moving up behind me, his face alert.

'We want it and we want to move in immediately.' Dave put a hand on my shoulder and squeezed, I held my breath.

The guy laughed, taken aback.

'Oh you can't do that. You'd have to see it first.'

I looked at Dave – he nodded and turned to the guy.

'No! It's OK. We don't need to see it, it sounds fine we'll take it.'

'Well I think someone else has the key to look at it and the key might be out for the weekend.'

My heart sank again. By this time we'd followed the guy into his office. Pas sat on the floor under his desk, talking to Big Doll.

'Keep quiet! I washin' face!' She was spitting on a tissue theatrically and rubbing hard.

'What's your name? OK! Steve, can't you get hold of the owner? Ask the owner if we can have it and move in on Saturday. Look it's really important, we've just arrived in Cape Town and we have to move out of where we're staying on Saturday morning.'

'Well I don't know… we usually take about a week to sign a contract….anyway you have to see the place first, that's definite.'

'Fine!' I said impatiently, 'But there's no key.' I looked at Dave again.

'I tell you what, we'll drive over, look at the outside and look in the windows.' Dave nodded enthusiastically.

'No, no you have to look at it properly. The owner will insist on that… hmm… let me see…'

Steve was beginning to catch on to our urgency and picked up the phone. We held our breath and after several attempts, got through to the owner. The owner instructed him to get hold of the people who had the key. We waited and waited.

About 3.30 he traced the key. He would fetch it and meet us over there - we had a 3-4 mile drive to the suburb of Mowbray. After driving around suburban streets, up and down, we finally found the street.

'Look Anna, you can see Table Mountain from the front porch! It looks so close!'

I was hugging myself, thinking - I can't bear it if we don't get it.

We drove down past a short row of white-washed tiny terraced cottages on a raised ledge with iron railings in front. We met the agent and he showed us the entrance which was at the back - a little white picket gate opened onto a small walled and paved patio, with a tall avocado tree in it. It was laden with large avocados. In Britain these were a rare luxury, so we gasped in delight. A big, wooden, stable-door opened onto a large, L-shaped room - sitting room to the left, kitchenette separated by a breakfast bar on the right. There was a bathroom at right angles to the kitchen area, which ran alongside the back patio, you could see the avocado tree through the window, and of course down the corridor facing the front door - a bedroom with a window looking on to the street, next to the front door.

It was all unfurnished of course - most lettings in Cape Town were - but it was perfect for us, absolutely perfect. From the front door looking left, there was Table Mountain with hazy cloud around its summit and blue sky behind – it looked so close. The patio with the avocado tree was a perfect play area for Pascale, sunny and private and I could watch her there from the kitchen and living room.

We drove back into Cape Town, to the estate agent's office. We were so tense we couldn't speak. Steve rang the owner, the owner was out - back in half an hour. We waited, pacing the office. Pas was getting tired now, she was bored of the few toys I had with me, crawling around the office and starting to grizzle loudly.

'Mummy want bokl!' I handed her the bottle of milk I'd brought. She held it up with both hands and sucked loudly.

Steve rang again, spoke to the owner, we watched his face closely as he spoke to him.

'Wull, Mr Van der Merwe, they hev to move from where they're staying on Saturday...' Clearly the owner was reluctant to allow us to move in so quickly. We stared hard at Steve and he looked at our tense imploring faces. 'Ja! Ja! Okay sir! I'll do thet!'

Suddenly he smiled and it was as if a black cloud had lifted from the room. The owner was at last agreeing, yes we could have it, we could move in on Saturday morning. We were ecstatic!

Now we had to face the next problem, how were we going to pay? The agents wanted one month's rent in advance, plus one month's rent as deposit c. R300. We had about R20 left. Dave and I had had a quick discussion in the car on the way back from the cottage.

Dave: 'How are we going to pay?'

Me: 'Write a cheque?'

Dave: 'But it'll bounce sky high'.

Me: 'We'll have the flat and be in it before they find that out. Besides, I have a plan....'

Dave: 'OK, let's go for it, we have to. What plan?'

I explained. 'That bank manager in Cape Town – he's a big fish in a large branch, yeh? To him, we're insignificant little insects, right?'

'Yeh – fucking bastard – I tried everything to get him to see reason.'

'Well, what if we try the manager of a small branch, the local branch in Mowbray? I'll dress up, wear a skirt, lots of eye make-up, yeh? I'll just have to do my feminine bit on him - eyes full of tears and all that? What d'you think? I think it might work?'

'Well, I don't know... that wanker I saw was the top man.' Dave was stomping up and down, waving his arms about.

'Maybe that was the problem. What have we got to lose – I'll give it a go, ok?'

'Well, it's worth a bash I suppose, it might work!' The stress was beginning to damp his optimism a little.

Usually I was not in favour of this type of approach – I was not an eye fluttering, high heels and frills type of woman. I lived in blue-denim jeans and T shirts. However, desperation and pragmatism combined. If it was going to get us the money we wanted, it was a matter of survival.

Dave wrote the cheque to the agents, neither of us daring to look at the other for fear of breaking into nervous laughter. We signed the contracts, trying to contain the almost hysterical joy we felt - the new home was so perfect, so delightful, so completely what we needed and wanted, we could hardly believe our luck.

We left the estate agents and hugged each other, hugged Pascale and jumped into the car in excitement. The bank doors were shut on the way past, but when we got back to 'our room', I phoned up and made an appointment for 2:30 next day. That night I cooked pasta and cheese, with a bottle of wine to celebrate.

Dave spent the evening, going over his audition pieces; I tested him until he was word perfect, which never took him long. His audition with the Cape Performing Arts Board (CAPAB) was at 11 am. So much depended on him getting this job, without which it was hard to see how we were going to stay in South Africa at all. We hadn't got work permits yet. There was no dole, no social security and worst of all no casual manual labour. It was all done either by black Africans or by local 'Cape Coloured' people. White people were overseers or white collar workers. That was the way it worked here.

Dave had always done any kind of manual labour at home, between acting jobs, or he'd signed on the dole. Everything hung on this audition the next day - everything. The job came with a three month contract and a small but reasonable salary. The work permit situation worried us. We had a one-month holiday visa stamped in our passports. What if they couldn't give him the job without the permit? We decided that he would keep quiet about it and see if he was offered the job and then work out what to do.

In that one week, we had faced more problems than in the previous 2 years. For now though we had found a place to live and it was just right. What we wanted was to be able to buy furniture and work out how we could stop all the cheques from bouncing until we could transfer some money from the UK and the first salary instalment had come in. That's all!

Chapter 6: The kindness of three strangers

Next day Dave took the car and went off for his audition. I worried about how he was doing. He was good – I knew he was good – he'd left RADA three years before and had been working as an actor consistently since then – but all small parts, because no one would try out a young actor in the bigger parts, there were strict hierarchies and who you knew was everything. One of our main reasons for being here, was to get away from the frustration of bit parts in England – he was too good an actor, to stay stuck in those kind of roles.

Meanwhile I had to think about the next problem – furniture. Our new place had no bed, table or chairs, no kitchen equipment, no cooker, no food and we had no money. Our long term future depended on Dave getting the job. Our short term prospects depended on persuading a bank manager to advance us some money. I went through the local paper and found a second-hand furniture place in Table View, on the other side of Cape Town. I phoned them up and went through the list.... yes they had everything we needed. As soon as Dave got back, we'd go there. My bank appointment was at 2.30 in the afternoon. Meanwhile I paced up and down wondering how the audition was going. Dave had been cheerful and confident going off, but I worried about what we'd do, if he didn't get the job.

Dave returned in high spirits, the audition had gone well.

'What happened?' I asked anxiously.

He laughed, 'Wait till I tell you', he said, 'you won't believe this. They called me in for the audition and I was all ready to do my pieces. As I walked in a voice said,

'Oh hello David!' I looked over and it was this director I'd worked with on a TV drama in London, Bill something. |"Oh! Hello!" I said, "What are you doing here?" He said he'd been asked to come over and direct this production.'

'What production?' I interrupted his flow.

'Oh er 'Anthony and Cleo!'

'Anthony and Cleo? Again!'

Dave had been in an RSC production of this in England, with Janette Suzman and Richard Johnson, directed by Trevor Nunn. He'd had a small part.

'Anyway, we had a bit of a chat, he asked me to read for the part of Dollabella. "That's fine!" he said, 'I was brilliant of course and that was it, they're letting me know Monday and if I've got it, I start next week, on Wednesday!'

'Wow!' I breathed out, I'd been holding my breath, 'That sounds great. Dolabella?'

'Yeh, Dolabella's quite a nice little part, quite a few lines.'

'Do you think ..?'

'Oh yes definitely', Dave said, 'I'm pretty sure I got it. Now, what's next?' He was looking at me expectantly.

'Furniture!' I said firmly. 'Don't forget I've got to see the bank manager at 2.30!'

At which point, Pas said 'Want my dolly!' and we spent the next ten minutes hunting for Big Doll.

'No! no,no, want my dolly', she wailed, refusing to go until we eventually found her hidden under a pile of washing in a bag under the bed. Big Doll was placed in her arms. Now we could go.

We finally drove to the furniture store at around 12.30. Pascale bounced cheerfully up and down on the back seat, chatting happily to her dolly.

At the store the man was very helpful. He was older, in his forties, wearing a brown shirt and with a pencil behind his ear. He had everything we asked for; a double mattress, a small table and two chairs, a cooker, a small fridge. There was even an ancient settee/put-you-up - we had to have somewhere to sit apart from the kitchen chairs! On the way there we'd discussed the question of money, or no money to be exact.

'So, we're going to do the bouncing cheque game again?' (Me)

'Yeh ... suppose so, got no choice have we?'

'The man sounded so nice on the phone', I sighed, 'I hate to ... but you're right we've no choice.'

When it came to a crisis I was always pragmatic.

'Well as soon as the money comes through we can repay him anyway'

'Yes, of course!'

All together it came to R120.

'Can you deliver the stuff to our new place? We need it tomorrow. We're just moving in'.

I waited nervously. He looked at me straight, 'Yew kids from England? '

'Yes'.

'Well,' he laughed, 'I wouldn't loike to see you sleeping on the floorboards on your first noit, not wuth a baby. Doan worry, ma men will load up the bakkie (open-backed truck) t'noit and I'll brung it over t'morrow. What toyme d'you get there?'

'Er,' I looked at Dave...

'About 2 o'clock,' he said firmly.

'OK, I'll see yew there, and good luck hey? Un your new home, eh?'

'Thanks!' I smiled at him, feeling guilty about the cheque. Then I realised, I couldn't just write out a cheque, that I knew would bounce and then leave. Not with him being so kind. I looked at Dave and then...

'Look!', I said 'We're waiting for funds to come through from England. 'Could you hold on to the cheque for a few days before putting it in the bank?'

I was afraid he would say no, we couldn't have the furniture. I held my breath.

'OK' he said and smiled – 'Ah'll hev to trust you won't I? I'll brung it all over in the ven t'morrow.' I smiled at him with relief, glad that I'd not deceived him.

We went back to our room at the house, feeling relieved. Another hurdle had been jumped – we had a bed to sleep on and a cooker to cook on, thanks to that nice man.

The next thing was to dress up for the bank manager! Neat dark blue skirt, pretty pink blouse, eye make-up, lipstick, the works. I drove myself there and walked in. The bank manager, a middle-aged man with greying temples and a moustache, stood up and smiled as I came into his office and held out his hand. I gave him my warmest smile in return. I could see at once we were going to get on. I told him the whole story, straight, including the cheques we'd written out, knowing they would be bounced. He was absolutely charming, concerned and fatherly.

'Hmm I can see you're in a bit of a pickle, aren't you my dear?' he smiled.

'Yes, but we've got money in England – it's just going to take a few days to come through. And my husband should have a job with CAPAB, starting next week.

'Well, I'm sure we can do something. It must be difficult for new arrivals to this country and I'm always glad to help young people get started... I have a daughter about your age. I'll tell you what I'll do, I'll arrange an overdraft, let's say for about 400 Rand – that should cover you until the money arrives?'

I looked at him stunned; he was going to give us the money. After the other bank manager, I was expecting to do a lot more persuading.

'That's really great, thank you so much,' I was so grateful, there were tears in my eyes. But then I thought of another problem. 'But we opened the account at the main branch...?'

'Don't worry about that. I'll ring them and get it transferred to this branch.'

'And then there's the agents, the property agents, what about them, we gave them a cheque, the main branch might bounce it?'

'Don't worry. You can tell them, that if the cheque is bounced, to re-present it. I'll give them my personal guarantee.'

I jumped up, shook his hand and thanked him profusely. Such a contrast to the cold indifference of the other manager would have been impossible to find - a very kind man. I came out of the bank, smiling with relief and excited about giving Dave the good news. He was waiting outside in the car with Pas. He was amazed.

'Wow! I can't believe that, how did you do it?'

'Oh you know, a bit of eyelash fluttering works wonders! And he was a nice man!'

'After that other bastard.... oh that's such a relief. We're going to be OK! Yippee!'

'Yippee! Yippee', Miss Echo was bouncing up and down on the back seat! We drove back talking excitedly all the way.

Next morning, I was still cheerful when I drove to the open street market held on Saturday mornings in the centre of Cape Town – I parked in the street, opposite the market and dashed round buying cheap things for the kitchen. Parking on the street was restricted, there was a yellow line, but I was only going to be five minutes. ..

I bought three plates, knives and forks, spoons, tea-pot, mugs and a couple of saucepans - the basics. With these items in a couple of carrier bags I dashed back to the car. It wasn't there - I ran up and down looking for it and slowly it dawned on me - it was gone - it couldn't have been stolen, not today of all days, when we had to move all our stuff, within the next two hours, out of one place to another 3-4 miles away! I spoke to some people in a bus queue, no they hadn't seen it - then suddenly one remembered - a blue VW beetle had been towed away a short while ago – it would go to the car pound, a long way away - on the other side of Cape Town.

Biting my lip to hold back the tears, Dave must be worried by now, as I hadn't returned, I took the bus across to the other side of town. A woman on the bus told me where to get off for the car pound. I saw it on the other side of the street, next to some big iron gates and a long Nissan hut. Inside were lots of cars parked in rows.

I steeled myself and walked up the ramp into the hut. Inside, there was a long corridor, with a bench on one side and on the opposite side, a policeman at a desk behind a walled office with an open window. Various big burly policemen were coming in and out of several doors along the corridor. I walked over to the window, feeling desperate by now.

'My car – a blue VW Beetle – I think it was towed away.' The desk officer was indifferent. 'Ja.' He was looking down a long list. 'We hev it here – you'll have to pay the fine if you want it bek – that's thirty-fahv rend.' I looked in my handbag and was pulling everything out, no, no it wasn't there, the cheque book wasn't there. Oh my god! I realised with horror that Dave had the cheque book and I only had a few rand on me. I would have to go back, by bus to the house, collect the cheque book and return to the pound - it would take hours. For the first time that week, I felt totally defeated. All the problems we'd had to overcome that week, suddenly crowded down on top of me and exploded over my head like a thunder burst. I sat down on the bench and to my embarrassment burst into tears and sobbed. I must have made plenty of noise, because the police captain came out of one of the doors further along..

I knew little about South African police at that time, but even in the short time we'd been there I'd heard a few stories about their indifference and occasional brutality, they were not renowned for IQs or empathy. This man had stripes on his sleeve and carried himself with an air of authority. He was tall, had chiselled features and was forty-something. He took me into his office and made me sit down and tell him the whole story - it all poured out, in between tears and sobs and he listened quietly and sympathetically.

'We're moving in to our new place in Mowbray this afternoon and the man's delivering our furniture in 2 hours' time and my husband and baby are waiting for me in Rondebosch to come back, so we can drive there with all our bags....'

He stood up. 'Now don't you worry young lady...Henny, Johann!' He was striding to the door and calling two patrolmen –

'I want you to take this young lady to Rondebosch to pick up her husband ...'

I looked at him in disbelief, my eyes red, 'Do you mean ...?'

'Ja, ja, your husband ken come bek here with the money, my men will give him a lift. Yew can stay there with your baby....'

He waved away my thanks. 'Never mand all thet, just go and... good luck in your new home, eh?' He escorted me to the patrol car, ushered me in to the back seat and closed the door. Blinking back tears still, I looked at him with relief and astonishment. No, he definitely did not match the stereotype.

They drove me back to the room and I stayed there with Pas while Dave was driven to the pound with the cheque book. At the pound, he handed over a cheque for thirty-five rand which we could ill afford, but the car was returned. He arrived back nearly an hour later. Oh and I nearly forgot to mention – they didn't ask him for his licence, which was just as well under the circumstances.

We loaded the car, leaving the room behind - we never saw the house or John again, he was out when we were leaving, so I left a brief thank-you note. We drove off, to our new home in Mowbray and arrived just in time, as the furniture van pulled up a few minutes later.

That night we sat at our own table, eating a hot meal, cooked in our own kitchen and then tucked Pascale up in her travel cot in our bedroom. We were euphoric. We had our own home, our own car, good prospects of work and enough to eat. We fell onto our mattress together exhausted, happy and slept soundly. The last few weeks had been a roller coaster and at last it felt like our life here was just beginning, everything would calm down now. What a hope!

Pas and me

Chapter 7: Mowbray and a jelly fish incident

Waking up next morning, I looked around with relief. Although we had few belongings, we had a place to stay and I felt safe at last. I set about making it look like home, cleaning out the kitchen cupboards and sweeping the floors. A bright patterned cloth from our suitcase was put over the settle and soon it began to look more homely. Next would be shopping – we needed to stock up the small second-hand fridge the furniture store man had found for us and the food cupboard, with some basics.

As I cleaned, Dave went off to find provisions, while Pas played under the shade of the avocado tree, with Big Doll. While he was out, I examined our cottage more closely – the L-shaped room, one side of which was the kitchen with a breakfast bar in front. The old settle filled the other side, it faced the door and the window looking over the small paved patio. At the bottom of this small paved area was a low white picket fence with a gate in the middle. On the left side of the patio was the avocado tree. The tree was laden with avocados, some already large. Such luxury!

On the other side of the apartment, if you stepped outside the front door and looked left, Table Mountain seemed near enough to touch almost, just a trick of the bright, clear African light. You couldn't see the flat top from here, just a hazy peak and high above it, blue sky.

Also outside the front door, was a tiny narrow raised-above-the-road porch with black cast iron railings, which continued on in front of the other three cottages in our row. We rarely used that door.

The back door however, which opened from the living area onto the small paved patio was always open. Although winter was slowly tailing into spring, the weather was mild in late August, temperatures 18—20C mostly.

When Dave got back he made toast and bacon and eggs for a late breakfast, while I finished off as much unpacking as I could. We still had nowhere to keep our clothes except the suitcase. We sat down at our little table, smiling and chatting about our plans.

After the weekend, Dave rang CAPAB and found out he'd got the contract and soon he was off all day rehearsing Anthony and Cleo. Sandra Prinsloo was playing Cleopatra this time, not Janet Suzman who had played the part in the film production in England. Generally the lead stars did not mix with those in the smaller parts. There was an unwritten but clearly demarcated hierarchy.

Meanwhile, I spent the days at home with Pascale who was now nearly two. Dave came home every night excited and stimulated, with funny stories about the other actors.

Mowbray was a small suburb about 2-3 miles from the centre of Cape Town. I could see, from walking around the area, that black and coloured people apparently did not live locally. If you saw them emerging from a house, the women were alone and wore headscarves tied at the back of the head. Black women tended to be short and stout with brightly coloured wraps around their sturdy bodies. Coloured women wore faded T shirts, lacy cardigans and skirts, but also the headscarves. They were nannies or domestic servants and the white South Africans called them 'maids'....'ma maid this,' 'ma maid that,' peppered their conversations. Sometimes you saw the 'maids' carrying their own babies on their backs – they were tied on with a large cloth – two ends of the cloth were tied above the bust and two lower down at waist level securing the babies legs and feet. You often saw women stopping to rearrange the whole bundle. I wondered what it would be like to carry Pas like that, but she was too heavy now. The little, stripy, fold-up umbrella pram was light, easy to push and take everywhere. I also discovered from talking to people we met that many of these 'maids' had their own children living with a relative in a rural township – often they only went home to see them once a month, travelling many hours on public transport to get there and back. I tried to imagine what it would be like, to see my child only once a month and puzzled over why white friends only gave their 'maids' such limited time off. It seemed to be just the way things were and no one questioned it, if you tried, you were met with puzzlement – it was what 'they' were used to. Besides, who would look after their children if the maid was away too often?

I heard that most areas that had once been mixed race were now 'whites only'. Mowbray was one of these and had been 'separate' for some time. It was not what we wanted, but there was little choice. We had to live somewhere for now.

Most of the houses in Mowbray were one storey bungalows with a small, wooden front 'stoep' or veranda, where you could sit out. In our row of cottages, with the stoep at the front, no one in the row used them - we all trotted round the back and visited each other there.

One evening I heard chanting and strange singing behind our cottage. Strolling out to investigate and make enquiries, I found a small mosque close by – every Friday and Saturday you would see a stream of brown faces going in to the small mosque and then the sounds of chanting and worship could be heard clearly in our front room. It was very soothing. I've always enjoyed the sound of chanting.

I was curious about the machinery of apartheid and what any new acquaintance made of it all, so asked when I got the chance. I hoped people were as opposed to it as we were, or it was difficult to see how we could all be friends. But we were wary of how to approach the topic at first.

Some days when Dave was rehearsing, Pas and I would drive to Sea Point to one of the beaches, taking a few snacks and a drink. This was winter in Cape Town and when we went to the beach we'd sit there, in grand solitude. South Africans probably thought we were mad, but coming from England, temperatures in the mid-sixties seemed warm enough.

One particular day, while Dave was at rehearsals, I decided to drive to the beach. Pascale need to be out in the fresh air and besides I wanted to get a closer look at the beaches I'd glimpsed just past Sea Point, on our first day in Cape Town. The road from Mowbray was a dual carriageway that skirted round the lower slopes of Table Mountain on the left. We swung past the docks on the right and the centre with its modern skyscrapers and shops. Then the road swung left, down into the wide streets of Sea Point and its tall pastel buildings along beside the ocean.

Just beyond Sea Point, I could see a beach on my right and found a place to park along the front. We walked down onto Clifton beach, a small sandy cove with white sand and rocky outcrops on both sides. I held Pascale's chubby little hand tight, in her other hand she clutched her bucket. As we walked across the sand, we could see that the rocky areas had pools of water – ideal for crabbing. My childhood summers had been spent with my brother and sister and cousins on the beaches of West Wales turning over rocks and collecting crabs, poking bright red anemones and chasing small catfish, which we rarely caught. Here was my chance to show Pascale some of the sea life on a rocky shore.

We paddled around, our trousers rolled up to the knees, lifting stones and watching small crabs scuttle sideways and catching one or two to put in her bucket. I saw a small blue balloon-like sac lying in the water near the rocks at the water's edge and went over to investigate it. I gave it a poke, but couldn't work out what it was and glanced up to call Pas who was busy looking into another pool a few yards away. She was calling

'Look, Mummy look! Wat dis?'

No one else was about on that stretch of beach. I moved across the pool towards her and my ankle brushed a long stringy thin blue thread which was floating across the water. Suddenly, searing pain shot up my leg and I bit my lip hard to stop myself from screaming out – my eyes were watering and I knew I had to get back to the sandy area fast and sit down and work out what to do. I must not above all, frighten Pascale. I grabbed her hand and said 'Come on baby' – she was resisting and saying 'No, no look mummy', pointing into the rock pool, but I just pulled her along and sat heavily on the sand.

I handed her the spade and said (between gritted teeth) 'Dig a hole for the crabs, baby,' sweat appearing on my forehead. Luckily, she didn't notice and quickly absorbed herself in this task, giving a running commentary.

'Dig hole, dig, dig. Now I put crabs in Mummy?'

I was now looking wildly up and down the beach for help. If this white hot pain continued, I would need help, but no one was near. I was rocking back and forth, clutching my leg trying not to moan out loud. I wondered if I would die and what would become of Pascale.

'Get some water in your bucket baby, from that pool, put it in the hole.' I managed to control my voice to speak.... For twenty minutes I sat there rocking, my vision misted with pain, my face sweating, while Pascale chatted and poked at her crabs in the hole.

'Mummy, look mummy, crabs go way, crabs get out, quick Mummy help get crabs.'

I felt helpless and terrified and could not respond except to nod and say

'In a minute, darling.' Gradually, after what seemed like aeons, I realised that the pain was subsiding. After a while, I was able to stand up at last.

'Come on Pas we're going home now.'

'No Mummy no, want crabs. Take home!'

'No darling the crabs live here, they have to go back in the sea now.'

I was exhausted by the pain and fright, but we took the crabs in a bucket to the nearest rock pool and tipped them in, Pascale shouting and pointing as they scuttled for cover.

Somehow, I got us to the car and we drove back to Mowbray, where I lay down on the settle breathing hard, but greatly relieved to be still alive and to have got Pas home safely. The pain was nearly gone now.

Later, when Dave got back from his rehearsals and Pas had gone to bed I told him all about it

'I wonder what stung you?' He came up and put his arms round me, sympathetically.

'I don't know, but I thought I was going to die on the beach and leave Pas on her own. It was horrible!'

'Well you're fine now...aren't you?'

'Oh yes, just a red mark on my leg, doesn't really hurt now!' I was bending down prodding it.

'Well, guess what happened in rehearsals today...'

....and soon he was telling me stories about the other actors, having me in fits of laughter, Robert the camp gay hatter, the lead actors and how they behaved as if they were something special and kept themselves apart from the more junior actors. And the nice actress called Pam, older than us, who was very down to earth and good fun. Dave was having a ball.

Although I loved to hear his stories and laughed and enjoyed them all, in some ways they only highlighted my isolation. Having only a toddler for company was not enough. Now that the excitement and drama of our journey had calmed down and life had fallen into a routine there was little to stimulate me in the daytime. I must somehow find friends of my own, adults to spend time with while Dave was at rehearsals. And he told me they were going on tour after the three week run in Cape Town. What would I do alone, while he was away?

Pas outside our front door. Table Mountain behind.

Chapter 8: CAPAB and meet the neighbours

Quite soon after we had moved in, Peter called by to investigate the new neighbours. He lived at the end of the four cottages, was about 6'4" tall, with shoulder length dark hair and beard.

I told him about the incident on Clifton beach.

'Ow! Sounds like you got stung by a Portuguese man-o-war! It's a jellyfish with a blue sac and a long tail! Nasty sting! You find them in rock pools.'

'Well, I thought I was a gonner, the pain was AWFUL!'

'Ja, their sting is very bad – it can even kill you I've heard in extreme cases.'

'Wow.' I looked down at my leg again, at the pink weal which throbbed faintly and thought thank God the tendril hadn't touched Pascale.

Dave filled up the kettle and lit the gas below, 'I'm just glad you and Pas got home safe. You got a nasty fright!'

I offered Peter a cup of tea - 'Have you got Rooibos?'

'No, what's that?'

'We drink it here - red bush – it grows all over the bush – I'll bring you some.'

'Great! You want ordinary tea now?' He smiled and nodded.

Dave explained that he was an actor, working for CAPAB and that he was writing a book . . .

'It's fantasy fiction - about an ordinary guy called Wilf, who works in a clerical job in London, he gets taken in to outer space and saves the Universe. I'll show you some later.'

I handed Peter his mug of tea. 'It's really good, get him to read you some. I love hearing the story out loud.'

Fantasy fiction had been all the rage since everyone started reading 'Lord of the Rings' in the late sixties and early seventies. I had read it three times. Peter's eyes lit up at the mention of writing,

'I write poetry, would you like to read some? I'll show you. I've started writing a play called 'Goldfields of South Africa'.

I'll bring it over later – maybe we can write some stuff together', he looked at Dave.

Dave laughed, 'And maybe we can share something else too.' He winked at Peter.

'I'll roll us a joint to help us think,' he was smiling. 'I got a little bit from one of the actors.'

Dave had been renowned in London for rolling joints about five inches long. I gave him a look...

'Don't worry, we'll be careful.' Dave looked at Peter. 'You like Red Leb?'

Peter had a big grin on his face. 'Good stuff, but my home-grown grass is better. I'll bring some over...later.'

'Only a little,' I added. 'Just remember, they put you in prison here for having a little bit of dope.'

'Yeh, I'll have to stash it somewhere.' Dave was looking around vaguely.

'I put mine in a tin, outside in a small hole.' Pete was watching Dave's large joint being put together and his smile grew wider. 'You can't keep it in the house.'

'That's a good idea.' I knew there was no way to stop Dave smoking dope and besides most people our age smoked it. The general consensus was that it made you 'mellow' and had a better effect than alcohol. I'd tried it myself and then stopped after a bad experience. Besides I didn't like the way it made me feel dopey for several days. 'I'll find a place outside,' thinking of a spot in a hole high up in the avocado tree ...

After that Peter became a regular visitor and gradually he explained to us that he had to have monthly injections for schizophrenia and had had phases of hospitalisation in the local mental institution, Valkenberg hospital. We had known a close neighbour in England with this condition, so had an idea what to expect. We knew it was important for him to keep taking his medication or he might start to behave strangely.

Peter and Dave's friendship soon developed - they were both bright, with a shared creative talent and would discuss ideas for writing stories late into the night. Peter often wrote a poem spontaneously in beautiful script and then handed it to me or Dave. I would pour over the poem and ponder about it, asking questions, but his answers were usually vague and enigmatic. His poetry reminded me of my favourite poet – Dylan Thomas – I had a picture of him on the wall, a cartoon drawn by a friend in Wales whose parents had known him well - it transpired that Peter was also a great fan.

One night, after we'd been there only a few weeks, I asked Peter about apartheid - I wanted to know more about how it operated here.

'Peter, we saw how it worked in Jo'burg – separate toilets, that sort of thing. It seems to be the same here too, right?'

'Ja, it's the same - take the beaches ...'

'I haven't seen any black people on the beaches I've been too.' I said, 'but it's winter so....'

'Well Sea Point and Clifton are beaches for whites only.'

'Separate beaches', I was astounded, 'No! Shit! Really? What about where people live, round here for example?'

'What do you mean?'

'Well I see black people walking about in Mowbray, but they don't seem to live here.'

He sighed, 'You have to understand, the government is Afrikaaner run, they brought in the Group Areas Act a few years ago – many Cape Town suburbs were mixed, every-one got on fine, but now... Any blacks in mixed areas have had to move out to townships like Guguletu and Langa, the Coloureds to Manenberg and Wynberg and other places. There aren't many parts of Cape Town left where different races can live together.'

'Which ones are left?' I was looking at Dave and thinking how we might move to one of these. We didn't want to stay in an all-white suburb, where black or coloured people were banned from living - the thought appalled me.

'Well there's a few left - District Six was the biggest – it's in Cape Town but they've been moving everyone out. Some to the Cape Flats. They're building a big new township for coloureds now on Mitchell's Plain.'

'Where's that?' He gestured vaguely to the east – 'about 10-20 kilometres away'.

'But, don't people work in Cape Town?'

'Ja, and in the suburbs.'

'… and they go by bus or train?'

He shrugged, 'Transport's segregated too.'

'What!' I was shocked, we hadn't used public transport yet as we had the car. 'How?'

'Well they have some carriages for only whites, and some for the blacks and coloureds.'

'Bloody hell!' Dave was just passing the large joint he'd made to Peter, who took a big draw. 'Good stuff Dave.'

I got up to make a cup of tea and then heard a little cry from the bedroom down the corridor. 'Mummy, mummy!'

'OK baby, Mummy's coming!' I hurried down to the bedroom.

'What baby?' I opened the door to find a wide awake child, standing up in her cot with arms lifted out to me, and a big wail rising.

'All right darling, shush, sh, sh, shoosh. I'll get you a bottle. Did you have a bad dream?' Now she was in my arms and getting a cuddle she was calming down. I groped around for her dummy that had fallen out of the cot and carried her out to the kitchen, with her legs wrapped around my waist and her arms around my neck. Then, sitting her on the kitchen surface next to me, I stuck the dummy under the tap and put it in her mouth. She sucked it, while I mixed her up a bottle of milk with hot water and milk. Dave came over and tickled her until she was shrieking with laughter, as I ran a cold tap over the bottle to cool it to the right temperature. She didn't have many bottles now – just one at night when she needed it.

'OK back to bed you!' I smiled at her and lifted her up, placing her on my hip and handed her the bottle. As we walked back down the corridor, I heard Dave ask,

'So what's the difference between black and coloured?'

'Well the Cape has a large population of mixed races, the coloureds have their own townships and they don't really mix with the blacks.'

'Why not, why don't they mix?'

He shrugged again, 'I suppose the coloureds feel closer to the whites and the government has encouraged it, by promising to give them a bit more political power. Besides the blacks have their tribes.'

'But where did the coloureds come from?'

'From the early sailors mixing with the local tribal women and workers from India and Malaya, workers brought in by the Dutch East India Company and the English and Germans. The Dutch called them 'Hottentots.'

I put Pascale back in her cot and stroked her face for a minute, while she sucked her bottle. Her eyes were closing and she turned over. I crept quietly from the room.

Peter was saying, 'They string the Coloured leaders along with talk of 'power-sharing' to keep them happy, but don't give them much.'

'Why do they make people live in townships?' I re-joined the conversation, while putting the kettle on in the kitchen area.

'Well, if there's trouble the police can seal off the townships quickly and keep them away from the white areas. There's usually one entrance to each township and so it's easy for the police to close it fast.'

'So what it boils down to,' Dave was pouring a beer into a glass, 'is that the whites are afraid of the revolution. 'Have a beer Peter?' who was nodding.

'Ja, thanks!' Pete swigged out of the bottle, 'Cheers! Ja! That's about it. You see the whites are a very small number compared to the blacks – there's only about 5 million.

'And how many blacks?' I asked

'About 20 million!' He smiled and took another swig from the bottle.

'Jesus!' Dave was rolling another joint, 'There's going to be a blood-bath one day.'

Peter shrugged. 'Obviously apartheid's not right, but the Cape's English speaking and liberal. Most people here don't want apartheid. What can we do? The government's run by Afrikaaners. Have you read the Cape Times yet?'

'No! Haven't had time to read a paper.' Dave was licking along the seam of another joint and sticking it down.

'You should get it. It's the only paper worth reading, the only one that stands up to them... censorship's heavy here. And we've got a good liberal MP in Cape Town – Helen Suzman – she and a few others try and fight against this stuff. But it's dangerous. The Afrikaners have a stranglehold on the government. If you make too much of a noise, the secret police start watching you. They're everywhere, they've got spies all over. If you're not careful you get picked up and end up in prison.'

'What on Robben Island like that Mandela guy? I heard about that place.'

'No, that's for the blacks and coloureds! The whites go to Polsmoor!'

'Oh really, I should have guessed! So where exactly is Robben Island?'

'Next time you go to Sea Point, look out to the South East – it's there, you can see it across the water - they keep politicals and criminals together. You can bet they don't treat them too good either. That guy got 25 years I think, that Mandela guy. They said he was plotting to start a revolution, that he's a terrorist.'

'And is he?'

'I don't know, I doubt it – they only give us their version of what's happening. Apartheid is everywhere. Not just the beaches, restaurants, theatres, trains, even park benches...'

'No!' My voice was a whisper now. 'You're joking?'

'No really, they even have park benches for 'Whites only' – you go to that park about a mile from here, you'll see them....'

'No thanks. I'm not going there.'

Dave and I looked at each other. What have we landed ourselves in, I thought to myself. What can we do to avoid being sucked in to this whole apartheid thing? When we'd left UK we'd heard about apartheid, but not that often, we hadn't absorbed the reality of it. It sometimes popped up in the UK media and sometimes you heard of demos outside the South African Embassy. Equity, the actor's union had been talking about banning actors from working in South Africa, but hadn't before we left. Before coming, Dave and I had resolved that Pascale should not grow up thinking some people could be treated differently because of skin colour. But if we lived here, it was going to be difficult once she went to school.

Dave went to the fridge and took out two more bottles of cold beer – he handed one to Pete. 'Well I didn't realise when I started, but most of our shows'll be in theatres in Cape Town with whites-only audiences. And the casts are all white, although when we go on tour in a few weeks, we'll be doing some shows in the black townships.'

'Yeh, that's because CAPAB's funded by the government,' said Pete. 'Apartheid is strictly enforced in the Arts too.'

'God, Dave! You can't stay in that company for long.' I was shocked at the reach of apartheid into every facet of life.

'I know, I'll do my three month contract and then see if I can find a mixed-race theatre group. I don't want to stay longer than I have to. For now though, it's our bread and butter.'

A week later, Peter brought his friend Steve to meet us. Steve was mid-20s, 5'9", wiry, intense and he had two sons Storm and Georgie. Storm was a few months older than Pascale, but Georgie was about nine months old. Storm and Pas got on well - it was great for her to have the occasional playmate at last. As Steve visited Peter regularly and often brought the kids, he became a regular visitor and Storm and Pascale became good playmates. They played together in the back patio while Steve and I chatted and drank rooibos. Steve and I hit it off at once and soon we were chatting like old friends, talking about every subject under the sun.

Soon after, while the kids were playing outside, Steve started to tell me a bit about himself and Lily,

'....you see after Storm was born, she kind of handed him over to me and I did the bottle feeding, nappy changing routine and then she was pregnant with Georgie again by the time Storm was 15 months old. Once he was born, she lost interest, didn't feel well and so I looked after them.

One day I went to get some money from our joint account and found it was all gone. When I asked her about it, she told me she needed some shoes for her modelling – she bought <u>ten</u> pairs. I went mad but she told me to 'fuck off, stop making such a fuss'. What could I do?'

I thought of a few things but kept them to myself. From what he was saying, it seemed that Lily was not keen on the mothering role – she largely left daily child care to Steve.

A week later, Lily came with him and stayed for a cool drink while Steve went to visit Peter. She was about 6 foot tall, slim, long blonde hair with striking looks. She had some of her professional modelling photos with her and showed me as we were chatting. Lily had a powerful presence, but an aloof manner, which made me a bit nervous around her.

'Wow! You look so fab! Just like Jerry Hall!'

'Oh thanks, everyone says that.'

'And do you get work, as a model I mean?'

'Oh yes, some,' she took a sip from her cold drink. 'I'd like more though, I'm a bit tied down with the kids.'

I thought about what Steve had told me but kept quiet. After a while she went to get Steve and he gathered up the boys, who were playing with Pas under the avocado tree.

Peter had told me that he, Lily and Steve were followers of a guru, an Indian Spiritual Master called Charang Singh and they had been 'initiated' and were called Satsangis. I was curious about their devotion to this guru – I was looking for a way to express my own spiritual beliefs and next time I saw Steve, I asked him questions about it, while the kids were playing outside.

'So what do you have to do to be a Satsangi?'

I was wondering what it would be like to join their group. I wanted more than conventional Christianity had to offer, a new spiritual focus.

'Well you have to stop eating meat.'

I'd never liked preparing or dealing with meat, so that would be all right.

'And fish and eggs and cheese'.

Whoa, I thought. That's taking it too far, I can't do that!

'Anything else?'

'Yes you have to meditate for one and a half hours a day and go to regular weekly study meetings. You can come along to an intro session if you like?'

'OK', I was wary. 'But it sounds quite heavy?'

Steve sighed, 'Yeh, 'specially with kids.' Georgie started howling right on cue – Storm had taken his bucket …Steve went out and got the bucket back for Georgie.

'Sounds a bit much for me, but I'd like to learn to meditate.'

'Well that's easy … ask Peter, he'll teach you.'

Steve and I had long talks about the teachings of his Swami and about spirituality in general. My Irish grand-mother had sent her children to Roman Catholic schools and my mother had followed suit – my brothers were taught by monks and me and my sister by nuns. I wanted to move away from the constrictions of my Catholic upbringing and explore other spiritual paths. The Beatles had led the way by following the teachings of the Mahareshi Mahesh Yogi and his teachings on Transcendental Meditation.

* * *

Life in Mowbray continued. Dave went to daily rehearsals and I stayed at home with Pas. We went for drives, went to small parks with swings, did the shopping or I cleaned the house. But apart from Peter and Steve, I knew no one and felt like everything was alien. I missed my family and friends in London and felt incredibly homesick.

I needed some friends of my own and I began to think about finding a nursery school for Pas as a way to give me some freedom and to meet other mothers.

Chapter 9: Unwanted guests and Angel

One morning, not many weeks after we'd moved into our new home, I was pottering around in the kitchen, wiping surfaces, putting things away. I was never a morning person, I have to have some tea and move about before I can fire on all cylinders. That doesn't happen much before 11. Pas was still in the bedroom playing with her dolly. I could hear her chatting way...

'Naughty dolly, sit down! Drink dis! (Clinking of dolly cup and teapot).... 'if you naughty, you get a smack!'

I peeped round the door grinning to myself. Pas liked smacking dolly when she was 'naughty'. You'd think (watching) that she had cruel parents who beat her - dolly got hard smacks quite a lot!

I made my tea and washed up a few dishes. Then I bent down to the cupboard to get some cornflakes out for our breakfast. As I put my hand on the top of the packet, something large and black leapt off the top and I gave a blood-curdling scream. I should mention that I was spider-phobic - severely. Being in a room alone, with a spider, usually caused me to freeze with utter terror. If it moved, I felt complete panic. This one had moved FAST. I ran out of the door yelling, 'Dave!' He had gone down to Peter's, to work with him on their play 'Goldfields of South Africa'– over a few joints no doubt. He and Peter appeared at the gate and ran in, thinking to find me with a machete through my skull at least. Pas appeared at the door to her bedroom, shouting 'Mummy, mummy what hap'd!'

When I had calmed down sufficiently, I'd sent Pas back to her room to play.

'It's all right darling, nothing to worry about, just a silly spider... ', I explained to Peter and Dave what I'd seen, 'It was a huge black spider, big as my hand and it jumped out of the cornflakes, must be still in the cupboard', I was gasping and shuddering.

Peter looked dubious, 'Are you sure it was a spider? Sounds more like a cockroach to me?'

'No, I've seen cockroaches, they don't come THAT big, no it must have been a spider...'

Dave and Peter went to the cupboard I was pointing to (from a safe distance). Peter pulled everything out and then reached in and pulled his hands out, cupped together.

He grinned as he walked calmly out the door and down the path:

'Not a spider – it's a cockroach', he said over his shoulder. He dropped it outside the gate and then stamped on it, hard...

'No, no,' I whispered to myself. 'Don't kill it, I can't bear to kill it,' but it was too late. I looked over the gate, shuddering – the cockroach was huge – about three inches long and an inch across, I was aghast that that thing had been in my food cupboard.

However as time passed, it became painfully obvious that this cockroach was not alone. There was a colony of them living in our apartment. And I had to overcome my squeamish feelings, about not wanting them dead. They never appeared during the day, only at night, when the lights were out. I suppose I must have become gradually desensitised from my phobia or I never could have slept at night. Dave and I had to adopt a set procedure before we went to bed. Pascale would be asleep in her cot in the bedroom, at around 7 pm. Her cot was one side of the room, our double bed was on the other. We would go to sleep around midnight.

'You ready – got your flip-flop ready?'

Dave would wave it at me, smiling grimly. I would be standing outside the door to the bedroom. It was my job to whip open the door really fast and put my hand round the corner and flick on the light switch. It was his job, to leap into the room with the flip-flop and start beating the scattering cockroaches, who the moment the lights went on would start running for cover from the centre of the room where they seemed to congregate. Every night he would get about eight to ten cockroaches and these were all big ones two to three inches long. I would fetch the dustpan and brush and hand it to Dave who would sweep them up and take them outside, right outside the garden gate and dump them on the roadside or in the car park outside. I insisted, they had to be way out of our territory. But no matter how many he got, a new group would be back the next night.

Something had to be done after a week or so of this. One Sunday, when Dave was at home, I knocked on our next-door neighbour Jane's door to explain the situation. I'd not really had a chance to chat to her when we'd passed on the way to our homes, as she was usually dashing to or from work. It was morning and Dave was half asleep and Pas was in bed next to him playing with a few toys.

The door was opened by a young woman a few years older than me – about twenty-seven, wearing an exotic head-scarf wrapped around her head and a yellow silk dressing gown.

'Hi, I'm Di,' she smiled warmly. 'Come in. Jane's not here but she'll be back soon, gone to get a paper and a few things. Would you like some tea, just made a cup?'

'Great!' I stepped inside, '... you've got an English accent? Where're you from?'

'Well, Kent originally, but I haven't lived there for a few years. Been living in Kenya.'

'Oh, how interesting. What made you go there?'

'Well I had an aunt who lived there originally, but one of my cousins still lives there. I'm actually a florist, same as Jane...that's how we met, working together years ago in London.'

'I didn't know Jane was a florist?'

'Yes she works at the Mount Nelson, it's one of the smart-est hotels in South Africa. It's down near Sea Point.'

We had sat down on a rather elegant cream sofa and as Di poured some tea I looked around the room. Jane's place was immaculate. Small fragile glass ornaments were on low tables and shelves, cream rugs were on the polished wood floor. I was glad that Pas was not with me. Also it didn't look like the sort of place ever to have a cockroach problem.

Di was scratching her bare legs, which seemed to have a lot of red weals on them.

'God what happened to your legs?'

'Oh, it's the Cape fleas – my legs are a mess with all the bites.'

'Oh! Is that what they are? We've all had some bites on our legs, we thought they were mozzie bites.'

Di sighed. 'I keep dabbing them with calamine, but they still itch like crazy. 'Anyway, tell me – how did you come to be here?'

Soon I was telling Di all about myself and we were chatting and laughing. I liked her at once, she was warm, down-to-earth, direct and full of fun. Then the door opened and Jane walked in. Her brown hair curled under and she was slim and attractive, smartly dressed. She had perfect nails, I noticed, making me look at my own ragged broken ones.

I stood up nervously. 'Hi Jane, I was just going actually - just popped round to ask what to do about the cockroaches, they're terrible in our flat.' I told her about our nightly ritual. Jane shook her head, 'There's not much you can do really except call in the pest control guys. I get them every 6 months. When they come here I go out and stay out all day - the fumes.'

'Sooo ... how much do they charge?'

'Oh about thirty or forty rand or so.' She was matter-of-fact.

'Quite a lot then.' In my head I was thinking - We can't afford it. We'll have to find some other way to deal with them. But what?

'Yes everyone along here gets it done, at least once a year.'

'Well, I'll have to see. Anyway it was nice to meet you and if either of you feel like popping next door for a chat? Always got a cup of tea going! Or a glass of wine, be lovely to see you!'

At least I've made some new friends, I thought to myself. I'd really liked Di in particular, she was fun. Jane might take a while to get to know as she was more reserved. I 'spose, I thought, we'll have to put up with the cockroaches for a while - can't pay out that kind of money.

One night, a few weeks later we went through the usual procedure, light switch, flip-flop, beating them to death on the floor. This time one of them in its panic to run away, ran straight up Dave's trouser leg. His face registered a split second of horror.

'Oh No! Oh my God it's going up my leg!' Then he was frantically fumbling with his flies and his trousers were off in a split second. Then he was jumping up and down in his boxers shouting, 'Eurrrgh! No!' batting at his legs!

* * *

Di became a regular visitor after that first meeting. She frequently dropped by and told me about her training as a florist and bits about her past life.

'I trained with Pulbrook and Gould in Bond Street, London – I used to go round the stately homes doing their flower displays.'

'God what a great job! I love flowers – I don't suppose you'd arrange some for me would you?'

She looked around the small kitchen/living area, 'Well OK. But I'll have to go out and cut some grasses and blossom. Uh! The flower arranging here.' She made a face.

'What in Cape Town?'

'No in South Africa, everywhere you go that's all you see - fucking triangles.'

'What are you talking about?'

'Flower arranging here – you look – anywhere you go, look at the shape of the display, God – so dated. Awful!'

I was laughing at her vehemence. And I'd not heard Di swear before.

'It's true,' she was laughing too. 'Here take a look at this magazine I bought today – same thing – triangles, triangles, fucking triangles.'

'I think I get the idea how you feel about 'fucking triangles!'

Di was laughing. 'Well I'm going now, but I'll pop back in a few hours to do you a display.'

Later, she came back with armfuls of hedge grasses, bits of shrub, small branches covered in blossom, clumps of leaves of various shades of green and a few roses she had bought. She pulled out her secateurs, stripped the stems and chopped off the bases, hit the last inch of each with a rolling pin and flung together, within a couple of minutes the most magnificent floral display I had ever seen in my life, which she placed on my kitchen table. I stood in awe of this amazing vision.

'Oh Di! They are absolutely fantastic I feel so spoilt. Well you can come anytime!' I said smiling.

A few weeks later, Di told me that she'd had a baby son when she was very young and he had been adopted. We were watching Pas rolling out some pink play dough I'd made for her. She was cutting out shapes while we chatted.

'Do you still think about him then?' I asked.

'Every day,' she looked at me, 'every day.' I felt sad for her, I couldn't imagine having to make such a decision at such a young age.

Sometimes Pas understood more than we realised, she must have been looking at Di's face.

'Look Di-di, I made you a doggie, coz you sad.' She handed Di a pink cut-out shape, vaguely dog-like. Pascale surprised us at times making observations about people and their emotions that most adults wouldn't notice.

Di smiled at her, but her eyes were bright with tears.

'Thanks darling,' she patted Pas's head.

'I couldn't have kept him,' she looked at me, 'I was so young – only 17, so was the father, I just couldn't do it, not then.'

'How terrible,' I said, putting my hand out to touch her arm and thinking, how can you go through something like that? Such an awful choice to make. But Di was amazingly pragmatic. She had talked it through with her parents and made a decision that was, they all felt, best for her and best for her baby.

'Well,' she said, getting up briskly. 'I must be off - so much to do, I'll see you tomorrow probably. Bye Pas, bye Anna'.

When Dave came back from rehearsals that evening, he noticed the flower display at once. It was so large, colourful and exuberant, it cheered the room up. I told him about Di and the baby. He had rolled a joint by now and was sitting back puffing it. I was stirring a large pot of stew, made with a ham hock and vegetables.

'That's sad', he was reflective. 'Giving up your baby – how can you do that?'

'Well I think she and her parents thought it was the only way, as she was so young.'

Dave was shaking his head and then changed the subject.

'They're taking Anthony and Cleo on tour soon. I'll be going away with them of course, so you and Pas will be on your own for a bit.'

I put a large bowl of the thick soup on the table for him. 'For how long?'

'About 4 weeks I think... It'll go quick don't worry.' I must have looked upset as he came over and put his arms round me.

'I don't want you to go away,' I said sadly, 'I'll be lonely, I'll have Pas but it's not the same.'

'Yeah, I'll miss you too – loads. Maybe we should get a dog for extra security, while I'm away.'

'A dog, what sort of a dog?'

'Anything. What about a puppy?'

'Well I don't know...' I pushed my soup away, I'd lost my appetite at the thought of Dave being gone for a whole month. I didn't want to think about it, I hardly knew anybody, what was I going to do with my time?

'Maybe a dog would be company too, I s'pose. Not any type of dog. I quite like bull terriers. They're kind of ugly but beautiful.... really short hair, so they don't moult all over the place and they're good guard dogs. My uncle used to have one, a white one - something like that perhaps.'

A few days later, I picked up a local newspaper and turned to the back pages, looked at the Pet's column and there it was, '...bull terrier cross puppies for sale to good homes, six weeks old'. When Dave got back that night, I showed him the advert. We rang and made an appointment for the next day, to see the pups. The woman said,

'... but they not pure bred, that's why ah'm selling them a but cheaper. They got a but of Ridgebek in them, OK? '

'OK,' I said not having the faintest idea what she was talking about. I saw Peter later and asked him.

'Oh Rhodesian Ridgebacks – they're these huge hairy dogs with the hair on their spines growing the wrong way - they often have them on farms, good guard dogs!'

Pas was very excited. I tried to tell her we might not get one, not today anyway but she ignored this.

'I want puppy, I want puppy,' she kept saying all the way there.

The Afrikaans woman showed us to a room at the back of her neat house, where the puppies were all scrambling over each other to get at the mother-dog's teats. I wanted a female, because it was likely to be gentler and more sweet-tempered which is important when you have a small child. The one we liked straightaway was white with a black patch over one eye and one black paw. I picked her up, the little legs scrambling in the air and told Pas to sit down on a chair. Now she could hold the little wriggling thing ... the puppy nuzzled into Pas's shoulder, and then curled up and went to sleep. She was captivated. Dave and I negotiated a price that we probably couldn't afford but somehow we would manage. The woman said we could take her home straight away, but we must keep her inside for a few more weeks until she'd had her injections. Pascale was ecstatic and we put the puppy next to her on the back seat of the car, where it sniffed around then curled up and went to sleep.

I'd read a book about a dog, called 'Angel' , set in Australia and therefore as our puppy with her pink eyes, pointed nose and black eye-patch looked more devilish than angelic I suggested we call her 'Angel'. I'd also got a book called 'How to Care for Your Puppy' from the library. It suggested in one of the early chapters that a wooden cage be obtained to keep your puppy safe at night (and your furniture intact). Dave was quite good at making things and next day he went out and got some wood. Then he constructed a large wooden hut with a wire-mesh front. We made it cosy with a warm blanket on one side, dried food and water in the middle. There were newspapers at the other end. We put the hut on our little patio by the back door.

The first few nights she cried and howled when she was put in there at bedtime. She was very young still and missing her mum and siblings, but after a few days she got used to it and settled down. If someone came to our door, she barked or growled loudly, I could see she was going to be a very good guard dog.

Every day she jumped into the car when I was going out, sitting on the back seat next to Pas. They were both happy to have company. If there was time after doing the shopping, we'd go down to one of the beaches and take her for a walk. Her little tail would be wagging and she'd run around following Pas, sniffing the stones, the sand, the seaweed, the water in the pool –everything had to be investigated. Pas caught a crab and put it on the sand to show her. She went up to sniff this strange thing and got a nip from a claw, so leapt back yelping and looked at us accusingly 'Why didn't you warn me,' the look said. We just laughed as she looked so funny.

As she was an intelligent puppy, she became house-trained quickly and if I was too busy to take her out for a walk, I'd open the picket gate and she'd wander off into the big empty car park nearby and sniff around there, perform her ablutions and then come back. She grew quickly and in a short time she was a medium-sized dog and part of the family.

It was great having Angel around, knowing that she'd bark if anyone walked past our back gate. But of course she was no substitute for real human company. Once Dave went off on tour a couple of weeks later, I often spent days without adults to talk to. We had no TV, which had not yet been introduced in South Africa, part of government strategy to keep media out of general South African society. The following year when the government relented and did permit TV, there was only one government-controlled channel, censorship must be upheld on everything. A few people bought one, but most English-speaking South Africans didn't want to listen to the pro-apartheid propaganda. This meant we all read a lot of books and socialised informally in the evenings. Pete dropped by occasionally for a chat and so did Di. But I needed other people to talk to in the daytime, people with children, other mothers or I would go stir-crazy.

Steve and Di outside our cottage

Me, Steve, Lily, Peter, Pas

Chapter 10: The Party

Before Anthony and Cleo went on tour it had a run in Cape Town for a few weeks at the main theatre. Dave had quickly made friends with the other actors and often went socialising with them, but he never did things by halves. He was in fact a bit of a hell-raiser. Moderation was not a word in Dave's vocabulary. Once he started to party, he wanted to be the last man standing. Meanwhile, I was at home baby-sitting, which was often OK with me as I was a light-weight when it came to drinking.

We were invited to a big party, in the main CAPAB building. It was to be a grand affair. Di agreed to baby-sit and we got all dressed up – I think we must have been a striking looking couple, Dave - six foot three, long limbed, straight blonde hair, blue eyes wearing his straight trousers and his favourite Ben Sherman shirt, cheesecloth with pink and white stripes. Me in a full length cotton dress that my Mum had sent me, white background, wine flowers all over, red-brown hair cut in a bob and big-eye make-up.

We drove to the centre of Cape Town, found the tall glass building and then went up in a lift to the second floor. The lift door opened onto a large room with thick pile wall-to-wall carpets and a long table, laid out with drinks and canapés. There were a few chairs against the walls and various groups of people milling about – actors, directors and theatre people.

Dave's eyes lit up as he saw the drinks table. I knew what he was thinking, 'Whooppee! Free booze!' I gave him a warning glance and followed him over to the table, where he poured himself a large glass of wine and asked what I wanted. I was a bit of a phenomenon in my family, who all liked to drink. You could almost call me the 'black sheep' of the family. I would have a couple of drinks occasionally but often I preferred a cup of tea. Family members had frequently tried to cure me of this nasty habit, but with limited success. I had learnt to disguise my poor drinking capacity, by always having a glass of wine or beer in my hand and sipping from it occasionally. This meant that drinkers felt comfortable and didn't notice that I wasn't drinking as much as them. Dave knew my lightweight capacity very well. It didn't seem to bother him or retard his progress.

'Yes thanks Dave, I'll have a small glass of wine,' I was saying as this very camp guy came up to us.

'So David, this is your wife?'

'Meet Anna, Robert. Anna, Robert works for the costume department – he makes hats! Robert keep her company, I'm going to talk to Ben over there.' Robert looked slightly disappointed but turned to me. Robert had an aquiline face, long thin nose, shoulder length hair and a foppish appearance.

I was well used to such company, I'd worked with a couple of gay guys for a theatre bookings agency in London a few years before as well as mixing with all Dave's theatrical crowd.

'So Robert, tell me about the actors here – which one's do you fancy?'

This broke the ice immediately and soon Robert was telling me the under-stairs gossip about some of the people in the room, who he considered 'talent' and who not. We were looking over at a small gaggle of actors and in the centre was CAPAB's leading actor Richard something, an ageing gay man wearing a white cardigan and white trousers.

'Look at him darling,' said Robert.' I don't know who he thinks he is, but he obviously thinks he's something!' We both giggled.

Richard put on a grand actorish voice,

'So I said to Peter, er Peter Hall I mean, look I can't take on Lear until next year, I'm just completely booked up. But of course I'd love to play him, who wouldn't my dear.'

The circle of acolytes around this leading actor appeared to be hanging on his every word. At that moment Dave reappeared,

'Robert was just telling me about the company's leading actor,' I was giggling. Dave glanced over.

'Oh him!' Dave was unenthusiastic. 'Tell you what I probably better introduce you to him, come on.'

'OK, bye Robert, see you later.'

Robert gave me a significant look, arching his eyebrows. We knew we were going to be friends.

We stood at the periphery of the little group for a few moments then Dave caught Richard's eye.

'Er ... Richard, this is my wife Anna.'

I smiled pleasantly and extended my hand.

'Charming.' He took my hand limply and his glance slid away from me without interest. Obviously I was nobody and female too. He walked past me to talk to someone more important. Dave didn't seem to notice. I looked over at him, he was by now talking to a slightly older blonde actress who had a pleasantly modulated English voice. His face was a little flushed and he sounded animated.

Uh- oh! I thought, how much has he had to drink...?

'Dave?'

'Meet my friend Pam,' his voice was slightly slurred, 'It's great to be working with you.'

'Oh hello,' she smiled at me, 'nice to meet a fellow Brit. Dave's always talking about you and your little girl, what's her name again?'

Pam was older than me and seemed incredibly mature (probably about 32). She had blonde, short-cut straight hair with a long fringe falling over direct, hazel eyes.

'So how come you're here in Cape Town, Pam?'

'Oh (husky voice), well thought I'd escape the bloody English weather for a bit and see the world. Had an old friend here, invited me over'.

'Male or female?'

'Male .....'

'Oh ....and what happened?'

'Didn't work out darling, now I'm open to offers!'

I laughed and immediately warmed to her frankness. We were to become good friends.

Dave and Pam started talking about the CAPAB company.

'Far as I can see, it takes years to get into leads. Like at home. But the good thing about here, is you can meet directors easily – not like London – over there they won't see you unless you've got a name.'

'Well the leading actors in CAPAB do seem to have a stranglehold on the main parts.' Pam spoke quietly. Dave agreed, then wandered off towards another group of actors, grabbing another glass of wine from the table on his way.

Pam pointed out the small group of older actors who'd been in CAPAB for years.

'Oh there's quite a hierarchy you know. We're far down the pecking order, that's the way it works in this company.'

I looked across at these leading CAPAB actors and wondered how long it was going to take Dave to move up into larger parts. Dave was called over by some of the other actors. I knew how important it was for him to work in good roles. He got bored otherwise.

Robert wandered over.

'Shall we have something to eat,' he said taking my arm. 'Let's take a look at the canapés, dahling.'

'OK I'm starving.' I followed him across to the table. 'So Robert, have you been in Cape Town long?'

'Oh, about six months, I came over on the QE2.'

'Really? What was that like?'

'Great, like one long party. I don't remember much of the journey.'

We started helping ourselves to food, small bite-sized pieces of this and that - pastries, sausages, pieces of cheese and melon on sticks. I looked up and down, I'd always had a large appetite which surprised people as I was so slim. But there was nothing here to fill you up.

'Yes,' Pam had wandered over, 'I came over on the same ship as Robert, there seemed to be a lot of big drinkers on board. I did quite a lot of reading. It was quite relaxing actually.'

'Oh you weren't joining in then?'

'Lord no, I wouldn't like to get that drunk. But I enjoyed watching everybody else.'

'And then you joined CAPAB?'

'Well,' she picked up a piece of pineapple and cheese on a stick, 'I was already invited. From England, someone who directed me there, came over to direct a play here. They were doing The Importance of Being Ernest and he wanted me to play Lady Bracknell.'

'But you're much too young for Lady Bracknell aren't you?'

'God, yes. It was obvious when I got here. The director offered me another part, I was here by then and I had to work, so I took it.'

'In spite of the apartheid!' I raised an eyebrow.

'Well Equity hasn't banned actors from working here yet have they?' The thing is one has to live and there's lots of English speaking theatre here.

I sighed, 'Yes, I know. ... and what do you think of it so far, the apartheid stuff I mean?'

'Ghastly isn't it', she spoke quietly looking round to make sure there were no South Africans close by.

'Yes it's hard to believe how far it reaches here and how much censorship there is. You just don't grasp that in the UK.'

'I know, you can't talk about it much here either. South Africans are quite sensitive about it. Even the liberals won't talk about it too often.'

'Well, maybe they get sick of talking about it with new people? And then there's the other problem - I'm told the secret police are everywhere.' I was munching a piece of melon and cherry ... we both looked round somewhat nervously.

We chatted sotto-voce about apartheid for a while. I asked about how it was applied in relation to CAPAB. Apparently, the audiences for CAPAB shows were almost exclusively white European although they did have the occasional nights in Cape Town when 'mixed' audiences were permitted. We looked at each other but there was nothing to say.

Dave came over, glass of wine in his hand and noticed Pam's glass was empty.

'Shall I get you one Pam?' His hand was making a drinking gesture.

'No thanks Dave. I've had enough for tonight. I feel a bit light-headed already.'

'Pam was telling me about CAPAB and how it all works,' I said glancing over at the clique across the room.

Dave started doing a take-off of the leading actor, in a very camp voice,

'Dahling, how lovely to see you, you look wonderful, yes I LOVED the show, you were fabulous dahling. Oh yes I'm playing in the spring, *such* a bore, I'll be *exhausted...* ' he flopped his hand theatrically and minced up and down.

I gave him a warning glance – the great man was coming in our direction. Dave downed another glass of wine, as the tray went past and Richard, obviously passing to talk to someone higher up the ladder, stopped rather grandly to bestow his pearls of wisdom on us, enroute.

'David isn't it? The new boy! What part have they given you? Oh, yes, so you've got a few lines...?'

Dave was holding a glass of red wine and I should have seen the warning signs – this was, 'I'm a genius and no one knows it'.

He didn't take kindly to being talked down to. If sober he would have just laughed it off, but he'd had a lot of wine by now.... suddenly without warning Dave's hand shot out and the glass of red wine shot over the Leading Man's white cardigan. A look of shock and horror crossed Richard's face - matched by mine, although somewhere in the back of my head I wanted to laugh. The fall out though was dreadful. People rushed over, but Dave's eyes were glazed and unrepentant. He had a silly grin on his face and his words were coming out slurred.

'Whatsh all the fussh about,' he was looking round for another glass.

Richard fixed me with a cold steely glare...as he and an acolyte dabbed at his cardigan.

'I think you'd better take your husband home, he's had too much to drink.' Everyone was looking at me. I wanted the ground to open up and swallow me. I grabbed Dave's arm firmly and grimly led him to the exit, he was protesting,

'Where are we going, I want another drink.'

I said, 'We have to go now, it's time to leave.' I got him out to the car somehow and drove us home. By the time we got home, Dave was beginning to sober a little. He tried to laugh it off. I kept thinking - they'll sack him, he'll be out of work and we'll have no money. What are we going to do?

I got him in to bed, but lay awake worrying. What will happen now? The scene kept replaying in my head in vivid detail - the red wine flying out of the glass onto the white cardigan. The humiliation of being asked to take him home - I was being held to account for him drinking too much. My face kept going hot with embarrassment and anger. How could we ever face those people again?

Next day, Dave woke with a slight hangover. He had a vast capacity for alcohol and a constitution like an ox. He made a quick recovery and shrugged off the incident. I recounted the incident back to him, but it seemed to have little impact...

'...and what did I do then? Oh...what did I say next?' (as if he couldn't remember). 'Oh... aha ...oh.'

He went to his evening performance somewhat sheepishly, I took Pas out to the beach to distract myself from worrying if he'd be sacked...

It all blew over somehow. Dave didn't mention if anything was said to him - not much I think. His blasé charm and humour pulled him through as always. As for me, well, somehow I could never stay cross with him for long. I worried about him, but his warmth and fun always made me forget the difficult times.

Soon after, Dave went off on his tour for about ten days with Anthony and Cleo – he went to strange places I'd never heard of, like Grahamstown. One day the actors went to somewhere called Oudtshoorn and visited an Ostrich farm there, they had their days free to visit places, as long as they were in the theatre for 'the half', or half an hour before the show. Pas and I had regular postcards back from him which helped. I missed him a great deal when he was away. His postcards arrived every few days – here's one dated 18/9/75:

Darling Anna & Pascale

The Monument Theatre at Grahamstown is very beautiful inside, lovely stage, excellent acoustics. Cango Caves were terrific apart from tourist coloured lights and bullshit [guided tour]. It's sunny and I'm sitting outside the Cathedral. I'm staying in a cheap but pleasant apartment - working well on Goldfields – tell Peter, he'll be pleased. I've been out-of-my-brain most nights – it's the only way to cope. We're staying in George on Sunday night and will probably arrive in Cape Town at 5 or 6 on Monday. I'll soon be back. I think of you and Passy constantly. Miss you and love you both very much. Dave

Dave's cards were full of info and kept me going whenever he was away. Meanwhile, Pas and I were alone together most days - we had long walks on the beach. I was lonely and irritable, although I saw Peter and Di sometimes but I couldn't wait for Dave's return and some adult conversation.

The weather was moving towards spring (Sept), not much rain now, but the South- Easterly winds – they were so strong in the Cape Town area in spring. There could be a clear blue sky, warm sun and a wind that you could lean in to it blew so hard.

CAPAB ENGLISH DRAMA
Presents

Antony and Cleopatra

by William Shakespeare

Directed by DAVID GILES

Set and Costumes designed by PETER CAZALET
Lighting designed by JOHN T. BAKER

First performed in 1759 at the Garrick Theatre, London
Nico Malan Theatre, Cape Town. 16 August, 1975

Pam

Chapter 11: Katrina

In our little back concrete patio, the avocado tree was soon full of avocados and as the weeks passed the fruit on the branches grew and ripened, until in the end many of them were the size of rugby balls. I've never seen avocados that size before or since - we had avocados for breakfast, lunch, snacks, supper. In England, avocados were an expensive luxury. We felt really spoilt at first, until like everything in excess, you get tired of it.

One clear sunny day while Dave was away on tour, Angel barked and I looked out past the avocado tree, past the little picket fence and there was a small, plump, coloured woman opening my gate. Her battered face had the suffering of the world upon it and yet she couldn't have been more than her early thirties. She wore an orange printed cotton skirt and a red cotton head-scarf tied at the back of the neck. I wondered what she could want and felt slightly irritated by the interruption as I was just about to go out.

'Hello?' I said

'Ah'm looking for werk, medam, any sort of werk, I'm alone you see with mah three kids, mah husband left us.'

'Where do you live?'

'We're livin in the hawse of an Undian family.' She pointed out the gate with a gesture that could have meant anything near or far.

'At night, we slip, well med'm, I don't lahk to tell yew this, but we all slip in the borthroom, me and the kids. '

'In the bathroom?' I said

'Yes – they say that's all there is....'

'Whereabouts do you sleep?'

'On the floor, medam... he guves us a blenket to lie on, sometimes I lie in the borth, so m' kids got more room. Please, med'm, ah need work so ah can buy food to tek home for the kids.'

What could I do? Unlike most white families in Cape Town, we could not afford the usual live-in nanny and cleaner. Our budget was on a shoe string. We had a roof over our heads and could run our battered old VW Beetle. But I had to go very carefully with the shopping and there certainly wasn't any money to spare for extras.

However I just couldn't turn Katrina away - the thought of children living in such appalling conditions waiting to be fed was too much. Besides, I loathed housework and it would be nice to have someone else do it. It would leave me free to go out and do other things.

'Well,' I said, looking round our small place. 'I suppose you could come once a week?'

'Oh no medem don't yew want someone every day?'

'No!' I said firmly. 'Once a week would be fine – for 3 hours.'

'Three hours? I werk very hard and Ah could do lots more, if I was here for four hours?'

'No! Three hours would be enough. How much do you want for 3 hours?'

Her shrewd eyes looked at me sideways. We haggled until a fair price was agreed and she knew I wasn't going to go up any further.

Katrina came erratically over the next few months and it soon became obvious that she had a serious alcohol problem. She often turned up in various stages of drink or smelling heavily of drink. But I kept her on and often bought large shopping bags of food for her - thinking of her poor kids.

Then one night a few months later, Dave was performing at the theatre and Peter from the end cottage came round to borrow a cup of sugar.

'Hi Peter – cup of Rooibos or a beer?'

'No, Rooibos would be great.'

'OK. What you doing this evening?'

'Nothing much.'

'Me neither.'

I was wondering what we could do and then I had an idea. I was bored and it was a few hours until Dave would be back.

'You want to play Ouija?'

I'd played it before in England once or twice, the glass had moved but sporadically and slowly then. I was interested in all things psychic and was fascinated by how it worked. Besides, Pas was in bed and it would while away the evening. We had no television and I'd read all my books.

'I don't mind. I've played before, the glass moved … we weren't touching it.'

So I wrote the letters of the alphabet on pieces of torn paper, set out the kitchen table, found a small jam-jar and up turned it in the middle of the table. It was dark outside by now so we lit a candle and turned the main light out. Peter was sipping his tea and then leaned forward and put his cup down.

'Who will we ask for?'

'What do you mean?'

'You're supposed to ask if anyone's there aren't you?'

'Oh yeh right, who shall we ask for?'

'Someone who's dead, do you know someone who's died, that you knew well?'

'Well ….my Auntie Maisie in Ireland died a few years ago, I was really fond of her.'

'Let's ask her to come then…'

I put down my cup and I put my finger lightly on the glass.

'No, not like that', Peter said. 'Like this.'

He put his finger an inch above the glass, hovering. I followed him, thinking nothing's going to happen, this can't work. Before Peter came round I'd been worrying about Katrina, what to do about her. I was worried about her drinking and her children and how I was always giving her money for this or that, money I could ill afford. I asked

'Is anyone there?'

At first nothing happened, we sat staring at the glass so I asked,

'Is Auntie Maisie there?'

Our fingers hovered above the glass and we waited. Nothing. After a few minutes of this I was just about to say, 'Oh well, we tried' and start putting it all away.

Suddenly there was a slight scratching sound and the glass started to scrape across the top of the wooden table, catching slightly on knots, but building up speed and becoming long swishing movements. My eyes widened in surprise – I'd never seen it go that fast before – I checked to see if Peter's finger was touching the glass, but there was space between his finger and the glass and mine was the same, opposite his. The hairs on the back of my neck prickled, in the warm summer evening air.

The glass swished to the M and then the A. It kept repeating 'MA,' 'MA.' I was holding my breath.

'Who's Ma?' Peter lifted his hand from the glass.

I breathed out....... 'Don't know, unless it's short for Maisie?'

'OK', I said 'I'll try another question.' We put our fingers back and I took a deep breath. 'What shall I do about Katrina?' I asked in a rush. The glass immediately started scraping to the letters in long swishing lines.

It spelt out 'SHOW HER THE DOOR.' I gulped, 'What does that mean?' I looked at Peter, he shrugged. 'OK I'll ask something else, shall I?' I spoke again to the table.

'What about her children?'

'NOT WITH HER,' it spelt.

I glanced at Peter. He frowned. 'This can't be', I thought. I got up, lit a cigarette and fetched an ashtray and sat down again, balancing the cigarette on the ashtray. We put our fingers back above the glass. I spoke again.

'Who do they live with then?'

HUSBAND.

'That can't be right' I said to Peter. 'They're with her she told me, he left her long ago. Mind you the way she drinks, I can't blame him! I'll ask another question.

Where does he live, her husband – where does he live?'

'ELSIES RIVER', it spelt out in sweeping strokes.

'Is there somewhere called that?' I said to Peter

'Yah. There's a coloured township on the other side of the Cape Flats called that'.

'Oh, so it's a real place, it really exists?'

He nodded.

'Wow, this can't be true can it?'

He shrugged, 'Why not?'

'Do you think I should *Show her the door*?'

He looked at me, 'I've always thought that.'

'But we weren't touching the glass were we? That's so weird! Katrina's coming tomorrow. What shall I do?'

'Tell her.'

'I can't very well say I found out from an Ouija board that you don't have the kids?'

'You don't have to say how you found out.'

'No, I can try it out and see what she says, but I don't think it can be true. It can't be. Ok, let's stop now. It's too freaky.'

'Goodbye Ma, and thank you for coming!' I said.

Our fingers were over the glass, again it started moving and spelt out 'SHOW HER THE DOOR' again, and then, 'GOODBYE' with those long sweeping strokes.

I shivered. Then we put away the letters, Peter said he had to go and I waited for Dave to come back from the theatre. When he came in, I told him what had happened.

'I wish I'd taped it, the sound of the glass scraping across the table!'

'Yeh, maybe next time', he said ... 'That does seem really weird.'

'Can it be real though?' I passed him a beer from the fridge and lit another cigarette.

'Ask her about it tomorrow, see what she says.'

'If it's true, that's it!' She can go, I don't want her here anymore.

'No, definitely,' he said. 'You've given her so much stuff for her kids.'

I was thinking about it now, while pouring Dave a beer in the kitchen. And about Auntie Maisie, who had always made a fuss of us when we had visited her in Lismore, in Ireland. She was my Gran's sister and lived opposite a sweet shop – heaven when we were kids. She had eloped as a young girl but her husband had gone off to the First World War and been killed. She had remained single for the rest of her life.

'At the beginning I asked for Auntie Maisie to come through?' I said as I handed him the beer and a ham sandwich'.

'And what happened?'

'It kept spelling 'M ... A', over and over. Oh just a minute, that's weird, I just remembered something. Yes. That was Mum's pet name for Auntie Maisie, I'd forgotten...Oh God, my Mum always called her – 'Ma'.'

'Now that's freaky!'

'Yeh, isn't it? Unreal, as they say here.' I got up and walked down the corridor to just check on Pas as I heard a little moaning sound. Quietly I opened the door, but she was just dreaming and I pulled up her blanket around her and crept out of the room.

In the kitchen, as I was making myself a cup of tea, I said 'How'd the show go tonight?'

'Oh, yeh, really good audience, laughed at all my funny bits. Except Mark nearly made me corpse in the middle with this look he does – then he said the line the wrong way round - on purpose – me and Steve, our shoulders were heaving.'

Dave's stories about the show always had us both laughing as he would be acting them out in front of me and doing all the facial expressions.

The next day Katrina turned up smelling strongly of alcohol, with the usual sob stories about the kids in the bathroom. She started cleaning the kitchen as she was talking but I didn't listen for long.

'Someone told me that your kids don't live with you - they live with your husband.' I was angry and launched right in, but still holding back in case it wasn't true, I was ready to listen to what she had to say and if she'd completely denied it and looked shocked, I'd have believed her.

She stopped cleaning the sink and turned to look at me.

'Who told yew thet?'

'Someone who knows you. ...;'

'Who? Who told yew?'

Then she started sobbing...gradually she admitted that the story about the 'kids-in-the-bathroom' was untrue.

'He took mah kids away,' she sobbed. 'He should niver have dun that – he's got them with her. He took mah kids away.'

'Where does he live?'

'Ah don't know, ah don't know where they moved to.'

'So you have got children then?'

'Yis,' she spoke angrily. 'I got 3 children, like I said med'm, I swear'

'Do they live in Elsie's River?'

She looked startled. 'I don't know med'm, ah don't know wir he took 'em,' she started sobbing theatrically. 'Who told yew, who told yew?'

Then I got angry, because I realised the Ouija was right. She had told me a pack of lies from the beginning. I'd been buying her food parcels for kids she didn't have and all the money I'd ever given her, had gone to one thing only – the bottle.

She had also told me that she was pregnant and I was worried, about the effects of her drinking on the baby. I knew that once she had the baby, she would have an even bigger hold on me. I went to the door and held it open,

'Go away Katrina and don't come back. I don't want to see you here anymore!'

Loudly protesting, Katrina left. I felt sad for her but also relieved not to have that drain on our small resources and my energy. For a while, I thought I'd seen the back of her.

Chapter 12: The Punch up

You'd think I really liked drama, because no sooner was one over, than another one arrived to take its place. Dave had come back from tour and left CAPAB. He was offered a part in a new company. The play was a murder/mystery called The Cat and the Canary – playing one of the suspects.

I hadn't seen Steve for over a week until one day he called round on his way to Peter's. I was cooking the evening meal and chopping vegetables on our breakfast bar. He seemed a bit on edge...

'How's things?' I asked

'Oh, OK I suppose.'

'Lily all right?'

'Um, well she's got herself a motorbike now',

'A motorbike', I said puzzled, thinking you can't take kids out on a motorbike.

'Yes, so she can get around for her modelling assignments',

'Oh, does she do many?'

'Well not yet but ... she's taking her photos around.'

'Yes I saw them, she looks fantastic doesn't she, like Jerry Hall?'

'Err... yes, everyone says that. Well I have to go or she'll be looking for me. I said I was calling round to Peter's for a short while.'

'Ok, but bring Storm round soon to play with Pascale. You can leave him here for a while if you like. He and Pas play so well together'.

'Well I'd have Georgie.'

'Well you could leave him too I suppose.' Oh dear! I was thinking, Georgie was a bit of a handful and still quite a baby.

'That'd be great,' he smiled and waved as he let himself out the white picket gate and turned right on his way down to Peter's.

* * *

The following week Peter called round to borrow some milk.

'Did you hear about Lily and the motorbike?'

'Oh no, she didn't have an accident?'

'Yes, sort of. Not a crash, she was trying to kick start the bike and her foot slipped off the pedal. She pulled a tendon in her ankle and it's all bandaged up. She has to use crutches for a bit.'

'Poor Lily', how's she going to find modelling work now?' I was thinking of Steve with Lily at home all the time – he would have to take care of her and the kids.

'I bet she'll make Steve wait on her hand and foot.' I wasn't very sympathetic.

'Yah,' said Peter, laughing, 'I went over there today. She has her leg up on the couch and keeps calling Steve to get her this and that. He's looking after the kids and she's shouting at the maid.'

'What maid?' I said surprised.

'Oh you know', Peter said casually, 'They have a maid that lives there half the week. I think they share her with someone.'

Of course, they had a maid, I thought to myself. Every South African household did. Steve hadn't even bothered to mention her, it was just what everyone had – so maybe his life wasn't so tough after all, someone did the washing and cleaning in his place.

'Well I've got to go', said Peter finishing his cup of rooibos and putting the mug down. 'Steve's coming over later.' Steve often visited Peter in the evenings, they might roll a joint and sit talking about their guru, as Peter too was a Satsangi with the same spiritual master. If I was on my own while Dave was at the theatre, I sometimes dropped by for a short while to join in the discussions.

That evening around 9 pm, I called over to 'borrow' some tea and stayed to chat for a few minutes. Then we heard clump, clump, clump outside - it was Lily on crutches. She stumped in angrily and she sat down on the edge of Peter's single bed which was in the living room. Peter was making tea. I wondered who was with the kids, she said she'd got a taxi here. I got up from my chair nervously and moved towards the front door:

'Thanks for the tea, I must be getting home.' I opened the front door.

Lily barely glanced at me and then turned back to Steve, 'Where've you been, you wanker, I've been waiting for you?'

'I came down to see Peter – I was coming home soon.'

'Oh so you've been off visiting your mates, while I'm stuck at home with the kids.'

'Well I was with them most of the day.'

'But you knew I had to go out this evening?'

'It wasn't definite and I've looked after them all week.'

'What do you mean, you fucking martyr!'

'You know how much I take care of the kids - you can do it for a few hours.'

I didn't hear what was said next by Lily – Peter came out of the kitchen and I turned away from the angry pair - Steve's usually quiet voice was getting louder, I turned back - he was standing over Lily, she was sitting on the bed facing him - suddenly she lunged at his crotch, he moved like lightning and smash, there was blood everywhere. Steve had punched Lily in the face, his expression black with rage that evaporated when he saw what he'd done. Lily had blood coursing down her face.

I rushed to the kitchen and brought out wads of tissues and cold flannels and rinsed what seemed like buckets of blood down the sink. Blood was everywhere - all over her face, shirt, everywhere, it gushed out. Lily's face was a mess and Steve was distraught at what he'd done. I was shocked - he was normally so calm and phlegmatic.

I drove Lily up to the hospital at Groote Schuur, holding a cold damp cloth and wedges of tissues to her nose. Dave was back from the theatre by then so I told him on the way past what had happened. We waited hours at the hospital – x-rays and so forth. Lily's nose was broken - she had to have it set and wear a bandage which covered most of her face. They asked the inevitable question – 'How did this happen?'

'My husband punched me in the face,' she had difficulty talking before the bandage was put on, and then her voice came out muffled.

No one commented, but they gave her sympathetic looks. The 'wife- beater' meanwhile had gone home to the kids who had been left on their own sleeping. Apparently they 'never' woke up once asleep.

I dropped Lily off and got home about 3-4 am, exhausted by it all. Pas would be awake by 8 a.m. Dave stirred sleepily.

'Oh! You're back! Is she alright?'

'Nose is broken – she's all bandaged up.'

'How you feeling?' he yawned.

I was taking my sandals off, then my shorts.

'Bloody exhausted, what happened to Steve?'

'He went back to the kids, he was really freaked out.'

'Yeh, we all were. Never thought Steve could explode like that. He must have been badly stressed.'

I got in to bed with my T-shirt and pants on and cuddled up to Dave's warm back. I drifted off to sleep with the image of Steve, leaning over Lily, and the blood, so much blood, like shock waves reverberating around my head. How was this going to affect our new circle of friends? An incident like that would have a big impact on all of us.

Chapter 13: The Mad Hatter, new friends

I didn't see Steve and Lily for a while, although I had regular bulletins from Peter. He would meet up with Steve once in a while. Lily's nose was bandaged for weeks and Steve stayed at home looking after her most of the time. It was sometime before Steve managed to visit again. I liked talking to him and adult company was sparse – so, in spite of what had happened I missed our chats - and Pas needed the company of other children. The other difficulty was that Lily was not someone I felt comfortable with. Lily was following the same spiritual path as Pete and Steve but she didn't seem to treat him very well and appeared casual about the kids. However, in a way that's hard to describe, Lily had a powerful spiritual presence. I never warmed to her though or found her easy company, unlike Steve whose company I always enjoyed.

Meanwhile we had made a few other friends. One was Robert - Robert and I had met at THE party. We met again at other social events, in less traumatic circumstances and he became a regular visitor to our home. We called him 'the Mad Hatter' – he made hats for CAPAB and he looked just like the drawings from the Alice in Wonderland story by Lewis Carroll. He was about 5 feet 8 inches tall, very slim and his face was thin and angular with a long thin autocratic nose. He always dressed immaculately, in what was then in fashion - tight fitting shirts with large collars – his had bold stripes and he wore a cravat. He was very camp and was the complete stereotype of a gay man. He had a very grand English accent and told us how he had been trained by Freddie Fox, who had been the hatter for the Queen. FF had taken him under his wing as a young man and Robert became very good at making top quality hats for famous people.

'So why did you leave England, Robert?'

'Oh dahling, you don't want to hear about that?'

'Yes I do, go on tell me.'

'Well dahling there was a man, we had a row, I left, and just jumped on a boat for Cape Town.'

'What man? What boat?'

'Oh I don't want to talk about him, we had an affair for a long time and we split up, that's all. I got on the QEII and here I am.'

'Were you living with him?' [My Welsh background made me very nosy].

'Oh! So many questions, no more now. No, I lived with my mother, he was older, found a younger model, dahling. He worked for the government. But that's ALL now. No more questions, pour me another glass of wine, sweetie.'

One night he invited me to go with him to a gay disco. In Cape Town there was a thriving gay community. Robert made me laugh; he was good company, said outrageous things and liked my droll, dead-pan humour too. Having worked in London with gay men and enjoyed their company and mixed with many in the theatre world, I was pleased to have a gay friend to go out with occasionally. Dave was still away on tour and it was difficult with a baby at home. As all the coloured and black population had to be back in their townships by nightfall every evening (unless they were for example, live-in nannies), it was hard to find anyone to babysit. Di, kindly agreed to baby-sit for a night. She didn't have far to come as she was right next door.

This disco was in the centre of Cape Town and was all muted soft colours and lighting. It had a large 'C' shaped bar and 70s dance music. As Robert and I walked in I just looked around and it was full of men, of all shapes and sizes, with a very small group of women in the distance in a seating area. Men were standing around the bar, dancing together on the dance floor, or sitting at tables. Some were all in leather, some in bright colours and some more soberly dressed. Some walked like Robert, others dressed and looked like straight men. All were looking around, checking each other out. When they met each other, the eyes flicked up and down and that glance took account of body shape, age, style of dress, cost of clothing and desirability, all in a millisecond. Heterosexuals do it too I suppose, but it seemed far more obvious here. I was fascinated as I had never been in a totally homosexual environment before.

Several guys came over to talk to Robert, he seemed to know many of them.

'Hi darling who's this then, you turning sweetie?' They looked me over critically.

I smiled and laughed and Robert kept up a running commentary about the different guys.

'....that's Jackie, he works in a hotel, I had a little thing with him for a while, he's embroidering a tea towel for his Mum. Can you believe it?'

'....that's the gorgeous, Filipe, look at those dark flashing eyes, stunning, he's a designer. I've been to his apartment – wonderful. You should see the size of HIS equipment darling. Outrageous!

Oh god! Don't look now, that's Gordon, he's an accountant, sooo ... boring, hope he hasn't seen me, I'll go mad if he comes over, oh no he's seen me, quick darling move over here...'

Oh, oh! Careful darling, here come the girls...' as a couple of lesbian women came up – one girl had a very short haircut and wore denim, the other had long brown curly hair, was petite and wore a floral print skirt...

Robert said, 'No girls, she's married, straight!' 'Oh!' they said, but we chatted for a while, until they went back to their friends.

Robert and I danced and had a few drinks and had a laugh. It was a lovely change for me to go out for the evening and as a married woman it felt like a safe way to spend a night out. The social scene in Cape Town was highly charged under the apartheid regime and often felt very alien to me. Most of my time was spent alone with a small child too. Getting out with Robert was great, made me feel like a human being, not just a mother. He was completely entertaining, fun and frivolous.

After a while Robert took me home in a taxi. It had been my first experience of a completely gay scene. Although interesting, the atmosphere had been highly charged with a big focus on 'pulling'. But, when I thought about it, much later, it must feel the same way for gay men and women when they're in a heterosexual disco setting.

Dave came back a few weeks later, much to my relief. He was full of stories about doing the show in the townships –

sometimes the shows were in old churches, with wooden seats for the congregation, other times in old barns. Anything could happen. In one such place, he was on stage, when two dogs strolled in and then started to rut right in front of the stage, people were shouting, yelling at them. A man came with a stick and chased them off as nothing else had worked.

He'd had been some odd looks from some of the CAPAB actors, as Dave made friends with the Cape Coloured crews who were driving the vans and putting up the sets. He said he often sat up drinking and smoking grass with them and ended up sleeping in the van with them a few times, too tired to go back to his digs. Although he'd had lots of wild times as usual, he was glad to come home. I told him about my night out with Robert which seemed quite tame by comparison.

Whenever we had friends over for a social evening, we would invite Robert, or he would ring up and drop by at short notice and I was always pleased to see him. Pam too would occasionally come over for an evening meal and a bottle of wine. We'd become friends after that first meeting at the party. Pam did well at CAPAB and was given some strong female roles, she was a good actress. We would discuss South African politics and share ideas.

One day she asked, 'So ... what do you think of it all here?'

'It's bloody awful of course! Dave wants to work in a mixed race theatre group as soon as he can.'

'Yes, it is difficult, but if we're here, we have to get on with it, don't we?'

'I know, but we don't have to like it.'

'Well, we have to keep quiet, it's not our country. This is the way they want to run things, so what can we do? Just be careful what you say to people.'

'What do you mean?'

'Well, Dave has to get work doesn't he, you have to watch what you say to people here, they don't like to talk about it. And they won't agree with you, a foreigner, interfering.'

I sighed, 'I suppose you're right, but I'm not very good at keeping my mouth shut.'

'I KNOW I'm right, keep a low profile, my dear. There's no Social Security if Dave can't get a job. He can't get fill-in labouring work, like actors do at home.'

She was right. With most local people, you couldn't talk about apartheid and what was going on politically. Apartheid and the effects of it, that we all experienced on a daily basis was not discussed in most social gatherings.

She introduced us to a friend of hers one day a guy called Mark –

'Mark's a music lecturer at South West University', she announced.

I was impressed, but a little apprehensive. I knew very little about classical music. In the 60s, classical music was listened to by parents, adults, 'straight' people, people we had nothing in common with. I did remember my father playing Beethoven very loud on his record player and Tchaikovsky and had enjoyed listening sometimes. A few times he'd taken me to the Brangwyn Hall, in Swansea for a big classical music concert and I'd enjoyed watching the violinists and the huge Kettle drums booming across the large hall.

'Gosh, you're a music expert, I'm afraid I know next to nothing about classical music. Where's the university where you work?'

'Oh its over in the Western Cape – in Stellenbosch, it's a university for coloured people you know.'

'Oh,' I said, blushing slightly, 'Excuse my ignorance, I'm from England, but does that mean….'

'Yes that's right,' he interrupted, 'No whites there, they go to University of Cape Town. I'm not allowed to teach there.'

'That's dreadful, how do you feel about that?'

He laughed, lighting a cigarette and puffing it slowly, 'No one's ever asked me that before.'

'Well,' I said hesitantly, 'Maybe it's because no one ever seems to talk about apartheid here.'

'That's right,' he said, 'I call it the 'Hippopotamus at the Table.' He twisted the glass of red wine in his hand and took a large sip.

'The Hippopotamus at the Table – it's like you're sitting down to dinner with a group of people and there's this big old hippo sitting there too, but everyone pretends it's not there. That's what the topic of apartheid's like here. It affects every aspect of our lives, but must never be mentioned.

In Cape Town, they see themselves as liberals, they're all against apartheid,' Mark stubbed out his cigarette in the ashtray. 'They're not like the Afrikaaner, they think. I get invited to parties by some of these 'liberals'. It's fashionable to have a 'non-white' at your party. This particular party I went to a few weeks ago, I was the only 'non-white' there. I was a token to show how liberal they were. There was some classical music playing in the background. An elderly woman came up to me, she smiled and put her head on one side.

'Do you know who this is, this music?' I said 'Yes lady, it's Dvorak's symphony No 4 in D minor, which he wrote in 1875. Now if you'll excuse me I have to get another drink.' He laughed. 'Now let's change the subject, tell me about yourself.'

I smiled, I didn't know how to respond to what he'd said, to just make some crass remark about how angry it all made me feel, it just wasn't enough. So I chatted away about how I had moved away from Christianity and felt the need for something else. He continued to look interested, so I carried on,

'I went in to a bookshop the other day and this book almost jumped out into my hands – it's a biography of Ena Twigg? Have you ever heard of her?'

Mark shook his head.

'Well apparently, she's this famous psychic medium in England, all sorts of well-known famous people have visited her. I've started reading it - when she was a child she could see people that weren't there, dead people. She went to a convent and kept going to sit in the chapel. When one of the nuns came in and asked why she wasn't out in the playground with the other kids, she told her she was with all her friends, the people in the chapel. The nun looked around and there was no one there. So they stopped her from going there on her own and she learnt to stop talking about what she could see. As an adult she eventually became a medium.'

Mark looked at me strangely, and I thought he probably thinks I'm mad, but he said: 'Well I'm psychic too, but in a different way.'

'Really.' Maybe he didn't think I was nuts, I thought. 'In what way?'

'Well I can see things that are going to happen before they happen'.

'Like what?'

'Usually when something bad is going to happen.'

'How do you mean 'see'?'

'Well it's like on a little TV screen in front of me, I just see it. I saw it before some friends of mine went for a drive round Chapman's Peak, I saw the car going over the cliff.'

'Did you tell them?'

'I tried to, I didn't like to say too much, but I said they should be careful or not go. They wouldn't listen though.'

'What happened?'

He shrugged. 'The car broke through a barrier and ... have you seen that road?'

I shook my head.

'It goes round the other side of Table Mountain, by the Twelve Apostles, that range of mountain crags. The road clings to the cliff side, huge drops down to the rocks and sea below – they went over and were all killed.'

'God how dreadful ... and scary, to see it beforehand and not be able to do anything. Have you seen things like that other times?'

'Yes a few times.'

'Wow,' I said, 'How weird. Does that mean you can see when someone's going to die?'

'It's not like that, it comes out of the blue, I can't tell when.'

My conversation with Mark, came at a time when my interest in the 'spiritual' side of my life, which had always been strong, was being rekindled and Cape Town at that time seemed to be a centre for all sorts of spiritual groups, gurus, etc. Many of my generation were searching for something more. Most of us had been brought up under some kind of rigid Christianity. We of the post-war generations had been rebelling against the establishment in the 60s and 70s. Many of us yearned to find a new framework for our spiritual life. Some went to India and joined the hippy trail. But Dave and I were in South Africa and strangely, under apartheid, religions of all sorts seemed to be flourishing, perhaps as a counterpoint to a whole political system based on skin colour. I went a few times to a Roman Catholic mass and even there found a church full of all age groups, strong anti-apartheid messages from the pulpit and a vibrancy within that had long ceased in the UK Christian churches.

Now I was moving towards my first forays into Christian Spiritualism. After this meeting with Mark, I would see him occasionally when he came to a show and we often chatted about his psychic gifts, spiritual matters and the current political scene.

* * *

One day a few weeks later, Steve came over with Storm and Georgie. It was great to see him again and Pascale was delighted to have Storm to play with once more, Georgie was still crawling. I gave the kids some peanut butter sandwiches and juice. Then Steve and I watched them playing with a ball in the front yard under the avocado tree.

'How's Lily's nose? Is she still wearing the bandages?'

'Yeh, but they're coming off this week.'

'Will her nose be alright?'

'Hope so,' he said glumly.

Steve seemed uncomfortable, he clearly had something on his mind.

'You OK though?'

He sighed, 'Well, it's a bit difficult to explain this but it's about Lily....'

'Yes?' I was unsure what was coming next.

'Well you see... er ...' He walked over to the avocado tree and put his hand on the trunk, looking up at the large avos growing there ... 'Lily's a bit jealous,' he turned to face me, ' ... of you.'

'What!' I said astonished, 'Why?'

'She thinks you and I are ... too close.'

'That's ridiculous.' I turned towards the kitchen and he followed, standing in the doorway watching me, as I filled the kettle and lit the gas. I was shocked by what he'd said and trying to think it through.

'I know, but she doesn't want me to come round here anymore ...'

'But Steve, look at the kids, they're playing so well together, how can she say that. And we're both married . . . we enjoy talking together, but that's all. How can she think...?'

How could she? I was thinking – Steve was a friend I could talk to and he was the only person I knew with kids of Pascale's age for her to play with.

'What are you going to do?' I handed him his tea and sat down cross-legged on the settle, where I had a clear view of the kids playing in the yard.

'Oh, watch out Steve – Georgie's pouring his juice all over the ground – he's going to get soaked...'

Steve picked up Georgie and put him on his knee, removing the feeder cup from his chubby little hand and bouncing him a little to distract him ...123 bouf! 123 bouf!' Soon Georgie was giggling and chuckling. Storm and Pas had come in now and were cutting out shapes with the playdough I'd made them and chatting.

'This one's a BIG dog and it's gonna bite you, ruff ruff!' Storm was saying.

Pas gave him a hard look, she was quite competitive. 'Well my dog's bigger and he'll bite your dog's head off!' But it was all good humoured, they were laughing.

'Look, I'll try talking to her but you don't understand what she's like when she gets things in her head.... anyway I have to go now – I'll probably bring the kids round again in the next few days if I can get away.'

Later that evening, I told Dave what Steve had said. He was amazed too,

'God she is weird, and he does all the childcare anyway. I thought they were glad to find a playmate for the kids, now she wants to end that? Perhaps it'll blow over.'

'I hope so', I said, but did not feel optimistic after the way Steve had described it - I was puzzled and upset. Lily seemed to have invented a scenario in her head which had nothing to do with reality. I wondered what effect it would have in the long term and whether Steve and I would be able to remain friends.

Looking back I was very naive, not to have foreseen this. But Dave and I had always had friends of both sexes and it would never occur to either of us that we had the right to interfere with each other's' friendship groups and they were often joint friends anyway. It would be a shame for Pas not to have Storm to play with anymore.

* * *

Around this time I noticed something else about our neighbourhood – groups of small boys standing at the 'robots' (traffic lights) every day, some looked as young as 6 or 7. They should not be in such a dangerous position with cars whizzing all around and them dodging in and out with bundles of newspapers. Was there no one to care for these boys?

Chapter 14: Martin the Paper boy

Whenever we stepped outside our front door, the mountain, often with its crown of clouds, was a living daily presence towering against a clear blue sky. It loomed possessively and maternally over the daily life of Cape Town.

Where we lived – Mowbray, was in a chain of suburbs, stretching from the city centre on the Atlantic coast, along a road that goes to Fish Hoek. If you carried on from there along the east coast, the Atlantic soon meets the Indian Ocean in the Eastern Cape. Many of these Cape Town suburbs had once been occupied by the multitude of races that made up the Southern African population.

Mowbray, as we'd discovered, was now mainly '*Whites only*', although just behind our group of cottages was the mosque, which Indian and Malay Muslims would attend. Presumably they had once lived in the area but now had to return to their 'township' areas after visiting their place of worship. '*Non-Whites*', apart from live-in domestic servants, were not permitted to be in the '*white*' areas after dark. 'Cape Coloured' people lived mainly in Manenberg, Table View and Wynberg. They travelled by train and by nightfall they returned to these townships.

However, there were those who slipped the net - the 'paper boys' aged 7/8 upwards, who were to be seen standing at '*robots*' (traffic-lights), all afternoon selling newspapers. At night you'd see them curled up in shop doorways, wrapped up in newspapers. And there they'd sleep all night, huddled together for warmth and security.

One day, I got talking to one of these boys, a boy of perhaps 9, tall and slim. I was pushing Pas in her pram, the stripy umbrella one.

'Hello medem, hev yew got something for me?'

'What do you want?' I asked, smiling at him.

'Hev you got sum sper chainj?'

'Well I tell you what, if you're hungry, I'll make you a sandwich, a cheese sandwich to eat.'

'Ok medem,' he said and trotted along beside me to our front door. He came in and looked around with curiosity. 'So, who luvs here wuth yew?'

'Well it's me, my husband and Pas,' I said, as I sat Pas down at the table and gave her a drink. He talked away as I got on with preparing food for the evening meal and I asked him some questions too.

'... end wair us he, your husband?'

'Oh he's working, he'll be back later. So what's your name?'

'Uts Martun...'

'Is that Martin?'

'Yis medem, that's roight.'

'And where do you sleep at night?'

'Wul, yew no wer those shops are on the mayn road? Yup those ones bar the bottle store? I slip there with my frins in a doorway, but uts cold now, we hev to all stay close ut noyt'.

I put out some paper and colouring pens on the table for Pas – she was making shapes and carefully colouring them in. Pas liked to be precise. Martin watched intently.

'You want to have a go?'

'Ah can't draw'.

'Well you could try, try a mouse, Martin look, like this.' I drew a quick sketch of a cartoon mouse, he tried to copy it.

'That's good Martin, really good.'

'Ken Ah stay here t'night, medem?'

'Well', I looked at him thoughtfully,

'I suppose so, you could sleep on the couch – just this once mind you......'

So Martin stayed in our cottage that night. When Dave came in, Martin went very quiet, but Dave soon made him laugh and he relaxed a bit. He went off next day and returned in the late afternoon, just before Dave left for the theatre. We pondered what to do, as he came with friends the second time. We fed them the usual cheese sandwiches and felt bad that we couldn't accommodate more than Martin.

The following day, I rang a couple of friends and asked what to do. They said 'Put him out, you're just causing more problems for yourself, you could get in trouble for having him stay in your house.' Apparently, there were some small charities that attempted to do something for the enormous problems of the poor in Cape Town. There appeared to be no Social Services of any description and yet the poverty of the non-white population reflected onto the children. These small charities and church organisations attempted to alleviate some of the worst problems, but their poorly funded efforts seemed to make little overall significance due to the magnitude of the situation.

I spoke to Peter and he said that there was a charity which might be able to help – they had a connection with the Black Sash - an organisation set up in the fifties, by the wives of some important figures in commerce and government to oppose apartheid. These brave women were able, some through the power of their husbands' positions and some being lawyers, doctors and professionals in their own right, to run schemes ranging from lobbying to legal aid, medical help and social work for the poor of South Africa. They were looked on with distaste by police and government, but generally allowed to continue their activities. They had powerful friends.

I decided to take Martin to the office of this charity and see if they could fix him up, perhaps in a children's home, perhaps sort out his background. I was worried about the Group Areas Act and what if the secret police found out he was staying with us. I persuaded him to come in the car with me, although I was sparing in my explanation.

'Where we going to, medem?'

'Well Martin we're going to see a nice lady to see if we can find you a better place to live?'

'Ah don't want to go, Medem. Ah just want to stay with yew!'

'We're only going to talk Martin, if you don't like it we'll just come back.'

We waited in a waiting room like a doctor's surgery, Martin becoming increasingly agitated, stayed very close to me. We were ushered into a room with two women counsellors – it was not unlike a Citizens Advice Bureau in England. Martin spoke little English, his main tongue being Afrikaans.

The women were business like and unsentimental....one of them, the older of the two sighed.

'These boys, there's not a lot you can do for them, they've often got into trouble and run away from home.'

'Well may be he had a reason to run away, perhaps he was being beaten or something?'

'It's possible, but often they start hanging about with these street kids because there's no one telling them what to do...'

'He keeps wanting to stay at my place and he's started to bring his friends.'

'You can't have that,' she was brisk. 'You'll get into all sorts of trouble – its illegal and against the Group Areas Act.'

'I know!' I sighed. 'That's why I've brought him here. I was hoping you can do something?'

She spoke to Martin in Afrikaans, he answered hesitantly. She was firing questions at him, he mumbled answers.

I didn't know what was being said but I could see that Martin was nervous, he kept his eyes on the floor and mumbled answers. She translated for me after a while.

'He says that he ran away from his mother's place, his Dad wasn't there anymore. He didn't like it at home, his Mum was always shouting at him. Then he was picked up by the police and they took him to his auntie's place. She agreed to have him. He stayed there for a while. But gradually he just started spending more and more time away from home. His auntie told him off but ...my guess is the streets were more exciting...'

I looked at Martin. He looked at the ground. He didn't look like any kind of wild street kid, just a sad little boy. But what did I know, I thought about the life he'd come from.

'So,' I said firmly 'What's to be done? He's a bright kid, surely he can't just be left on the streets.'

'Well,' the other woman sighed. 'There's a boy's home run by a priest, where boys can stay if they want to. The priest doesn't make it like a prison or anything, but he does expect them to make a commitment to staying. He will interview them and see what they will agree to. If they want to stay, well then they're given food and shelter and education.'

'The trouble is,' the first woman said, 'he probably won't agree to it, but even if we do get him there, he'll probably run away again.'

'Well, I'd like to try,' I smiled at Martin who was watching me carefully. 'Let me talk to him.'

'You'd best just leave him with us and we'll arrange to get him over there,' the first woman said.

'Wouldn't it be better if I took him there? He trusts me.'

'No my dear, we know how to handle these boys, you leave him with us – we'll get him taken to Father John's place a bit later.'

I tried to explain about the boy's home to Martin,

'... and it's really nice there Martin – you get 3 meals a day, you'll be with other boys, Father John will be kind to you, you don't have to stay there if you don't like it,. Just go for a look. These ladies are going to get someone to take you there from here. I have to go, but I'll come and visit you tomorrow.'

I just hoped that if he went there and saw that he would be looked after, that he could learn some skills, get an education, he might decide to stay.

But all he could hear was that I, who he had come to trust, was deserting him, leaving him with these white strangers. He wept and clung to me.

'No medem, don't leave me, don't leave me, I want to come home with you.'

'Martin you can't, you must give this a try, see if you like it...'

It was hopeless, I knew this was a chance for Martin and may be the only chance he would have. Looking back now, I wish that I had been firm about taking him to the boy's home myself. But the women were insistent, that the sooner he detached himself from me the better and that anyway it was illegal for him to stay at my house. Gently, but firmly they pulled the sobbing boy away from me and I walked out - one part of me sad and confused, feeling like a betrayer, another part of me perhaps, relieved that a problem of great magnitude had been taken from my shoulders.

That evening, I was walking back from the shop when I saw Martin again on the loose with a group of other kids. He rushed up to me and I questioned him about the boy's home and why he wasn't there. He said he hadn't liked it, but I knew he hadn't been there long enough to decide. I tried to persuade him to go back, but his friends started pulling him away, whispering to him.

'Martin, Martin come with me. I'll take you back there, we'll talk to Father John...just stay there for a few days, try it out .....' But it was hopeless, the other kids dragged him off and when I tried to follow them, they all ran away.

After that I hardly ever saw Martin again, except in the distance. Those kids viewed me as some kind of white authority figure trying to reform them I suppose. I felt sad whenever I thought of Martin - and all the other children - lost souls, unloved and uncared for by parents or a state that seemed to care nothing for a large part of the population. The wide spread effects of apartheid were adding stress to our lives too, resulting in feelings of frustration and helplessness.

Chapter 15: The Pink Lady

As time passed it became increasingly obvious that although I tried to take Pas out every day, to the sea or to playgrounds, she needed to have the stimulation of other children to play with. I asked around the few people I knew and eventually someone told me about a little nursery school called Brooksfield.   I rang and made an appointment with the woman who ran it, called Melissa.

Melissa opened the door to a large old house – one of the few with two-storeys that I had seen in the Cape. She was an attractive brunette, with a wide smile and dressed all in pink - pink slacks, pink blouse with frilly cuffs. As someone who rarely wears pink and never frills, I was a little wary at first, but her wide smile and easy vivacious manner soon put me at ease. She didn't make a fuss of Pascale or pretend to be someone who adored children, just let her be – putting out a few toys and children's books for her while we sat chatting on the large, leather couch.

'I started the school about two years ago and I like to provide plenty of stimulation and interest for the children. We teach art and crafts and creative play and we have thirty-five minute sessions. Then they switch to a different teacher.' She smiled, 'I generally don't take kids under three though – how old is Pascale?'

'She's two and three quarters' (I added on a few months,) 'but she's potty trained and very bright.'

'You're not from South Africa are you?'

'No, from the UK – we've been here more than six months now. Pas really needs to be with other kids, she has no one to play with all day.'

'Well, I don't know, she's a bit young; maybe you should wait a few months?'

'Why don't you try her out?' I could feel my freedom pass slipping away. 'I'd need to stay with her for the first few sessions of course, she's not used to being away from me, but I'm sure she'll be fine once she has other kids to play with.'

I was holding my breath, it was hard to find a local nursery school and I had discovered to my horror that children in S Africa did not start school until they were seven.

Melissa frowned and looked at Pascale. She had a packet of cigarettes on the table in front of her. She took one out with slim fingers and polished pink nails, then held the packet out to me. She smiled,

'Smoke?'

'Yes thanks.' I took one out, my hand shaking a little and lit it. I took a long draw and exhaled slowly, thinking about what was I going to do if she said no.

'Have you got kids?'

'Yis, Two big ones and a little one - second marriage!'

'Oh!' I was surprised, '...your second marriage?'

'Well, I was widowed,' she looked away.

'Oh, sorry. Was that a while ago?' I was amazed that this young woman could already be widowed.

'A few years', she said drily, in a tone which discouraged further questions on the subject.

'You South African?'

'Not really' she said, 'I grew up in Northern Rhodesia, it's called Zambia now.'

'Oh I was born in Southern Rhodesia,' I said.

'Really,' Now she was surprised, 'Whereabouts?'

'In Bulawayo, my parents left there when I was three and went back to Wales. What do you think then, will you take her?' I couldn't bear the suspense any more.

'I suppose we could give it a try.' She paused, thoughtfully and gave me a cool appraising look through a cloud of cigarette smoke that was escaping from her pink mouth.

'Well,' she said briskly, suddenly stubbing out her cigarette and standing up.

'Bring her in next Monday and we'll give it a few days trial, see how she gets on.'

I stood up smiling with relief and glanced at Pas who was by now playing with a doll she'd found near the bookcase, talking to herself and undressing it.

'Do you want to have a look around the school?' Melissa moved towards the door at the back of the room. 'The kids aren't here at this time so you can look in all the classrooms.'

'That would be great! Pas come and look at your new school.' I held out my hand.

The school was a long L-shaped one-storey building, an annexe at the back of the house, with a playground at the side. Each of the three large rooms was bright and colourful, with children's paintings on the walls. Pascale held my hand tightly but when she saw the toys and small tables and chairs laid out, she pulled away from me. She wanted to play with them at once.

'Not now Pas – but we'll come back and you can play with the toys and the other children then....'

'Want play now,' she tugged my hand.

'No darling. Not today, we'll come back very soon!'

I took her hand as we walked back to the front door. I didn't know it then but Melissa was to become my dearest friend in Cape Town, with whom I was to share much.

'See you Monday then,' she smiled, holding out her manicured hand. I shook it and knew there and then that our lives would be intertwined.

We came back on Monday at 9 a.m. I didn't know how Pas was going to react to being left, but I thought that maybe once she got involved with playing with other kids, she wouldn't notice my departure. But she had always been quite clingy and never liked to be left with anyone. It was not just insecurity caused by the travelling though – she'd been like that before we left UK. From two weeks old Passy had refused to have anyone but me hold her. We'd moved from Hampton-on-Thames, when we sold our house, prior to our departure and she had, when the removers arrived, clung to the chair that I used to sit on to give her a bottle – a chair given to me by my grandfather – and wept copiously.

Therefore when we got to Mel's nursery I was prepared for a fuss to be made. A few times, I edged towards the door when I saw her involved in sand play or painting. She had a sixth sense though and would spot me trying to slip out and a loud wail would start, so I would have to rush back in to stop the racket. The teacher tried hard to involve her, but after a few attempts her suspicions were aroused and she ran after me and constantly kept me in her sights. Finally, with a sigh I gave up. I took her out telling the teacher we'd come back the next day.

I tried talking to her in the car,

'Pas wouldn't you like to stay in school and play with the other children?'

'Mummy come too.'

'But Mummy has to go to the shops and get food for our supper. You can stay with the other children for a little while can't you?'

'Mummy come too.' Pas was immovable when she'd made up her mind.

The next day the same pattern repeated itself. I stayed for an hour and tried to sneak out when she wasn't looking. But now she was watching me all the time. I was not going to be allowed out of her sight.

I talked it over with Dave that night when he got back. Anthony and Cleopatra was ending in a week or so and he was starting to look around for his next job. We both decided that tomorrow would be the last day of trying to settle her. She just wasn't ready yet.

The next day, Mel saw me arrive and observed the pattern happen again – Pas starting to play, me trying to slip out, loud wails and running after me. She decided to take matters in hand. She told me that this time, I must go for an hour and she'd see what she could do. She took Pas's hand firmly and took her over to the book corner and pulled out a picture book. Pas loved books, so her attention was momentarily diverted. Mel looked over her head at me and nodded and I slipped out. Pas of course noticed almost immediately and I heard the wail and wanted desperately to go back. But Mel had told me that on no account was I to do that. With my hands over my ears I ran out of the playground, through the gates and jumped in the car and drove away, feeling like a monster, tears pouring down my face. I resolved that if she was in a bad way when I got back then we'd have to postpone her start date until she was older. However, I also felt that I badly needed some time on my own to do things that didn't involve a toddler and it felt liberating just to do the shopping on my own.

An hour later, I came back, resigned to hearing continuous wails as I entered the school gates. But to my surprise there was nothing – just the sound of children chatting and playing and a teacher's voice over the top. I looked cautiously through the window of the classroom to find Pas listening quietly beside the teacher to a story with all the rest of the class in a semi-circle, sitting on the floor. Mel saw me from the house and quietly beckoned me in. She took me to the kitchen and asked her maid Lena to make us some tea. We went up the large staircase to the lounge and soon we were smoking and chatting and she told me what had happened:

'When you left, she was making a lot of noise, crying and trying to get out. It was disrupting the whole class. So I picked her up, with some books and took her up to the main house. I put her down in the study on the floor and told her quite clearly,

'If you make that noise, you can't play with the other children. You can stay here on your own while you're crying, with these books to look at, until Mummy gets back. It won't be long. If you stop crying I'll come and get you and you can go back in the class with the other children.'

Pas continued crying loudly, 'I want my mummy.'

Mel repeated what she'd said and then walked out the door and closed it behind her. She waited a few minutes, listening outside the door. At first the crying got louder, and then it subsided and stopped. She waited another minute and then opened the door.

'Have you stopped crying now? If you have you can go back with the other children. OK?'

Pascale looked down at the floor and nodded. She knew when the game was up and she'd met her match. She stood up, Mel scooped up the books and held out her hand. Pas took her hand meekly and they went back to the classroom.

As Mel told me the story, I looked at her admiringly. Wow, she'd accomplished something quite dramatic in one quick morning. I'd thought we'd be dealing with this for weeks and had been afraid that, due to Pas's age, Mel would tell me to come back when Pas was older. Out would go my small dreams of freedom and Pas's chances of mixing with other children.

I didn't quite believe it would continue to work though. Next day we went to the school and I had to be quite firm when we got to the classroom.

'No, Pas (she was holding my hand very tightly), in you go and play with the other kids. I'm going shopping, but I'll come and get you very soon. Give Mummy a kiss.' I bent down and the small arms came round my neck tight and my face got kissed a dozen times before I said,

'Go and play darling. I'll be back soon.' Reluctantly, while she was waving her small hand at me I walked off, with her eyes fixed on me. The teacher was calling to her to come and put on an apron and 'help' with the washing up, irresistible for Pas who loved water play.

This time I stayed away on Mel's instruction for a full three hours. What bliss to have three whole hours all to myself – I drove to Sea Point and sat at a pavement cafe looking at the sea with a cup of tea. Lovely.

When I got back, I peeped through the window, Pas was next to a blonde girl-child in the tiny play kitchen and they were 'making tea'.

'This one for my Mummy, this one for Daddy,' Pas was pouring from a little china teapot.

'An here's some cake too'. They had laid out a table with cups and saucers and side plates, a jug (of pretend milk) and a bowl of (pretend) sugar.

'How many sugars?' the blonde child was saying in her best grown-up voice.

'Ermm, two for Daddy and one for Mummy.'

And so Pas settled into a routine of nursery school, at first 3 mornings a week and then 5 mornings. I had three hours a day to myself. Luxury. Although of course these hours soon got filled with chores at home – washing, cleaning and preparing food for later. Sometimes though I would curl up on the sofa with a book and relax. Bliss!

You might ask how we paid for this nursery school – it was not publicly funded. Anthony and Cleopatra had been a great success in Cape Town. Dave and I had discussed his continued working for CAPAB – this policy of whites-only casts and segregated audiences (other races had set nights they could come) was not tolerable for Dave. He got himself another job in the Labia Theatre – a small company – the production was 'The Cat and the Canary,' a murder mystery involving a haunted house and the reading of an old man's will to relatives. The play had a three week run, and rehearsals started the week after Anthony and Cleo finished. He had a lead part, which of course meant reasonable money.

He was also doing other work, as he was free in the day once rehearsals were over. Now he was doing radio dramas for the Cape Town radio station, they clearly appreciated his microphone technique – there were about two to three a month. These paid quite well and he was in hot demand as a private drama teacher for groups of teenagers from various private schools around Cape Town. Dave had, it seemed, a talent for teaching – he was thoughtful, supportive and inspiring – his classes were most of all fun. He was always asked back - teenagers loved him. He had a teenage group, one afternoon a week. The other groups were ad hoc and occasional. The extra income meant that we could pay Pas's school fees. Sometimes, he'd be asked to come and entertain groups of younger kids. His favourite source material was Spike Milligan's children's stories. He'd use the microphone to make all sorts of sounds, train sounds, popping sounds. He'd practice the stories and sound effects at home to me and Pas. Our favourite was the story about the children who shrunk and went down a drain... they came out on a patch of grass with a big sign 'Beware the Dangerous Rabbit'...

'Hello children,' said a voice. The children looked up and saw a large white rabbit.

'Who are you?' The children said,

'I'm the Dangerous Rabbit,' said the rabbit.

'But rabbits aren't dangerous,' they said. 'Why are you dangerous?'

'I'm dangerous to grass,' said the rabbit, 'I EAT GRASS'.

We'd be laughing so much, hugging ourselves. As Dave would say about comedy, 'It's t-t-timing', quoting some comedian. His comic timing was always spot on.

* * *

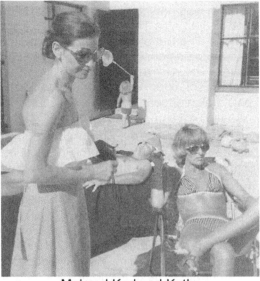
Mel and Karl and Kathy

Chapter 16: Tommy, Mel and Son of Man

Towards the end of the Cat and the Canary run, Dave began looking around for more acting work – he called up the various theatre producers and directors. He really wanted to work for The Space, which was innovative, daring and challenging – but somehow it never worked out – he went to see the director there but they had no parts coming up, that he would be suitable for. The director told him about an interesting theatre group at St George's Cathedral – Jo Dunstan was the director and she was putting on some new plays that quietly challenged the political system, because the theatre group was under the auspices of the church council, which was chaired by Jo's husband, who was vicar of St George's. She was, therefore, given more or less free reign – except each play had to have a loosely religious (Christian) theme. And the usual cast and audience rules in regard to apartheid were able to be suspended, as the stage for this theatre group was in the cathedral and the audience sat in pews.

Dave went to see Jo and they got on at once. Jo was delighted to have found a professional, someone who could 'carry' the rest of the cast. As it was coming up to Christmas, the first production was going to be 'The Nativity', a short run. After that she was talking about a full season of plays. It was unusual, in those days, for professional actors to mix with amateurs in a production, but Dave was game for anything. Besides, the salary was reasonable – a bit less than CAPAB, but we could manage, just. We were both delighted – the cast was mixed, some 'coloured' guys, a few whites and some black. Our old friend Mark the music research lecturer was one, another was John, an administrator at the cathedral. Soon Dave was heavily into rehearsals again, from 9-5 every day, for 3 weeks and after that, nightly performances at the cathedral.

I was very relieved that Dave had been offered another part so quickly – there was, as Pam had previously pointed out, no fall-back position here. If he didn't work, we didn't eat or pay the rent, it was as simple as that. My life settled back again into the routine - taking Pas to nursery school, coming home, doing a few chores, shopping, washing, then fetching her from school again, taking her home, cooking food and putting her to bed. While Dave was rehearsing, he would be home in the evenings. While he was performing, he'd be up late, home in the day, and out every evening for the show.

* * *

It was hot the day Tommy showed up, that first time. The sun was a white, hot ball in a metallic blue sky. Pas was at nursery, Dave was doing a radio play and I was in the bathroom, bending over the bath which contained all the week's wash – jeans, shorts T-shirts etc. We had no washing machine and no means of paying for one, so I bought Sunlight Soap, a large, square, green bar, which smelt of carbolic. Then I scrubbed and rubbed with soap each item, then rinsed and rinsed. My back would be aching by the time all the washing was hanging on the line in the yard. It was so hot that they'd all be dry in little more than an hour.

On this occasion I took a break in the middle, as I was so hot, strolling into the kitchen and taking some lemon squash from the fridge to make myself a drink. I glanced up as the gate creaked and Angel started barking. There he was, all 5 foot 2 inches of him. The hump on his back was pronounced. When he turned to close the gate behind him, he turned his whole body. As he approached my door, I saw the bright inquisitive look on his lively dark face – it did not require sympathy.

'Can ah yev a gloss of warter, medem?' His voice was surprisingly deep.

'Of course,' I grabbed Angel's collar, she was growling and asked him to wait a minute as I shut her in the back yard.

'Come in and sit at the table.' I made him the usual doorstep cheese and tomato sandwich. Hospitality, taking care of visitors were part of the training by my Irish grandmother. It just never occurred to her that guests were not only given a drink (preferably tea), but something substantial to eat too.

Soon, Tommy was chatting away, between gulps of lemon squash and chunks of sandwich. For me it was a welcome break from the routine, the clothes washing, the chores and good to have some adult conversation. The disparity in our circumstances was never referred to directly by Tommy. Much later I discovered that he lived at a squatter camp called Crossroads. What I did know, was that I was drawn to his intelligence and energy and he became a regular visitor.

120

We could talk for hours about any subject, politics, religion - we both had strong opinions and I learnt much from Tommy. Maybe we were both lonely, in our different ways, needing company.

It was his contention that most black people, in the North of the country at least, grew up hating whites. Perhaps it was naivety on my part, but I was shocked by this, not surprised, but shocked. It felt depressing to be part of a group so hated. Yet strangely, here we were Tommy and I, one black, one white, standing outside this situation and talking about it as observers, not participants in this great divide. The outside world did come in and slap us back to reality from time to time though.

One time, Tommy brought with him a couple of other guys he knew – but they took advantage of my hospitality – one walked up to my fridge, opened the door and started to pick things up and put them down again. The other was strolling round, touching our few possessions. I looked at Tommy and walked over to the fridge and said firmly,

'Please, if you want something, just ask and I'll see what I can do – would you like a drink? A sandwich? Sit here please.'

Tommy made some excuse for leaving quite quickly and never brought them again. On another occasion, Tommy turned up unexpectedly. Pas and her little blonde friend Caroline were with me and I had promised to take them to the swimming pool near Rondebosch. The pool was a public one, set in gardens and I sometimes took the kids for a picnic there. But I also knew, that it was for 'whites only' because there was a sign near the entrance saying so. This was an awkward situation, but I had to just come out and say it,

'Tommy, we're going out to the pool near Rondebosch, sorry!'

'Ken ah come too?'

In my head I pictured the heads turning at the pool all staring at this strange little group, how the girls might feel, what would happen if some official came up and demanded that Tommy leave, how that would make Tommy feel, how I would feel (very angry mostly). Our little picnic outing would turn into a great huge scene. No! No I couldn't face it.

Embarrassed, I told him about the policy and the sign.

'So what,' he spoke angrily. I sighed, inwardly,

'Look Tommy, I don't like it either, but if I hadn't promised the girls to go, we could do something else. But they're really looking forward to a swim in the pool. I'll see you another day, I can't take you with us there.'

The reality was that there was no where I could take Tommy as an equal, not to beaches or any public area, not to most of the Brooksfield parents' places. The best place to spend time with Tommy was in my own home.

I gave Tommy a drink and a sandwich in his hand that day and went off with the girls in our little blue Volkswagen. Sitting there by the pool under my beach umbrella, I looked around at the well-kept lawns, the well-spaced groups and felt sad, terribly sad, that Tommy couldn't be with us.

* * *

While Dave was in 'The Nativity, he met up with someone who'd been ahead of him in RADA and who he'd known there, although not well - Henry Goodman. This meeting was to end up in a long collaboration and some significant shows together.

Towards the end of the run, Henry who was also in the cast, told Dave that Jo Dunstan had asked him to direct the next production for The Centre, at St Georges. He was thinking of putting on a Denis Potter play and he asked Dave if he'd like to read for the main part. Dave came home bouncing, around midnight.

'Henry told me tonight – the next show is 'Son of Man' by Dennis Potter. And guess what part he's asked me to read for?'

I looked blank, and asked what it was about.

'The life of Jesus, ending in the crucifixion. But it's different, it's fantastic! And I'm reading for it for Henry, tomorrow afternoon.'

'Wow!' Have you got the script, let me see....'

He was flicking through and I was reading over his shoulder, it was dynamic. I felt delighted that at last he was getting considered for the sort of part he'd always wanted, but also scared – would he get it? Could he pull it off?

We checked it through, page by page, for the character's dialogue, as we always did. Usually it was a few lines here and a few there, but this part was massive, Jesus was on every page and in some sections he had pages of monologue. We looked at each other in awe. It was the sort of part he had always dreamed of and could not have hoped to do in England, where it would have been played by someone well-known or famous.

I sat down beside him, we read chunks together. In the play, Jesus was not represented as some saintly holy man at all. He was a real human being, riven by self-doubt. He was also an orator who knew how to hold his audience in the palm of his hand while putting across his message. In this extract he is addressing a large crowd.

Jesus: 'Hate your enemy. But love your own kind. Your own sort of people. Your own crowd....

But what – tell me then, dear, safe, cosy, smug people – what is so extraordinary about holding the hands of your own brothers and sisters? Mmmm? Do you want me to congratulate you for loving those who love you? Eh? Eh?

[*Silence*]

Love your enemies.

[*Pause*]

Love your enemies! Yes. I say it again. Love your enemies. It is all that is left to us. It is all that can save us. Love – the hardest, toughest, most challenging, most invincible force of all. Love your enemies. Love those who hate you.'

It was stunning, the script was so powerful. I looked at Dave to see if he was frightened by the magnitude of this part, but his eyes were sparkling,

'I'm going to get it.' His voice was firm, he was relishing the challenge.

I pointed to one monologue, it was four pages long. It was a lot to learn, although Dave had a phenomenal memory for lines.

'Yeh, I know.' He was flicking through the script, grinning. I was shaking my head from side to side in disbelief.

'So you think you can do it then?' His enthusiasm was infectious, I was smiling broadly. My question was ironical, as the answer was written all over his face.

'Bloody hell!' I was shaking my head at the number of pages of lines to learn. 'Well, let's see if you get it before we get excited. When's rehearsals start?'

'Next week! First week in January, three weeks rehearsal.' He glanced up at me and laughed.

'And you know what else? They're gonna do the crucifixion scene by the altar in St George's, look there's a scene at the end where they put me on a crucifix.'

'Christ Almighty!' I gasped, '... er perhaps that's not the right way to put it.... Wow!'

Next day, I held my breath, until Dave came home from his meeting with Henry.

'It went well, I think I've got it.' He looked cheerful. Sue Parker, Henry's wife had been in the next room. She'd come in smiling, when he finished doing the reading and shook his hand.

'I'm in with a good chance anyway.' By the look on his face, he clearly felt he'd done a good reading.

Months later, Henry told him that he hadn't been sure after the reading, but that Sue, who'd heard it all from the next room, had felt that Dave was right for the part. She'd persuaded Henry to offer it to Dave. Henry had then gone to Jo Dunstan and agreed to direct it, but told her that he wanted Dave to play Jesus. Jo wasn't sure, she'd only seen Dave do a smallish part in The Nativity and had reservations, but Henry had overruled them.

A few days later, as I was dropping Pas off to Brooksfield, I bumped in to Melissa. She invited me up to her sitting room and asked her 'maid' Lena to get us a cup of tea. Soon, we were chatting away and smoking Mel's king size cigarettes.

Henry had told Dave he wanted him for the part, the day before. I was excited for him, so told Mel all about it.

She said, that was wonderful, lit another cigarette and poured us both a glass of wine to celebrate. She clapped her hands and seemed genuinely impressed. I told her about him going up on the cross at the end of the play and we both laughed,

'Well he's a bit wild,' I sighed. 'He doesn't have much resemblance to Jesus! Maybe that's why he'll be good at it?'

There was something about Mel's lively attractive face and world-weary manner that always held me in thrall. I looked up to her like an older sister. I wanted to know all about her. She had told me about being widowed but much later I discovered that she was not widowed at all – she'd just told people she was, to fend off questions about an unhappy marriage. Brought up in 'Northern Rhodesia' (i.e. Zambia), her father had been a doctor. She had two children by this marriage – Errol and Noelle. Noelle was coming up to fourteen and Errol was 11. She had a little one by her present husband, Werner, called Gabrielle or Gabby. When talking about her childhood, she mentioned 'the munts' several times – I frowned and looked at her, puzzled. 'What's 'the munts?'

'Oh, it's what we called the blacks in Rhodesia.' Her tone was casual.

'God what a horrible word.' I hoped that my reaction would make her stop using it. I knew she'd been brought up with it, but she had to know that it was degrading to use such a term. She gave me a strange look (years later she told me that it had never occurred to her before and I don't remember her using it after that).

I told her a bit about myself – my middle-class upbringing in Wales, my rather strict (English) father and his occasional bouts of explosive rage. We smoked quite a bit that morning until it was time to dash off to the shops before school was over for the morning.

She told me about her husband Werner - they'd been married for six years and her third child Gabby was his. He was German and most of his friends were also – there was a large German community in Cape Town. They would all meet up regularly, in the evening, at the German Club, in the centre of Cape Town.

'Would you like to come and have lunch one day? Ma maid, Lena, can take Pas and Gabby off somewhere, maybe you can meet a friend of mine – Dieter, I'll ask him too.'

'Yes,' I smiled, '… that would me lovely.' Oh! It was lovely, I was thinking, to have a new friend like Mel.

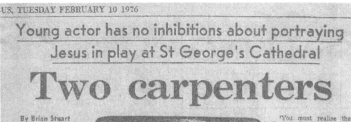

Young actor has no inhibitions about portraying Jesus in play at St George's Cathedral

Two carpenters

By Brian Stuart

THE one facet of his life which David Janes feels most people will not believe, is that his hobby is carpentry. For he is the young British actor who will portray Jesus in Dennis Potter's play, Son of Man, at St George's Cathedral this month.

'I do a lot of carpentry — I like working with wood,' David Janes said when we spoke about his role as Jesus.

'I am an actor, but there are times I need to earn money between jobs, so I have sold some of my carpentry, such as bookcases. My daughter Pascale sleeps on a bed I made.'

The slender, tanned young actor — he is 26, which is younger than the Jesus he will portray — is growing a small beard for the part. 'Not a big bushy thing, but enough to suggest a bearded Jesus,' he remarked.

'ON THE RUN'

He started life in Hong Kong, the son of a physics lecturer whose teaching profession has taken him and his family around the world — he is now in Singapore. So the young David was educated 'on the run,' partly in Nigeria and Uganda, before ending in his native Wales.

DAVID JANES, who will portray Jesus in a modern play at St George's Cathedral.

It was a school production of Shakespeare's Much Ado About Nothing that fired his interest in acting and led to his training at the Royal Academy of Dramatic Arts. And it was his travels with his father which created his desire to return to Africa with his wife and child last June.

An intense, articulate person who pours himself out, even in ordinary conversation, David has no inhibitions about playing Jesus.

'I am called on to play the part of a man, a carpenter, not the Christ,' he says. 'He has his doubts, frustrations and human qualities, he is completely human, but at the same time has what the Welsh call the hwyl.'

He had a moment's difficulty describing a 'hwyl' to a non-Welshman. 'Well, it's a spirit thing — a spiritual filling. You know, the sort of thing that floods a Welshman at a rugby match at Cardiff Arms Park. It is stirring.

'You must realise that Dennis Potter has not ripped away the majesty of Jesus. He is man of spiritual strength. There are moments in the play when the realisation that he is the Chosen One floods him.

'PRECONCEPTIONS'

'But I am not nervous about this role. Oh, I have the usual nerves an actor has about his part. But I am not afraid of the reaction from an audience in which individuals may have their own preconceptions about Jesus, because I feel that what Potter says does not in any way detract from the teachings of Jesus. To me, they become more understandable.

'After all, what I am doing in the role is to put across the teaching which is found in the Gospels, but without the barrier of the pulpit. That is the thing — I have to speak, in ordinary language, directly to the person in my audience.'

He pauses for a moment. 'Playing this part, I think I am growing within myself. You know, Henry Goodman (the director) and I have even studied modern translations of the Gospels.'

Son of Man will be presented by the Arts and Drama Department of The Centre at St George's Cathedral in Cape Town from February 25.

Chapter 17: The visitors

The rules of apartheid were strict. You found them out as you went along. You didn't see them written down anywhere. Punishment for breaking those rules was swift and severe, not just for 'non-whites'. No 'non-whites' except live-in maids must be outside of their township after dark, usually around 6 pm.

A couple of times our cleaner, Katrina, babysat for us. Dave drove her back afterwards to Wynberg, the coloured township where she lived. She, of course, could not sit next to him – a white driver – she must sit in the back. She should not be abroad in a white area after dark. There were other implications for a black/coloured women sitting next to a white man in his car, implications that neither of us considered, in our naivety.

Besides, for Dave it was as if apartheid did not exist. It would not have occurred to him to treat someone differently because of skin colour. He grew up in mixed-race schools in Uganda and Nigeria. He ignored apartheid as if it was not there. And somehow, in spite of my upbringing in largely white Wales, with all the racist attitudes of the 50s and 60s, born of ignorance, I was the same.

Dave came home one evening from rehearsals and said one of the stagehands had asked if we could put up a black musician and his white girlfriend, for a couple of nights. He was a friend of a friend.

Apparently, they had nowhere to go, they'd come down from Jo'burg, looking for work. They couldn't stay together in either black or white areas. It was against the law and it would put whoever they stayed with, in danger from the secret police. Dave looked at me.

'Of course they can stay.' Dave smiled, 'I assumed you'd say that.'

'You mean you've already told them they can stay?'

Dave went to the fridge and took out a bottle of beer, picked up the bottle opener and click, fizz! He sipped from the bottle.

'Yep!'

'When are they coming?'

'Tonight, about midnight.'

'Bloody hell! Where are we going to put them?' I leapt to my feet and looked round wildly. I glanced at the wall clock. It said 11 pm.

'They'll have to go in Pas's room, we can bring her cot into our room.' There was a single bed in there for Di or anyone else who came to visit.

'It's gonna be a bit of a squash, two of them in a single bed . . .?'

'Yeh well. It'll have to do.'

'... and how long are they staying?'

'Well, he had to see someone in Cape Town today about fixing up a gig and then they're off to Durban for another gig. Not long I think, one night? Two? ...'

'OK come and help me carry the cot into our room.'

We crept in there - Pas woke so easily, we whispered and walked on tiptoe. I picked up armfuls of clean washing from the spare bed, looking for clean sheets and a blanket . . .

When we were back in the living room, Dave started chatting about his rehearsals in St George's Cathedral.

Then I heard the gate squeak, Angel gave a low growl and there was a soft knock on the door. I grabbed Angel's collar.

The couple on the doorstep looked nervous -- he was tall and thin, with hollow cheeks, a straggly beard, short wiry black hair, old blue jeans. He was older than us, perhaps about 30. She had long light-coloured hair, tied back in a po-nytail. She wore blue bellbottoms on her slim figure, her skin pale. The guy carried an old rucksack and a guitar case.

I opened the door wide and they stepped inside. They introduced themselves - Sam and Jeany. Dave handed him a bottle of cold lager, she just wanted a cup of Rooibos tea, so I had one too. Soon Dave was cracking jokes and making them laugh. He had a great gift for putting people at their ease. I was curious and so asked questions. They both looked quite tense but were beginning to relax.

'So where have you travelled from today?' I said.

'We stayed in Beaufort West last night.' Sam answered, sitting forward on the settle. 'My cousin lives there, but it was awkward for him. Beaufort West is a small place and so's the township.'

'Yes, we stayed there ourselves, when we came down from Jo burg.'

He looked at Dave sideways. They did not stay where we stayed.

'You stayed in the township?' I asked.

'Yes of course, I can't go into the white areas. And she can't be seen with me. In the township, a white woman stands out, so we had to smuggle her in and then she had to stay hidden indoors.'

I let that sink in, and felt for their situation.

'I've made some soup,' ...changing the subject, I was already on my feet, cutting large slices of wholemeal bread, while waiting for the soup to heat up - a thick vegetable broth made with a hock of ham from the butchers and carrots, onions, potatoes and herbs.

I passed them well-filled bowls, with the bread.

They had second helpings of the soup and were soon smiling and chatting. Sam came from a township near Pretoria. As he was talking, I pictured small concrete huts with corrugated tin roofs, long dusty streets with grubby children playing outside, we'd driven past quite a few. Did his mother work as a live-in maid in a white suburb? I wondered how he became a musician, must have been hard....

But in fact my picture was quite wrong. It seemed his father was a doctor and they lived in the better part of the township. His father was always busy, the area he covered was huge and the funding low. He was not pleased with his son's choice of career. I knew what that was like – I'd dropped out of my law degree a few years before and got married to Dave – my parents hadn't been too pleased either. Sam's lifestyle was wandering, nomadic, going from gig to gig ... and made doubly hard by being with a white girl.

There was a knock on our front door and we all jumped, Sam and Jeanie looked nervously at the door. I went around to the bathroom and looked out of the window to see who it was.

'It's okay,' I called, 'It's only Peter, he's fine.'

Peter came in and was soon chatting away to both of them. It seemed Jeanie was from the suburbs near Jo'burg. Sam was performing at a nightclub in Jo'burg when they met and they've been together ever since. But apartheid made it very stressful and difficult. Sam had been arrested twice by different police and taken away from Jeanie for a night in a police station. He didn't say much, but I was sure he'd not been treated well.

I explained about the bed arrangements and that Pascale got up early, so they might get woken up. Jeanie said she was tired and would anybody mind if she went to bed? I took her into the bedroom and showed her the bed.

'I'm afraid it's a single bed.'

'It's fine, believe me this is luxury compared to some of the places we've had to stay.'

Alone in the bedroom, she relaxed and started telling me a bit about the life style they were leading. If the police saw them together, they'd be watched or stopped and questioned. Interracial relationships were forbidden under the rules of apartheid.

'And Sam gets angry with them so easily,' she sighed. 'I keep telling him to keep his cool, not to antagonise them, but he won't listen.'

I nodded sympathetically, but didn't know what to say. That's the way it was here and although I often felt outraged, I couldn't do much about it.

Jeanie lay down wearily on top of the unmade bed as I unfolded the sheets.

'Do you think Sam might like to play his guitar? I'd love to hear him.'

'Oh yeah, you ask him,' she was yawning again. 'He'd like that, he loves to play for people.'

She helped me make the bed with the sheets. It was a warm night, so blankets weren't needed. I showed her the bathroom and then the kettle, teabags and cups in the kitchen. She went over to Sam and kissed him, then back to the bedroom, shutting the door, leaving me with the three guys. She had told me Sam parked their car, an old battered Morris minor, in the car park, close to our back lane. When they travel, she drives and he sits in the back, in case they're stopped. Then they can pretend, he's the gardener and she's driving him somewhere, to pick up supplies for the garden.

I asked Sam if he'd play for us and he picked up his guitar. Most musicians will play for even a small audience, I find. For a while, he gave us an impromptu performance of his music and singing. I was transported by the beauty of our own private concert and felt privileged to hear it. Sam had a deep voice and a raw quality to his singing which was moving.

Peter K had scored some 'ganja' from his local source, so he was rolling a big joint and soon Sam put down his guitar. Dave told stories about the cast of the Nativity and the rehearsals for Son of Man. I left the three guys to pass the joint around and 'shoot the breeze', about music, writing and poetry ... and crawled into bed.

Next day, I rose reasonably early, but they were already both up and Dave had made them tea. I gave them some cornflakes and toast and they smiled and we all shook hands. We walked them out to their car and they told us they were driving up towards Somerset West and then to a gig in Hermanus ... I watched them driving off and felt sad that this is how they lived and that's what it's like here.

'Dave! We have to get out of this fucking country soon, I can't stand it.'

'I know, but at least I'm working for a mixed-race theatre group now. We'll have to see how it goes for a bit longer...'

'Pas can't grow up thinking this is normal, can she?

I felt a kind of impotent rage and frustration about the stupidity of it all. But you couldn't talk about it here.

I drove Pas to school and went upstairs with Mel for some tea and a cigarette. I looked at her, thinking - she's used to all this, apartheid seems normal to her, I suppose.

* * *

Dave's rehearsals for Son of Man were going well, although he said that if Henry was giving him director's notes, he would often turn his back on him – Henry had a habit of acting out his own directions and Dave told him frequently to stop. The part had to be his own interpretation, not a copy of Henry's.

Jo and the stage hands started working out how to get him up on the cross at the end of the show. The logistics were difficult, the dying Jesus had to put his hands through looped ropes. The cross was attached to a pillar, with a small platform to stand on. He would have to access it, via the steps next to the pulpit.

A nun from St George's was coming every day, to watch the rehearsals and she was spending quite a lot of time chatting to Dave. The final scene was Jesus on the cross, taking his last breath and saying 'It – is – ACCOMPLISHED.'

I had spent all my school life in convents, although this was an Anglican nun. My convents had been Roman Catholic, Ursuline order and most of the nuns had been Irish. Every day he came back with tales of long conversations Sister Maria had had with him. Dave was six foot two with eyes of blue, good looking and charismatic, especially in that part. I began to suspect that the nun, the bride of Christ, had developed a crush on him and kept teasing him about it.

'Seen Sister Maria today?'

'Yes she came by as I was getting down from the cross, actually.' He was looking at me warily, waiting for the punch line.....

'Well, Jesus saves, I suppose... did she ask you to perform any miracles. Mention loaves and fishes, walking on water? No? .... Strange ...'

We both laughed.

Di and Jane were coming to the opening night on February 10th. Peter and Steve had also said they were coming. I arranged for Pas to stay the night at Mel's -- Lena was babysitting for her and Gabby, so I was going to leave the car there and Mel was going to drive us.. Pam couldn't come as she was away on tour with CAPAB that week. Robert, my mad hatter friend, wouldn't come to the show until a few days later. It was going to be quite a turnout. It was all getting very exciting and although confident Dave could pull it off, I felt nervous for him. We were going over his lines every night before the show. Dave was more or less word perfect by a week before, even the long, four-page monologues.

Chapter 18: A Spiritual search

Perhaps it was one of the hidden effects of apartheid that made me embark on my own spiritual quest with renewed vigour. The feelings of anger and lack of control towards a government so often cruel and uncaring about the effects of its policies on everyone in South Africa. While Dave was involved with 'Son of Man', which was stretching him to his mental limits, my mental focus turned to a spiritual search.

I was brought up a Roman Catholic and after a devout phase in my early teenage years, boys and parties had become the main focus of my attention, until I met Dave. When we arrived in South Africa, I was still nominally a Catholic, so at first, once we had settled in Cape Town, I looked for a Roman Catholic Church. The one I went to was packed with young people and a guitar-playing priest led the service. Peace and love was talked of from the pulpit and breaking down the racial barriers. However the church was in a white area and obviously black and coloured people were not much in evidence – they would have had too far to travel.

My spiritual yearnings had moved on from Christianity and I soon discovered through friends, like Peter and Steve, a complete smorgasbord of gurus and spiritual paths which bore investigation. Peter and Steve's guru, Charang Singh was interesting, but a hard path to follow - becoming a vegan, giving up all intoxicants and meditating for an hour and a half each day was too much for me, I thought.

The local library and bookshops had books about reincarnation, spiritualism and leaflets about other 'gurus' coming to Cape Town to give staged events to introduce their path or practise. I went to a few of these events and looked with a critical eye, as pictures and artefacts were on display at high prices. To me the spiritual life should not be a money-making venture.

One evening, I went to a public event in a church hall. It showed a film about an Indian swami, who was apparently able to spontaneously produce, large, semi-precious jewels (ready-faceted) from various orifices in his body. Mainly they were reported to be gulped up from his throat and his disciples vied with each other to purchase these jewels, for highly inflated prices – they were claimed to have magical properties and would be a link between you and your guru-swami. I had no money and anyway was not interested in a spiritual life that focused on raising cash. So I moved on swiftly to the next one.

One of the books I was reading, as I mentioned earlier, was an autobiography of a then famous British psychic called Ena Twigg. She had been 'seeing dead people,' since early childhood and the book was fascinating. As there was no television until 1976 in South Africa (and even then, only one State sponsored, censored channel), in the evening, when not socialising, I read, read, read. Those who say there's no evidence about reincarnation and psychic phenomena have not really looked. There are hundreds of books out there – of varying quality admittedly - the library had a whole section. I was devouring them all. There were many convincing case histories and personal stories. I read enough books to convince me that there's evidence out there, if you want to find it. If you don't that's your choice.

One day I heard about a psychic, who lived outside Cape Town towards Simonstown (about 30 miles away) and telephoned to make an appointment to visit her. I should add that although I became convinced by the evidence for reincarnation, I retained scepticism and examined credentials and evidence carefully. I say this, as those who don't believe, always think that us seekers are gullible idiots, which has always struck me as arrogant and patronising.

I drove up to an old battered Cape Dutch cottage in a small suburb, on a rather unkempt plot of land. A small plump woman in a brown knee length skirt and cream blouse, opened the door. She had short brown curly hair and looked ordinary and rather homely. She sat me down with a cup of Rooibos tea in her living room which had polished wood and lace doilies everywhere.

'So my dear, why have you come to see me?'

I didn't know how to answer the question, I knew that Dave and I were going through a difficult patch, his drinking was sometimes problematical. Our friend Pam had said to me once,

'Why is Dave such a lovely guy when he's sober and then after he's been drinking for a while...'

She'd trailed off. We both knew what she meant.

I'd brushed it off with excuses. But social events could be difficult for me, as I'd never know how much he was going to drink (he could drink most people under the table) and the result could mean he became difficult or even unpleasant at times.

'Well, I'm not sure really, just thought I'd see what the future holds.'

She closed her eyes for a moment, then opened them again.

'There's a man standing behind you....how can I describe him - a short man with a large stomach and a waistcoat on....reminds me of Winston Churchill, he's smoking a big cigar...'

This was an uncannily accurate portrait of my maternal grandfather Dr TGH James, who'd died a year before I was born. I was startled.

'...and there's a woman, dark, slim, big brown eyes – looks a bit like you'. (This had to be my father's mother, Missy, who'd died when I was small), she's telling me, she visits your child in her cot sometimes, talks to her. Has she ever talked about people who aren't there?'

I was surprised, 'No,' I wracked my brain, 'No she hasn't...'

'Well, listen out for it, she might...'

'...and what about my husband. Do they say anything?'

She paused, then gave a long sigh....

'I really don't know why you two are together... so different... I'll give you a picture that comes to my mind about him... you can lead a horse to water... You understand what I'm saying?'

'Yes... I think so.' I thought of the number of times I'd recounted to Dave what he'd done when he was drinking – said something unpleasant to someone that I'd had to cover up, got really drunk at a party and become difficult to deal with, falling about, arguing about going home...

'But you can't make it drink,' she said firmly shaking her head.

I nodded, Dave was the nicest, warmest, funniest guy, but when it came to alcohol and drugs – he just gravitated towards them, like a moth to a flame. No matter how many warnings he had, he ignored them all. Once, he told me that in his two and a half years in RADA, (when we were married and without me knowing) he'd taken acid (LSD) numerous times, as well as daily alcohol and marijuana. Of course many of his fellow students were doing the same, some of whom are well known actors today.

I gave the woman her money and reflected on what she'd said on the way home. I wondered if Pas would speak of her 'ghostly visitations' by my grandmother and I thought about Dave and our relationship. He was my husband, my lover and my best friend, as well as Pas's father. Leaving him was out of the question for me, we would just have to carry on for the moment.

A few nights later, Peter came round. I told him about my visit to the psychic. He pondered for a bit then said,

'Have you asked Pas if she's seen anyone?'

'Yeh...she just ignored me and carried on playing with Big Doll. I tried again later... she didn't seem to have a clue what I was talking about... so I gave up. Maybe it's true, maybe it isn't – who knows. Still it was weird the way the woman described my grandfather – couldn't have been a better description. And Missy, my grandmother.

I changed the subject. 'Tell me more about your guru, Peter? What's he like? And Steve said that I should ask you to teach me how to meditate....'

He talked quietly for a bit about his Indian guru, saying that he believed it was the right path for him to follow and that meditation helped his mental problems a great deal.

'You want to try meditation? That's easy. First sit down on a cushion, see if you can do the lotus position - otherwise just sit cross legged.'

As sitting cross-legged had always been comfortable for me, I found that I could manage the lotus-position quite easily.

'Now,' said Peter 'I'm going to give you a mantra to say in your head. You close your eyes and just keep repeating it over and over.'

I wondered if this was like Transcendental Meditation that the Beatles had been practising for the last few years. George Harrison was a follower of the Maharishi. He'd grown his hair long and was learning to play the sitar from Ravi Shankar.

I sat quietly on my cushion on the floor and Peter sat next to me. He said, 'We'll just do twenty minutes,' then stop. Alright, first you learn to count your breath.'

He showed me how to breathe deeply and slowly, in ... out, in ... out - in blocks of ten. Then we talked about a mantra, a word you focused on and repeated in your head.

'Will you be saying the same mantra as me?'

'No, we get given our own mantra when we commit ourselves to Charan Singh, to following his path. You don't tell anyone else your mantra.'

'What mantra shall I say then?'

'Radha Swami, just say that, repeat it over and over in your head. The purpose of meditation is to quieten down all the thinking. Rest your mind.'

'OK. What does it mean? Radha Swami?'

'It means Lord of Souls.'

I liked the sound of it, the meaning of it too. I tried it out. Radha Swami, Radha Swami. Yes. I was going to meditate every day if I could. Peter said the benefits of meditation were enormous, it could change your life.

'And don't tell anyone your mantra, keep it to yourself, hey?'

'Why not?' I felt conspiratorial, pleased with myself. It was my mantra, my secret.

'Because it reduces its power'.

Of course intention and reality are often two different things aren't they? I had a 2 year old, a husband and a busy social life. So although I had phases of regularly practising meditation over the next year, faithfully repeating my mantra, these phases ebbed and flowed like the Sea Point tides.

Dave as Jesus in Son of Man by Samuel Beckett

Dave on the cross as Jesus

Chapter 19: Katrina returns

Son of Man opened to great notices from the Cape Town press on Feb 8th 1976 - reviews came out a few days later. The Cape Times said

'He has a part of literally superhuman difficulty. He plays him simply as a troubled man, an honest carpenter, with fears and doubts and anguish, all a part of the burden he has elected to share with humanity, but with a constant awareness of the Godhead within him. Last night he held the audience from his appearance in the wilderness to the Crucifixion, conveying with quiet power, exhaustion, exultation and fear.'

We sat and read the reviews together and looked at each other, smiling.

'You were fantastic, you know, everyone said. I told you. I'm so pleased that you're playing a part like this at last.'

Dave waved his hand dismissively, but I threw my arms round him and hugged him,

'Well done, can I have your autograph now?' We both laughed.

'Actually, there were a few people waiting at the Stage door tonight, wanting me to sign their programme.'

'Wow, autographs, that's fab, you'd never have got anywhere near a part like that in the UK.'

'I know, I know, I've been very lucky here.'

'Luck's got nothing to do with it, you were thrown a magnificent part and you rose to it.'

He grinned, shy (for once) and then changed the subject.

'What's for lunch?'

* * *

A few weeks later, Dave finished his run of Son of Man. Henry was putting on another play - The Lovers, by Brian Friel, which he'd managed to get some funding for. Henry was directing again. It was a play in two halves – The Lovers and The Losers, Dave was in the second half. So now, Dave was out all day again at rehearsals.

One of those days, I was sorting the washing in the back bedroom, when I heard a familiar voice....

'Medem, medem, are yew there?'

The top of the stable door to our place was always open, to let in the light and the cool breeze. My heart sank, as I hurried up the passageway back to the kitchen.   Katrina stood on the other side of the door, grinning her gap-toothed smile, a bright scarf tied round her head and a blanket tied above and below her bust – the familiar African way to carry a baby.

So, she'd had the baby.

'Katrina! What a surprise! You've had the baby then!'

She was opening the bottom half of the door, before I could say anymore and undoing the blanket.   She un-wrapped the tiniest cutest little baby – thick curly hair, big eyes and tiny sweet mouth.

'Look medem, she's four wiks old now, why don't yew hold her?'

Katrina was shrewd, she knew I would melt at sight of the baby and holding her in my arms would cement it. As I took the baby, the big brown eyes fixed on me and the little thing cooed and I was captivated. I noticed wet patches around the nappy area of the Babygro.

'Katrina, this baby needs changing…?'

''Yis medem, ah no….'

'Have you got a spare nappy?'

'Er no, medem, none left…'

There was an awkward silence… I groaned silently to my-self, no money for nappies and probably none for milk either - a trap had been sprung and I was caught, well and truly.

'I'll go and get some.'

'Yis medem, tenk yew medem. And maybe some milk for the baby too while yew in the shop'.

'You mean baby-milk powder? Which one? Which for-mula?'

Katrina looked blank and a discussion ensued where it be-came clear she hadn't any idea. I would have to check on the tin, that I got the right one for a baby this age.

At that moment Pas woke up from her afternoon nap in the bedroom and wandered in, rubbing her eyes, which lit up, as she saw the baby.

'Mum, mum, mum, baby, baby, me hold, me hold!'

I lifted her on to the settle and put the baby into her little arms, which just about came round the baby, so I held on too. It wasn't safe for her do it on her own. She looked at the baby's face with a rapt expression and I showed her the tiny hands – next to which Pas's, which had always seemed so little, were huge!

Katrina wrapped the baby back onto her back, while Pas and I went to the supermarket. When I returned, Katrina was cleaning the sink and she handed me the baby again. Soon, I was changing the baby's nappy, boiling a kettle, measuring the milk formula into the bottle that Katrina had just washed out.

'Why aren't you breast-feeding, it's cheaper?'

'Yis medem, but ah hed this problem with ma breasts, it was very sore, I couldn't do it yew see...'

'Oh I see.' I began to worry about what she lived on now, how the baby was being fed and cared for, was Katrina still drinking? She looked clear-headed today.

'Where are you staying now?' I shot her a glance, 'The truth please?'

Katrina started talking. One thing she did well was talk, she had the gift of the gab all right.

'You see medem, I gotta room now in thus house over un Wahnberg.'

'Oh yes.' I sighed to myself.

'And now I got the baby, ut's expensive medem, so if you can give me some work medem?' I sighed again

'OK Katrina, but I don't want to see you drinking or turning up with alcohol on your breath.'

'Oh no, medem, Ah got the baby to think about now.' She was not looking at me. She was already sweeping the floor and looking around with a practised eye. She knew how to clean my place from past experience that was the one thing she was good at.

Over the next few weeks Katrina came more or less weekly, each time chatting away, asking questions. Each time I found myself taking the baby, who was adorable, bathing her, changing her sodden nappy (after buying a new packet), using Pas's old Babygros. Pas loved to see Caroline, as she was called and would sit with her, as she lay on the settle and talk to her and make her laugh.

The alcohol abstinence didn't last of course. A few times I could smell it on Katrina's breath and then later even smell it from the pores of her skin. I worried about the baby more and more. There was no proper social services here as I'd found out when dealing with Martin. The women from the Black Sash, that I had taken Martin to see, had run a little charity for lost children. I didn't think they'd want to handle this situation. I tried ringing them. It was difficult to explain – there were so many domestic servants with problems.

'Does she want to have the child adopted?' I didn't know as had not dared to broach the subject with Katrina. She'd already lost 3 children.

Then one day, she again turned up smelling of drink. Caroline's nappy was sodden and she was quieter than usual. She was now 6 weeks old. I took the wet clothes and nappy off. I started to clean her up and that's when I noticed the bruises – there were large black bruises on her buttocks. Oh my god, I thought, this can't be true. I know Katrina can be careless and drinks too much... but this. My heart sank.

'Katrina!' I said, 'Can you come and look at this.' I pointed to the bruises.

Her voice went shrill, 'No medem, ah know what yew thunking, but it wan't me, it was thet wummin, I was leaving her with, so ah could werk. Ah caym bek to mah room two days ago and found this. Ah dudn't know what to do. I hed a argument wuth her 'And ah told her... I took Kerolahn away 'n went round looking for another room. See, she was the wun ah rented the room from, I was giving her a little of mah munnee... oh medem, yew gotta believe me, ut wasn't me it was her.'

I looked at Katrina dubiously, whoever had done it, this meant one thing only. Katrina was not capable of looking after the baby any more. Something had to be done. I suspected Katrina had got very drunk and had done it herself, but I couldn't be sure. Her stories were all so plausible.

'Katrina, if any more harm comes to this baby, you are in big trouble.'

'No medem, no. Ah won't leave her wuth that witch again, for sure.'

Soon afterwards she left, Caroline strapped to her back. I sat down and did some hard thinking. That night I went to see Jane and Di next door. Jane was from Cape Town and she was practical. Maybe she'd have some idea what to do. I explained the situation.

'How terrible,' said Di immediately, 'We must do something.'

'I know, but what?'

Jane said, 'Well, I can ask around in work, my assistant is from Retreat [a coloured township], she might know someone.'

'Oh thanks, Jane that'd be great.'

'Well something must be done for sure.'

'I wish I could adopt the baby myself, but it's impossible here. How could I bring her up in a white's only area? Or maybe I could take her to the UK? But how? How could I get her out?'

'No, no, no, it's not possible.' Jane was shaking her head firmly. 'Let me make some enquiries at the hotel.'

I sighed, I had never come across such a situation and it was a huge burden that I felt had been placed on me alone. I already had to run a small home on a shoestring budget, and take care of my own child. Also I was still suffering from cluster migraines and my health and energy were often poor as a result. If I got a bad one, I was out of action for three days. I'd be doped up with Doloxene in order to get out of bed, feed Pas and take her to nursery. Then I'd go home, do some cleaning and if the migraine lifted carry on. Otherwise take another Doloxene and try and sleep it off until it was time to pick Pas up at lunchtime, bring her home and feed her.

We had no television, so I hoped that Steve would come round with his kids to play. Then I could talk over the Katrina situation with him. But that week, I didn't see him and his kids, so I made some play-dough to keep Pas occupied, she loved making shapes with the cutter. Her favourite game at home was water play – she loved that – standing on a stool by the sink with a plastic apron on, 'doing the washing up'. But today we concentrated on the play-dough shapes, while I turned over and over in my mind what to do.

My days had formed a pattern, which I tried to manage while dealing with the migraines. Now suddenly Katrina had thrown a firework into the middle and somehow I had to put it out.

The next evening, there was a knock on my door about 8 in the evening, I'd just put Pas to bed and was cleaning up the kitchen before settling down with a good book. Dave had left a few hours before to go the theatre. It was Jane.

'Come in, come in – have a glass of wine or a cup of tea?'

'I won't luvvy. I've got Herman coming over, I just wanted to let you know that I spoke to Joan, my assistant – she's got a 15 year old daughter, who's a bit of a handful, goes out a lot. She said she's missing having a little girl around and was thinking about whether to have another child. I explained the situation and she said she might be interested in adopting. If she got pregnant, she wouldn't be able to carry on working and she can't manage without her job.'

'Oh, that sounds good, is she OK? How long have you known her?

'She's very reliable, works hard. She's worked with me for two years now.

'What do you think? She sounds great and she knows what babies are like if she's got a teenage daughter. When will she let you know?'

'Well... I won't see her tomorrow. I'll see her again on Monday, that's when she's next on shift.' [It was now Friday]. And after what you told me ... well it seems like a better situation for a baby.'

This was very good news - if Joan decided to go ahead...

'Well fingers crossed eh?' Jane was edging towards the door. 'Anyway I have to go. Bye for now.'

I could see that Jane was rushing to get out – Herman her fiancé was coming round, and they did everything together. They were planning to get married next year. For Jane, it was not really her problem - such things happened here. 'These people' must sort out their own problems. But the reality of this situation had shocked her and she'd felt compelled to do something. If it could be sorted with minimum intervention by her, then that was OK.

'Anyway, thanks for your help Jane. You're a lifesaver. Where's Di tonight?'

'Oh, you know Di! Out with one of her guys'. She smiled and left with a toss of her neat flicked-up brown hair.

I was left thinking, Oh no! I'll be worrying about this all weekend. It was going to be difficult either way. If Jane's assistant said 'No', what would I do? If Jane's assistant said 'Yes', then what? I would have to talk to Katrina and persuade her to give up the baby, persuade her it would be best for her and the baby. How was I going to do that? Katrina wasn't coming until Tuesday, I hoped I'd have an answer my then.

Joan did say yes, as Jane reported to me on Monday evening, which was very good news. Now it was down to me to manage a meeting between her and Katrina and she was coming the next day. I talked over how to approach Katrina, with Dave when he got back from rehearsals.

'Well, just go on about how it's best for the baby and she'll have a better life... don't you think...? '

'I'll try, I just have to see what she says. She must know that her drinking and carrying round a baby isn't good. Not for her or the baby. If she refuses I might contact the Black Sash or something, see what they can come up with...I can't just leave it, no! I never thought I'd see that, bruises on a six week old baby.' I was shaking my head.

Katrina came the next day and as usual set to work, while talking and talking. She was at the sink washing and as usual I'd taken Caroline. Me and Pas (watching and handing me things) had taken off the sodden nappy and were bathing her. Pas was tickling her little feet and making Caroline gurgle with delight. There were no more bruises and Katrina was talking on and on about how she would never leave her with 'that wumin' again. But I'd smelt alcohol on her breathe when she walked in and her eyes were puffy. I made up a bottle for the baby and sat down to give it to her. She was so cute and her eyes fixed on my face, as she sucked the bottle. I wished I could adopt her, it would be good for Pas to have a little sister and I wracked my brains, about how I could do it. I'd been trying for another baby for two years now and nothing had happened. The only way would be if we could somehow get her out of the country. But without papers and passport, it was impossible. I sighed and decided just to say it how it was.

'Katrina, come and sit down here. We need to talk about something.'

Katrina looked at me warily. She pulled out a chair from the table and sat down heavily. So I told her all about it, about me speaking to Jane next door, about Jane's work as a florist at the Mount Nelson, about her assistant Joan and Joan's circumstances, about her wanting another baby. Katrina's eyes stayed on my face and for once she didn't talk, just listened. I spoke about her drinking and her struggle with money and accommodation and what sort of life she could offer to a baby? When I'd finished, I asked her what she thought...

"No medem, ah doan know, ah doan know. Ah doan know if ah ken do that. Ah cahnt give up mah baby, ah loss mah other three already. Ah doan know,' her eyes filled with tears.

'Don't decide right now,' I said. 'Think about it for a few days. That lady, Joan, told Jane that she could come here on Friday to look at the baby, before she would decide for sure. Think about it. Joan has her own place and an older teenage girl. She knows someone who could look after Caroline, while she's at work. Someone reliable. Think about it tonight and come and tell me what you've decided tomorrow. Then I'll tell Jane.'

Katrina came back the next day and gave me her decision. She decided that she would give up Caroline, she wasn't managing and the decision weighed heavily on her, I could see. I let Jane know and on the Friday morning Katrina came round and left Caroline with me for an hour. She didn't want to meet Joan that would have been too much for her to bear. Joan of course was immediately captivated by sweet little Caroline, and on the Monday, Jane let me know that Joan wanted to go ahead.

The handover was arranged for a few days later. Again Katrina left Caroline with me, for the last time. She just handed her over with a set look on her face, and probably went off to get drunk somewhere.

I washed her, fed her and changed her into the new Baby-gro I'd bought and wrapped her in the clean shawl that Katrina had left. Pas and I kissed her goodbye and for a while we had regular bulletins from Jane.

That was not the end of it though. Not for Katrina. The pain of loss and grief that she was going through became too much and within a week, she was back, very drunk, crying outside my door. I brought her in and listened for a while to the alcohol-fuelled ramblings. She was sobbing, rocking back and forth and saying over and over,

'I want my baby back, I want my baby back.'

I went over the reasons why she had given up the baby again and again and again. Then I told her she had to leave, but she could come back and talk to me when she was sober. Then, if she'd decided to stop drinking, I would speak to Joan and tell her that Katrina wanted her baby returned. This happened three to four times over the next few weeks.

The last time, Katrina turned up late in the evening, wailing and shouting outside my door, very drunk. I brought her in, but this time having talked it over with Dave and Peter and Jane, I told her that if she came back again, I would call the police. Poor Katrina, I felt so sorry for her, but there was nothing else to do. This torture had to stop. It was impossible for her to keep on drinking and take care of a baby.

Katrina cried into the early hours and fell asleep on the couch. I went to bed and when I woke up in the morning she was gone. The stress of it all had been enormous , I felt that I'd done what I had to for the baby, but it had been so much more complex than I'd bargained for, dealing with Katrina's pain. Perhaps if I'd known how hard it was going to be for all of us, I would never have started. But to see a 6 week old baby with bruises, was just too much. I just felt I had to do something.

I never saw Katrina (or Caroline) again. I thought about her often though and wondered how she was. I heard occasionally from Jean (the adoptive mother) via Jane. Jean too worked full time so had to leave Caroline with a child minder, but at least a properly paid, properly monitored one. I hope she thrived.

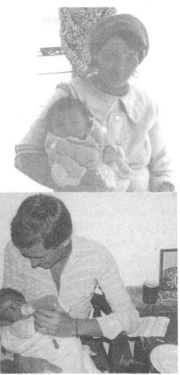

Katrina and Caroline/ Dave feeding Caroline

Chapter 20: Throwing stones to meet you

Throwing stones to meet you

A stranger at the gates
cast this spell on me
as I was wandering in the dawn.
I am crippled by his spell
which forbids me all contact
with my evil and twin nature.
In such a vacuum I must live
as shakes each dear pebble
from my hand though I would
cast it far over the water to you.
So here I stand on the soft shore
waiting for a stranger to release
my emptiness from the pain
that forbids me to reach you.

© Peter Kantey

The summer was drawing to an end but there were still hot days. After picking Pas up from Brooksfield, we'd often drive down to Clifton beach. Usually, we'd take Gabby too – the girl's would play with their bucket and spades and I'd walk down to the water's edge with them and have a towel ready for when they wanted to come out of the water. The Atlantic Ocean was usually very cold so I only went in when it was really hot.

On one of these days, we picked up Dave from the rehearsal rooms on the way back. He was now rehearsing for Playboy of the Western World, a play by John Millington Synge, in which CAPAB had offered him a good part and as we had to eat and pay our rent, he'd taken it. It was opening for a short run in the Arena theatre and then part of the run was going to be another tour the townships from early May for about four weeks

We were chatting as I made Pas her supper - I sat her down with mash and butternut and sausage. Then I went to the bathroom and sitting on the loo, I noticed that in the bath was a packet of spaghetti. How weird, I thought, how did that get there? I called out to Dave as I was buttoning up my blue shorts,

'Dave, how did a packet of spaghetti get in the bath?'

'What?'

He walked to the bathroom and we both stared at it.

'Pas did you get some spaghetti out of the cupboard,' Dave called out to Pas, she was sitting in the other room at the table. She got down from her chair and came in the bathroom as I was washing my hands.

'What that in bath for?' She said and leaned over and grabbed it. I caught her T-shirt just in time, to stop her falling in the bath.

'Give that to me,' I said firmly '...and go and finish your supper.'

Pas had no appearance of guilt or recognition. This was not going to be an easy mystery to solve. We were still puzzling about it for the next few days, the spaghetti-in-the-bath mystery.

Then one day the mystery was solved - Peter came round to see Dave. His hair was slightly wild and his beard unkempt, he was wearing an old T-shirt with holes in. He began talking intently to Dave about the play they were working on together. I walked in carrying some washing to fold.

'So when Goldfields goes into the mountains, he meets...' He looked up, 'oh hi Anna, did you get the spaghetti?'

We stared at him.

'What?' I put the washing down on the settle.

'I threw it in through the bathroom window? I'm not sure where it landed....'

[Our bathroom joined to the kitchen/living room at right angles, running along the side of our front yard.]

Light began to dawn...

'Oh! It was you, we couldn't work it out.'

'I thought you'd like a present, something to cook for supper.'

'Oh..., er yes, thanks.' I looked closely at him, his face was flushed and eager. I frowned slightly. Dave and I glanced at each other, but kept our faces neutral.

Over the next few days it became obvious that Peter was beginning to behave oddly in other ways. I came out of the house through our back patio, opened the small picket gate and walked round to the front, to get the car. Peter was outside by his car, with only his thin cotton boxer shorts on and holding an aerosol can of spray.

'What you doing Pete?' His face was animated, purposeful. 'Oh,' he looked distracted, there seemed to be yellow spray marks on his blue car.

'... painting yellow crosses on my car,' he dropped his voice. 'Keeping the spirits away.'

'Ohhh...,' I was thinking, oh shit, he's losing the plot. We'd had a woman friend in London who suffered from schizophrenia, she'd lived in one of the bedsits in some house where we'd stayed for a while. I knew, that when Delphine was not taking her medication, she started to behave very strangely. She told me that a psychiatrist had put metal bits in her ears, to program her thoughts. Then, they would get her on to this heavy drug called Largactyl, but that would make her dopey all the time. I didn't agree with this heavy medication regime for schizophrenics, which turned them docile and quiet. But on the other hand, something was required, to stop the slow slide into that strange world they go into without it, where they can become a danger to themselves, or even very occasionally to others.

'Would you like me to do your car, when I finish mine?' he asked.

'No thanks, Peter, I like my car the way it is.'

'Are you sure?' his voice was enthusiastic.

'Peter,' I said, 'You've been taking your medication, haven't you?'

'I don't need that stuff anymore,' he said dismissively. 'I feel much better without it.'

'Ah!' I said, thinking - Oh dear, that explains it.

I saw his mother, a very smartly dressed woman, coming to see him next day. I knew she lived in the very expensive suburb of Constantia. I stopped her as she passed my gate on her way to see him –

'I think Peter's going a bit funny,' I said, 'I'm not sure if he's been taking his medication...'

'Oh! I think he is,' she said firmly, looking me up and down with a kind of, do I know you, why are you interfering, kind of look.

'Well, I just thought I'd let you know.' I shrugged and walked back in my door.

Peter had told us previously, that in the past, while naked he had chased his Dad round their smart garden in Constantia with a carving knife and that on another occasion he had bent the iron railings outside his front door with his bare hands. He was nearly as tall as Dave but several stone heavier, well built. I wasn't scared of him though, I don't know why.

Life went on and there were a few more bizarre incidents with Peter. Then one day I came home and Jane and Di were in the lane at the back. Jane knew Peter's mother quite well having grown up locally.

'Have you heard about Peter?' Di asked.

'No... what?'

'An ambulance came this afternoon and took him to Valkenburg hospital. Apparently he had to be restrained.'

'What does that mean?' Diane crossed her arms across her waist.

'Oh no! Poor Peter,' I said, feeling sad for him, but also relieved that he was getting treatment at last.

He was in Valkenburg hospital for 2 weeks, until the medication had re-stabilised his condition. He told me later how they had put him in a straight-jacket, in a padded room and how frightening that had been. When he came out he was different - quiet, sleepy, his spark extinguished. But after a week or so he was back to normal again. He would come round regularly to see me in the evenings and chat until Dave got home. Then I'd go to bed and he and Dave would have a few beers and share a joint. They'd talk about ' Goldfields', the play they were working on together, into the early hours.

For a while Peter stuck to his regime of monthly injections. The next time he was due for one, I offered to drive him to the hospital. On the way there he explained the effects...

'I hate the injections, they make me sleep – I sleep for days and days after each one, I hate it and I have to take pills too.'

I waited outside in the landscaped gardens and afterwards drove him home. He went straight to bed.

In spite of all Peter's mental health problems, he was highly intelligent, sensitive and wrote brilliant poetry. His favourite poet was also mine - Dylan Thomas. I always felt that Peter's madness touched on the edge of genius.

We wouldn't have Peter next-door much longer though - or Di and Jane. We had decided to move on from Mowbray, we fancied a more rural lifestyle for a while. I kept thinking about the chicken farm we'd stayed in near Jo'burg and the quiet country lifestyle, the sound of the cock crowing and the grasshoppers humming. Not too far though, Dave had to get into Cape Town for his work and I wanted to be able to drive in and meet up with all our new friends. I started checking the newspapers for rentals further out.

Chapter 21: The Good Life

The great thing about renting was that you could up sticks at short notice and move quickly, which is what we decided to do. We'd leave city life behind and get out into the countryside, or in this case the bush. We had an idealised version of a life lived in the open, growing our own vegetables, clean air, keeping poultry and gathering fresh eggs etc. It didn't turn out quite like that though.

Dave's tour of the townships, starting in Somerset West was now looming. I was upset that he was going away for a month and leaving me on my own again, but we had bills to pay. While he was still in rehearsals, I found the place in Philippi, from an advert in a local paper.

We went to see it. There was a large, airy bungalow, well two next to each other, the other was unoccupied. They were set in 8 hectares of land (19 acres) about 7 miles out from the suburbs where we'd been living. You drove off the main road onto a winding road and a few miles along, there was a dirt track, which wound up a slope and down to the two bungalows. The nearest other dwelling around was a large pig farm with industrial-size, corrugated-iron and concrete sheds, about a mile away.

The two bungalows, shared a large concrete yard at the back, where cars could park. At the front, the cottages were built into an incline and a stepped front 'garden' was divided by crude stone steps between the two cottages. It was rough ground, poor soil - sandy and stony. It was going to be arduous work to improve the soil quality, in order to grow our own vegetables. We liked it immediately, it was peaceful and the sun was shining that day, although by now it was nearly .May and winter had begun. Still although it was cooler and wetter, many days were still warm and sunny. The bungalow was large and the open space all around was fantastic.

In the UK, we'd had our own garden at the back of our small house in Hampton-on-Thames. At the bottom, we'd grown our own tomatoes, green beans and lettuce. A small plastic greenhouse had been used by Dave to grow his own marijuana plants, which grew to be over 6 foot, until my lawyer Dad saw them and made Dave cut them down (he dried them in the attic).

Mr Schmidt, the owner of the bungalow, met us there, showed us around and explained things in his heavy German accent. He was a short, stocky, grizzled man in his sixties with eyes narrow and creased from a lifetime of squinting into the sun. He wore old khaki shorts and the kind of short-back-and-sides haircut that men had had in the fifties. He looked us over shrewdly then took us inside.

'Here iz ze basroom,' he opened the door with a flourish – it looked fine, having the usual toilet, bath and sink in pastel green. I went over and turned on the hot water bath tap – nothing happened.

'Er, yes, ve are vaiting for ze boiler to arrive and zen ze plumbing vill be arranged.'

'And when will that be?' Dave enquired.

'It vill be in ze next few weeks.' Mr Schmidt said firmly.

'So how will we bathe and have hot water?' I asked.

He led us out into the back yard and pointed to a large oil drum, cut in half, on a metal stand. Underneath it, was the remains of a fire – blackened logs.

'Iz very simple,' he said 'You carry a few buckets of water from ze house, pour into ze drum and make ze fire under. Very qvickly, ze wasser is hot, then you carry ze buckets back to ze bath'.

'Oh, right.' I avoided looking at Dave.

In spite of these 'minor' details, we decided to give it a go and moved in within a few weeks, saying 'Goodbye' to Mowbray and the suburbs, full of enthusiasm for our new rural lifestyle. This was Africa, out in the bush, miles from anywhere and apparently there were wild Duika (like miniature deer) all around the area. Don't imagine this was some kind of safari park though or that there was any big game here – those had all been hunted to extinction many years before. All around, were large expanses of sky, rolling slopes of dry, sandy soil, scrub-grass bushes and very few people. Yet it was near enough to Cape Town for Dave to commute every evening for the shows he was in and to stay in touch with our friends in Mowbray. When the van we'd hired was loaded up, Peter and Diana came and waved us goodbye, promising to come visit soon.

We were excited by the prospect of growing our own food, rearing egg-laying hens and getting some geese – we'd been told that they make very good 'guard-dogs'. Our other 'guard' dog, Angel - thought she'd died and gone to heaven. She was out running around in the bush all day, nose to the ground, sniffing and whimpering with excitement. After a few weeks, new neighbours moved in to the cottage next-door and they had a large Alsatian - so Angel had a pal to romp and play with.

A few days later, on a rehearsal break, Dave was out on the stony slopes at the back of the house, turning over the garden soil – it was dry and stony. We would have to get a huge garden sieve and gradually make a plot with some reasonably stone-free, top-soil so we could grow our vegetables. I went in to cook a meal, Pascale was playing with home-made play-dough on the kitchen table, cutting out shapes.

'This one for Mummy, this one for Daddy.'

Then I heard a shout from Dave,

'Anna! Come and look at this!'

'What is it?

'Come and see, it's a spider, but look what it's doing!'

'You know I hate spiders, I'm not coming to look at one',

'No, look, just come, it's weird!'

I sighed and put down my chopping knife.

'OK just coming.'

'Make some for Gabby darling, I'm just going to see what Daddy wants.'

When I got there, Dave was holding the garden fork gingerly in front of him and there was a largish black spider on the ground. I was very spider phobic but if they were outside, they didn't bother me quite so much. This spider was about the size of a dessert spoon without the handle, not extraordinary then, but it was not the size that was strange. This spider was not scuttling away, like most spiders I'd ever seen. This spider had sat back on its haunches and was using its two front fore-legs, like a crab uses its claws. Below its eyes was a red line like a mouth. It was clicking into the attack against the rungs of the fork, darting forward aggressively with a pincer movement. We watched it for a while with Dave poking at it with the fork, then it scuttled away. Dave got on with his digging and I went back to the kitchen. Later we found that it was called a boboyani or baboon spider, that they could jump six feet and had a nasty bite. They were often much bigger than the one Dave found – sometimes as big as a tarantula.

This spider was not the only creature that Dave uncovered in the soil. He also turned over several scorpions and that was on the first day's dig. He kept his boots on from then on whenever he was outside digging.

We had had this idea that we would keep geese – it was remote there and we'd heard stories of people on farmsteads, out in the bush, being burgled and attacked. Security was important – black townships like Guguletu and Langa were close to Philippi and poverty was rife in them.

We heard that a farm a few miles down the road sold geese. There was a large chicken wire pen at the back of our yard, about 6 by 5 foot and 5 foot high. We could keep a few geese in there for a while, until they got used to their new home and then let them out in the day to peck around. For three geese we negotiated a price with this farmer. The man said we would have to keep them in for a while or they would fly straight back, but if they turned up back there he would keep them until we arrived to fetch them.

The geese were trussed up in the back of the car with strips of cloth around their beaks, wings and ankles. They were not happy with this arrangement to say the least. When we got home, we carried the struggling geese quickly to the pens and started to remove the cloth strips that had been keeping them quiet. It soon became clear, that these birds were not quiet or tame, as soon as one's head was free, he started hissing and pecking wildly. I leapt back smartly, but Dave was not so fast...

'Ow! You bastard.' He dropped the bird on the ground and was hopping around nursing his finger and swearing loudly.

'Are you OK?'

'Yes!' he snapped. 'Let's get the bloody birds in their pen.'

A lot more carefully now, with only Dave going into the pen, we untrussed each goose, first untying the feet and wings and then last the beaks, then chucking each in the pen one by one, quick before it pecked us to bits. Dave then leapt back out of the pen each time as they hissed and spat angrily, and closed the gate smartly before they attacked. Geese are big birds when you're up close and their wings are quite large and powerful.

'Bloody hell!' Dave was tying up the gate of the pen with wire, 'I knew they were supposed to be good at guarding places but I wouldn't like to be shut in there with them. Well they'll probably settle down in a few days, once they get used to the place. Then we can let them out.'

I looked at them warily. Pascale was not at all keen on them, after seeing one of them bite Dad's finger. Now that they were in their pen, however, she came up and looked at them with more interest. Not too close though – they hissed ferociously if you got near.

Next morning, Dave brought me a cup of tea in bed.

'Bad news I'm afraid, you know we had three geese? Yeah well, now we only have two....'

'What, you're joking! Where's it gone?' I jumped out of bed.

'Was the gate still shut?' I was pulling on my shorts and rushing out the door.

'Yup!' Dave strode after me. 'But I found a hole by the side at the back – looks like something dug under the fence and got one of them and took it out.' We reached the pen and he pointed to the back. I walked round and looked – a hole had been scooped or scraped out....

'What could get one of those geese? They're pretty fierce!'

'Well unless it got out itself and flew back to the farm?'

'Possible I suppose, but that hole......'

'Yeah, could be a fox or something? It doesn't look hopeful. We could call by the farm and ask just in case...?'

'OK, maybe later.'

Meanwhile Dave repaired the hole and put a few rocks round the fence.

The following morning, we got up early and went to look at the pen. There was only one goose left. Dave opened the gate to take in a bowl of grain and change the water for the last goose. Big mistake. The goose flew at him knocking him sprawling onto his back and flew over his head and out the gate. He yelled for help and I ran out and helped him up. We tried to catch it, we were all running round the yard, but it flew off into the bush and was gone. Those geese were much larger than we had realised and much more fierce. We drove over to the farm later, on the off chance one or two of them had turned up, but no luck. The man there suggested that they would end up in someone's pot if they were found out in the bush. I'd like to have seen anyone try to catch the bloody things.

We never saw them again or knew what happened to them. Dave said perhaps it was a scam by the farmer and that they regularly sold the geese to unsuspecting customers. He knew they would escape and fly back home so he could sell them again to the next sucker. I was not too sure of that – what had made the hole at the side of the pen after all?

Our next venture was the chicks that were going to grow into laying hens.

'It would be great to have hens pecking around the place, collecting our own fresh eggs', I said.

'Yeh well we'll have to rear them ourselves' said Dave, he'd asked our new neighbours Jakub and Dawn.

'Ready laying hens are too expensive.'

'How long do they take to grow to laying age?'

'Well, Jakub said a couple of months.'

'OK, how many should we get?'

'Well maybe half a dozen to start with?'

We heard about a farm down the road that had incubators with hundreds of chicks for sale. So we drove over there and looked at the big long glass-sided incubators full of little yellow fluffy chicks. Some of them appeared to be dead, which was distressing to see, but the farm hands seemed matter of fact about that - sentiment does not come in to the farming mentality. We bought six live cheeping chicks. Pascale held the cardboard box carefully on the back seat of the car, her face rapt with fascination and delight.

When we got home we cleared out a space on a low shelf in the stable at the side of the house, we made a hole at the side of the box so they could get out and run around if they wanted, and put out a saucer of water and bread crumbs soaked in milk. The stable had a split door, the bottom half had a bolt – so in the day we could leave the top of the door open. No animals could get in as the bottom half of the door was c. five feet in height. It was a solid structure, we checked around the concrete floor – there were no holes. They were quite safe. I went in to the kitchen to give Pascale her lunch. Dave went to the lounge with a bottle of beer and his script, to learn his lines.

About an hour later, I strolled over to check on them. There was only five in the box. I hunted high and low – there was no sign of the sixth chick. Where could it have gone? I shouted for Dave to come – we emptied out the stable – but it was nowhere.

That afternoon we had to go out for a few hours – we shut the doors and bolted them – maybe the chick would turn up later....I returned later and started to make some scones for tea for myself and Pascale. Dave went off to the theatre. We had opened the top of the stable door again to let in light and air for the chicks, first checking on them – they were fine. Now I glanced in on them again and could only count four chicks. There was no sign of the missing chicks, no blood or remains either. It was weird. I checked the stable thoroughly again for holes or gaps round the concrete floor – but there was nothing. It must be a rat or something, but where was it getting in? So I locked them up for the night with the stable door bolted shut, top and bottom.

The next day, the chicks were still there, whatever had got the other two seemed to be leaving them alone. We thought it must be either a fox or a rat. But by lunch time two more went missing - the four was now down to two. Again, no remains. I was thoroughly fed up now, furious in fact, so was Dave. He had to go to the theatre in a couple of hours, at this rate there'd be none left by then. He decided to keep a sly watch on the doorway from the kitchen door, which was

5 metres away from the stable door, the stable being joined to the side of the house.

Suddenly he saw something move and looked over just in time to see the Alsatian from next door jumping OUT of the stable, clearing the 5 foot door with ease. It had jumped in so quick Dave had not seen it. We ran to the stable hurling curses and yelling at the dog, but we were too late. The last two chicks were gone and we had to come to the inescapable conclusion, as there was no blood or body parts that he had swallowed them whole! The dog ran away and kept out of our sight for the rest of the day – there were lots of hiding places in the bush. Besides, what could we do – it was too late to save the chicks! Pascale was a bit upset as she had enjoyed looking after the little fluffy chicks and smoothing them. It was hard to explain what had happened – the concept of death is difficult for a three year old, so I just told her the truth – she had seen much of the commotion when we ran into the yard to catch the dog and found all our chicks gone.

'Where's the chickies Mummy?'

"Naughty Timmy ate the chicks, baby.'

'Why he do that?'

Under my breath I said to myself, 'Because he's a fucking bastard and I'm going to kill him when I find that pig of a dog,' but out loud, I said,

'I don't know darling, maybe he was hungry?'

Perhaps we began to lose heart after that, I don't know. It was hard to dig in the dry, stony, inhospitable soil too and I was worried about Pas wandering about with snakes and scorpions and boboyani at large. We spoke to Mr Schmidt about our fears.

'Vat you need is a cet.' I looked puzzled. 'To ketch ze scorps.' His tone was firm, he was nodding to himself.

'But a scorpion would sting a cat too wouldn't it?'

'Nah, ze cet knows to jump awt the way of a scorp's tail... git yourself a cet – zat'll solve ze problem.' Meekly we went down to the animal refuge and picked the biggest cat we could find - a very large male tabby – he should be able to deal with any scorpions or poisonous insects that got too near the house shouldn't he?

From day one of his arrival, Big Cat insisted on using a cat litter tray. We were surrounded by miles of sandy bush – he would have none of it. If we put his tray outside the door a few feet, he would not use it – he would then use the waste paper basket. We tried all sorts of inducements to persuade Big Cat to perform outdoors. NOTHING worked. In the end I gave up and returned the litter tray to the inside, or I would have to keep cleaning out stinking waste paper baskets – male cat urine is not pleasant. He never caught so much as a small house spider in all the time we had him and when later we moved back into the suburbs, he obviously felt a lot happier, in the small front garden.

While we lived in Philippi, as I had in Mowbray, I washed our clothes in the bath with a block of Sunlight soap, it was hard and back-breaking work. As there was no hot water, it had to be heated in the cut-in-half, giant oil drum in the yard. The new boiler that Mr Schmidt had mentioned as 'coming very soon', when we first rented the cottage, never materialised.

First, you'd carry buckets of water from the bathroom to fill the drum, just as Mr Schmidt had described. Then you must gather twigs and logs for the fire underneath, twist up bits of newspaper, light the fire and wait for the water to get hot enough. Now you must carry the steaming hot water back to the sink or bath in the heavy buckets. After you'd washed and rinsed the clothes, hung them out on the line, within two hours they were bone-dry in the hot African sun. I did get used to it, accepted that this was part of living a rural life and that's what we had wanted.

Towards the end of April, Dave brought home the tour schedule - it was starting on May 5th. Amongst other venues, they would be travelling round the South African townships. The tour would start in Grahamstown, which is about 500 miles from Cape Town. He'd been there before with the Anthony and Cleo tour. The cast would be 'bussed' to Grahamstown travelling along the reputedly spectacular scenery of the Garden Route. Then on to East London, Port Elizabeth and end in Swellendam. It sounded like a fabulous route. The last tour to Grahamstown had gone a different way – inland.

This one was largely following the coast. I felt quite jealous, I'd love to have seen the famous Garden Route.

'How long's the tour?'

'Oh, they said, it'll be around four weeks.'

'But you will come back sometimes? You'll get breaks?'

'No, it's too far - they say we won't.'

'Oh Dave, four weeks!' I was upset, even though I was expecting it. He came over and put his arms round me.

'Don't worry, we'll manage somehow, we have to don't we?'

I thought of me and Pas alone all that time, with few friends and no other kids for her to play with. I was from a big family and was not used to long periods on my own. His other tours had been a week long and then he'd come home for a few days until the next one.

'What's the play about anyway?'

'It's an Irish play set in a pub in County Mayo around 1900.'

'An Irish play - for the townships? That'll be... interesting.'

'Yes, I don't know how it'll go down, but I think we can make it work.'

He looked at me - 'Look, don't worry; I'll phone you lots, write postcards. You'll have Di ... and Peter.'

'Yeah,' I said, trying to sound enthusiastic but I was feeling anxious already about the time apart. I'd be out in the sticks on my own for a month. I was glad to have our dog Angel with me. And it was a six mile drive back to Mowbray to see Di or Peter.

Then the new neighbours arrived, they moved into the semi-detached cottage next door. They would share the back yard with us. And they had a small boy! Good news for Pas. They parked a pick-up truck in the front yard next to our old blue beetle. What would they be like?

Capab English Drama presents:

J.M.SYNGE'S
THE
PLAYBOY
OF THE
WESTERN WORLD

Directed by DAVID CRICHTON
Designers: PETER KRUMMECK (set & costumes)
JOHN T. BAKER (lighting)

308 Arena Theatre. 10 April, 1976.

Chapter 22: Poor Whites

Dawn and Jakub spoke heavily-accented English, as their first language was Afrikaans. They seemed to have lived a gypsy/traveller lifestyle for quite a few years. Dawn was outspoken and blunt; Jakub was quiet and said very little. Dawn was about 5 foot 3 inches tall, slim and wore tight trousers, loose T-shirts, disguising a large bust. Her dark hair was always pulled back in a tight pony tail. She and Jakub were about our age and their son was 4 years old. Markus was quiet and shy like his Dad.

Pas was delighted - another kid to play with. The fact that Markus spoke no English did not bother her. She followed him around, played games with him and generally organised him around her play world, whenever he and his parents were home. She spent much time in Dawn's kitchen, listening and chatting and within three months, in that easy way small children have, she spoke fluent Afrikaans. She switched with ease, when she and Markus were in our kitchen from Afrikaans to him, then English to me or her Dad. She and Markus played outdoors much of the time, mostly in the backyard or sometimes, with the dogs in tow, wandering a little outside the yard into the bush – but within calling distance.

Dave and I were pleased and excited that Pas had learnt another language so quickly – another sign of our child's precocious intelligence.

Sometimes, Dawn and I would be out in the yard and she'd tell me stories of what sounded like a very much hand-to-mouth existence, living on the fringes of 'white' areas and often close to the edges of black or coloured townships, or even squatter camps. She'd lived a life very much like many poor blacks, in outlying areas where apartheid was generally ignored. Neither she nor Jakub had had much schooling and one day, Dawn told me about her experience of giving birth to Markus.

'Ah went to the med centre win Ah was twenty-eight weeks', she said, 'Ah was heving a few problems see? They sed Ah shud come in to hospital straight, but Ah sed No! Ah don't hold with such places see. So then Ah was in the bakkie with Jakub and ma waters broke, but Ah was jus thirty weeks. He took me bek to the med centre and the pains were coming bed, real fawst. So then Markus came out. Men, he was so tiny, he futted in the palm of mah yand. Mah god, you shuld hev seen um... so they put him in one of those things yah - unkubator whad-yew-call-ut and kep him there for a few wiks. Then Jakub cayme for us in the bekkie and sed 'we're goin home.' So I took the beby, wrep him up – they made a fuss, yurra! Sed his lungs weren't reddy. But Jakub jus sed no men, we're goin now. Those fus few wiks, I thort he wudn't mek it, he was so tarny and wik. He was wrepped to me day and naht in the truck. But in the yend he made it men.' She glanced round for Markus who was play-ing tag with Pas. She was shrieking with delight. As he dodged under her arm, Dawn cuffed his ear with her other practised hand.

'Hey yew! Git in now fa yew tea, men.'

'OK Pas, you too, time for supper ... in the kitchen now!'

Dawn and Jakub were in the motorway pick-up trade. In their old bakkie, they would, with Markus wrapped up asleep behind them, go out most evenings and hang about the ma-jor roads in the hope of a breakdown by some motorist. They would park up and listen in, on their walkie-talkie, to police radio frequencies – then speed up to get there before any other garage or pick-up truck and collect a fee for towing the driver to the garage of their choice. That's how they made a small living.

Sometimes, I discovered after a while, Markus was left at home to sleep. If I was home, Dawn would knock on my door before they left.

'He's sleeping men, he never wakes, OK? Just telling yew ay?'

'Oh, OK, Dawn,' I'd say, and she was right, I never heard him wake up, Markus seemed to sleep through anything.

I was friendly enough with Dawn when I saw her. She was, after all our only neighbour. We both had a child and shared info about Mr Schmidt our landlord, who was some-times difficult. Jakub was quiet and rarely spoke to me, alt-hough he would exchange a few words with Dave some-times. Both Dawn and Jakub had a low opinion of Mr Schmidt, our landlord. When we got an astronomical water bill a month or so later, Jakub explained it was because Mr Schmidt (saving money on pipes) had so many crude joints on the pipes leading to the mains supply down by the main road and most of them leaked.

Dave's play had now opened at the Arena Theatre in Cape Town six nights a week. Before he went on tour, we decided to throw a Sunday (Dave's only night off), braai (barbecue) for our friends. We realised that we must also invite our nearest neighbours, as it would be held in our shared back yard. Even so, they seemed surprised to be asked.

Dave asked Jakub the best way to do the barbecue and Jakub pointed out an old, half, oil-drum, cut lengthways, that was lying over by the 'goose' cage. He and Dave carried it onto the yard and raised it onto a rough stand, made of crossed metal poles lashed together. Dave then organised some bags of charcoal and bought a few dozen bottles of beer and a box of wine. We could not afford much so we asked our guests to bring a bottle and their own meat for the braai, this was common practice anyway. We bought some boereworst sausage – big fat rolls of spiced-sausage meat – a couple of metres long, cheap and 'lekker' as they said in South Africa, meaning 'yummy'. We also decided on a trip to Fish Hoek, to get a large snoek – a tasty fish, common in S Africa, which could be cut into steaks. Snoek was not expensive and a whole snoek could feed a largish group.

We decided to drive to Fish Hoek on the Sunday a week before the braai, as it was Dave's day off. We got out the map and worked out a route. We would drive on the main road southeast towards Simonstown where the naval base was. Fish Hoek was between a place called Muizenburg and Simonstown.

As we got closer to Muizenburg, rolling hills and green vistas opened up before us – the road turned left towards the coast and the back suburbs of Muizenburg town. We began to see old colonial type houses - some unusually several storeys high, painted pink and blue. I wanted to stop and look but we didn't have time. In the distance, we could see that the town, which looked like a 1950s English seafront, faced on to a long white-sandy beach with large breakers sweeping in. The sea looked beautiful but wild – of course it was winter in the Cape, nearing the end of April 1976. The road wound along the coast about a mile or so further and we could see signs for Kalk Bay and Fish Hoek and a little old stone harbour soon appeared. The sea had a choppy grey swell that day and clouds scudded across the open sky.

We drove towards the harbour which was sheltered from the strong breeze by a sea wall and then on to the harbour itself to park the car. Small painted wooden fishing boats were gathered inside the harbour, their catches on board and some of the seamen were hauling crates full of fish up onto the jetty. Cape Coloured men and women were busy with the fish or threading through the crowd, customers were examining the fish-filled crates. Everyone was shouting and haggling and waving their arms. Pas was fascinated by it all pointing to the fish and the boats, but I kept her close – it would be easy for her to get lost amongst all those people, or to slip on fish scales and fall over the jetty. We stopped to ask a fisherman about buying a snoek and Dave began haggling until he had struck a good deal. I asked the man if we could get the fish cleaned and prepared – a job I didn't want (I couldn't bear heads and eyes) and he pointed at the Cape-coloured women further down, some leaning against the stone walls, in groups gossiping.

'The scolly wumin will do it for yew,' he said 'Chorge yew about fufty cents a fish.'

I now noticed that some of these women were working on old wooden tables with sharp knives in their hands, quickly and expertly preparing the fish for customers. They had battered faces, head-scarves tied at the back and floral aprons covered in blood and fish-scales. They all had no front teeth and talked Afrikaans or heavily accented English. We took our large snoek – about 30 inches long to one of these and the woman lisped her price, then set to work, removing the head and tail and cutting the snoek into about twenty small steaks and wrapping it in newspaper for us to take home and put in the freezer.

* * *

Next Sunday, I woke early and looked out the window – it was dry, the sun was rising and although cool, it promised to get warmer. The Cape Town winter is a bit like the average English summer – changeable. It could, in winter, be sunny and warm by day, cool at night. In a bad year, it might be cloudy, cool and rain quite a bit. Often it might rain for an hour or two then be dry and warm for the rest of the day. Quite unpredictable at times, rather like the way that day turned out.

Dave was still fast asleep, he'd come home late from the theatre and then sat up writing until well into the night. He'd been working on his fantasy fiction book, he jokingly called Warty Wilf, after its main character. He often came home from the theatre on high adrenalin and then it was impossible for him to sleep for several hours.

I got up, and started cooking bacon, eggs, tomatoes, mushrooms and toast. The smell, wafting through the kitchen to the bedroom, soon woke Dave up. Pas was already at the table and as he walked into the kitchen I placed his egg sunny side up, as he liked it, on his laden plate and handed it to him as he walked past.

After breakfast Dave went outside to prepare the oil drum, half filling it with charcoal, putting bottles of beer in the bath with ice cubes, detrosting the snoek that we'd bought. Pas was out in the yard playing with Marcus. Angel and Max, next-door's Alsatian, were running about in a state of excitement and annoying us, by barking at nothing in particular.

As I was putting the finishing touches to a big bowl of salad and mixing mayonnaise into the potatoes, the first guests started to arrive. Diana and her latest boyfriend drove up in a Mustang, Peter came with Steve, Lily and the two boys in their beat up old Austin, Pam got a lift with a few of the actors from 'Fall and Redemption' and apparently Jo the director was coming along later with her husband the vicar at St George's cathedral. Some of the cast from 'Playboy' were coming too.

After a while, Dawn and Jakub came out and hovered around the braai. Dave handed Jakub a bottle of beer and told him to help himself to more beer when he needed a refill. Dawn just wanted juice and I gave them plates to help themselves to salad and bread to go with the meat from the braai. Everyone was busy chatting and laughing. We had the tape deck outside near the kitchen door, playing Moody Blues,

Pink Floyd and some of Dave's slow jazz LPs, Minnie Ripperton was one of his favourites. The day went well; some people had brought their own steaks or large chops, everyone enjoyed the snoek steaks and the Boereworst sausage and quite a bit of alcohol was drunk by all. People were leaving by about 7 p.m.

Pas and Marcus ran around playing with Storm, and Georgie toddled around after them trying to keep up.

Dave was busy with the braai all day and entertaining everyone with funny stories. He was drinking lots of beer and wine as usual, but was more careful since the "white cardigan incident". Even Jakub seemed to be enjoying himself, chatting to people here and there in his stilted English.

After the last guest had gone, Dawn started helping me to clear the plates and do the washing up, Dave put left-over meat and snoek steaks back in the freezer and doused the braai with a jug of water. Jakub disappeared with Marcus back into their cottage.

Sometime later, after I had put Pas to bed, I heard shouting and yelling coming from next door. Dave and I looked at each other, oh dear what was happening? Then suddenly there was a frantic knocking at our front door – I opened it quickly and there was Dawn. She seemed frightened and was looking over her shoulder. She came in fast.

"Quick men, lock the door!' I did as she asked. She pushed the bolt into place also.

'Is the other door open too? You gotta lock ut.' I walked quickly to the front door (at the back) and made sure the bolt was in place.

'What is it Dawn? What are you afraid of?'

'Ut's Jakub.' She was sobbing, 'You doan know what he's lahk when he's hed a drunk. Thet's why Ah don't let him, he goes med. He carn't hold ut.'

Now she tells me, I thought. I looked at her more closely and saw that one side of her face was red and swollen.

'You mean he hits you.' Her sobs got louder. 'Where's Markus? Is he awake?

'Nah Markus us farn. He's asleep, he woan wake up. He woan touch Markus.'

Just then, there was a loud knocking on the door, we all jumped and Jakub's voice shouted,

'Dawn, yew in there? Come awt now or ah'll break thus fuckin door dahn.' This was a side to the usually quiet and meek Jakub that was astonishing. I looked at Dave, thinking Fuck! Just what we need. He went over to the door to listen.

'Doan open the door,' she sobbed. 'Doan open it, pleez.' She backed across the kitchen. The banging was getting louder. Dave and I looked at each other nervously. Jakub was yelling again about breaking the door down. Luckily it was a solid wooden door with a stout bolt.

I was tired and wanted to go to bed, it had been a good day. How the hell had it turned into this.

'It's all right Dawn, we're not going to let him in. We're not going to let him hurt you'.

'Yew doan know him men, yew don't know what he's lark. He woan stop tul he gits me.'

Dave was looking out the window by the door. Jakub had gone quiet for a while and then,

'Oh Shit! Jakub's got an axe, oh fuck!'

There was a thud on the front door, and then another. Dave and I had a rapid conversation:

'I'm going out there.'

'Are you mad? He's got an axe.'

'He won't use it on me and besides I'm much bigger than him.'

'No, no, he might attack you with it.'

'It's okay, I'll be fine.' Thud, thud on the door.

'Look I have to, there's no other choice, I'm going to open the door, jump out and I want you to lock it quickly behind me. Don't worry I can run faster than him anyway. Remember I was a sprinter for Carmarthen.' He smiled.

Thud, thud. The door shook with the impact. It was a wonder that Pascale hadn't woken up with the noise. Dawn was sobbing,

'Ah'm going awt there men, he won't give up. He'll chop yew door down, ah swear.'

'No,' I steadied my voice, 'Dave's gonna go out and talk to him.'

Dave walked quickly to the door and I rushed up behind him. He shouted to Jakub that he was coming out, yanked open the door and I slammed it shut behind him, pushing back the heavy bolt. I was shaking and praying that Dave would be all right, glad that Pas was asleep in the back and hadn't woken up with all the noise. I poured myself a glass of wine, trying to stop it slopping over the brim as my hand shook, and took a large swig to calm my nerves. Dawn was sitting at the table sobbing and saying,

'Let me go awt to him. Ah'll talk to him, he'll calm down after a but.'

I took a deep breath and another swig of wine, before I answered. 'No, Dawn, I'm not gonna let him hit you. Dave's out there. Let him sort it out.'

'Ah'm jus sceered he's gonna hurt him. He maht hit Dave.'

'Well Dave's a big chap and he can run pretty fast too. Besides he's good at talking to people.'

I was not feeling as confident as I sounded. Dave was not a fighter, he was not well-built and he was dealing with some-one who had probably been fighting all his life, even if he was quite a bit shorter. I had a great fear of axes – when I was a child, the older teenage boy next door had pretended he was going to chop off my younger brother's head with one to scare me. He'd got him to put his head on a chair and held the axe over his neck until I started crying.

I went to the window and looked out. Another man, I hadn't seen before, had appeared and I called Dawn over to ask who he was. This man was medium height, with short hair and a moustache – he was dark and swarthy looking. Dawn said,

'Thet's Jakub's bruther, Henne. He'll stop Jakub. Ah'll be OK now, he ken knock him dahn uf he hes to.'

Henne disappeared from sight and then I saw Dave walking back rapidly, holding his nose, there was blood on his hands. I opened the door quickly and Dawn said,

'Ah'll go now, ut'll be OK now Henne's here. Look thenks, OK, thenks for everything men,' then she was gone. She slipped out the door before I could stop her.

As Dave came in, I shut the door and locked it. There was a swelling on his face just above the bridge of his nose.

Shit! I thought, but at a glance it didn't look broken, just bruised. I thought of Astrid and the gallons of blood when her nose was broken. No, it wasn't that bad. Dave sat down heavily at the table - I was already opening the freezer and bringing out a packet of frozen peas, wrapping them in a cloth. He took it and held it to the swelling. He explained what had happened.

'I was talking him down. I got him to put down the axe, but his eyes were glazed and he kept saying he was 'gonna git Dawn awt.' Then, I talked him down again, but he started all over again. He started shouting at me, because I said he couldn't hit Dawn. Then he slung a punch at me, I dodged it, luckily he's quite drunk. I was going to punch him back, when I heard this shout behind me. I turned and this guy punched me in the face and knocked me down. I found out he was Jakub's brother Henne. I was talking to him, holding my nose, trying to explain what happened. But he kept saying, he couldn't let anyone hit his brother. Bloody hell! That guy's got fists of steel. I was explaining it to him, but he wasn't listening.'

It was a relief that Dawn and the rest of them were out of our house and Dave was safe inside. I was still shaking. I poured Dave a large glass of wine which he drank quickly and sipped mine more slowly. He was worried that he'd have to go on stage again on Tuesday, with his face badly bruised.

'It was very brave of you to go out there, with the mad axe man. Don't ever do that again, I was really scared that something would happen to you.'

Dave was grinning now, holding his head back with the frozen peas.

'Oh I'm quite tough you know,' he was pleased with himself, now it was all over.

'No you're not, you're not a fighter - your height fools people!'

'I hope Dawn's all right?' He was gingerly prodding around his nose.

'You hear any shouting or yelling?' He sounded like he had a heavy cold. He put his head back and put the wrapped frozen peas back on his nose.

'Nope...Well she must be OK then, yeh?'

We went to bed and cuddled up close. Dave had to lie on his back, so his face wasn't touching the pillow. I had my arm across him. What a night, I thought. From now on, I'm keeping my distance, as long as Dawn's not being hit... then I'd have to do something. I sighed, at least Dave's safe, we're safe for tonight.

Next week he was going away on the first leg of the big tour of Playboy of the Western World, lasting a month, starting in Somerset West and up into the mountains to Beaufort West. Then it was back across the Eastern Cape past Durban into Zulu country at Umtata, a town in the Transkei – one of the so-called homelands that the government had created to place large groups of tribal black people outside of South African citizenship. A performance was scheduled there and afterwards back through PE (Port Elizabeth) along the coast to Swellendam, where the tour was to end. He'd return to Cape Town for a few weeks until it was time to go off again in early July for the next production for CAPAB – Richard III – this tour would start in Grahamstown.

Chapter 23: There's a riot going on

June 17 1976

Angel woke me that morning. She came dashing into the bedroom helter-skelter, barking and growling. Dave groaned and turned over. I opened my eyes a crack.

'Get out,' I said. She knew she wasn't allowed in the bedroom, so giving one more yap, she slunk out looking crestfallen in that way that dogs do. I barely noticed. I've never been a morning person - it takes a few hours awake for my brain to fire up. I sat up, yawned and stretched, then climbed out of bed, pulling on my old, blue shorts and slipping my feet into my flip-flops. I could hear our daughter, chatting to herself in the room next door.

'Pas!' I called yawning again.

'Breakfast!' I poured milk onto her cornflakes, and she climbed on her chair with Big Doll under her arm, chatting in between mouthfuls.

I strolled over to the doorway and looked across the back yard. On the far side of the yard was the empty chicken-wire coop, the one our geese had escaped from and next to it, another old, rusty, oil drum. Past that was bush in all directions, with low dust-green shrubs, sandy soil and a few small twisted trees as far as you could see into the distance.

I yawned and stretched again, then remembered Angel barking. What had set her off this time? I looked round for her - she was lying by Pas's feet, one eye shut, the other looking up at me. There's nothing different outside, no one about, I thought to myself.

Dave was fast asleep still. He'd returned from his tour of Playboy in early June and had a two week break before rehearsals were starting on Richard III. It was opening in Cape Town followed by a big 'jamboree' in Grahamstown starting on July 7th. Lots of other theatre groups would be showcasing their plays for this event and CAPAB's contribution was Richard III. He was playing Cardinal Bourchier, Archbishop of Canterbury, a small but significant part in the proceedings.

After Grahamstown, they were doing two more weeks touring the townships before returning to Cape Town in the last week of July.

'Come on Pas, time to get dressed for school!' I pulled a clean T-shirt and shorts over her chubby arms and legs. Big Doll sat next to her on the bed.

'Dolly come school.'

'No sweetie, leave dolly at home. Let's tuck her into bed! Dolly sleep, yes?'

She kissed Dolly's cheek, leaning over on tiptoes and then ran out the door without a backward glance.

I started the car in the yard and put it into second gear for driving down the dusty track, to the tarmac road. I was thinking about shopping I had to do in the three hours that Pas was at school. As the car came to the intersection of track and road, I glanced left and right and stopped. There was a police patrol car just down to the right, sitting in a small junction about fifty yards down on the other side of the road. It was a little known side entrance to the black township of Guguletu or so I'd heard. I'd never attempted to go through that entrance, whites weren't generally permitted in the townships. It was slightly puzzling because as far as I knew, each township only had one entrance, so they could be sealed off quickly in the event of trouble. The main entrance was miles away to the North. I'd rarely seen anyone using this side entrance.

I wondered what the police car was doing and why they were there. Perhaps Angel had heard the car and that was why she'd been barking earlier.

I stared for a minute, then turned away to the left and drove off down the road and left again onto the main highway towards Cape Town. During the 6-mile drive to the suburb of Rondebosch, I chatted to Pas, about seeing Gabby at school. Pas was coming up to her third birthday in a few weeks and could now talk in longer sentences and understand more.

'After school today, we can go for a walk on the beach, yes?'

'Yes, yes, yes!' She was bouncing up and down on the seat.

'Gab come too, Mummy? Gab come too?

We'll see.' I answered absently, still thinking about the police car. It was odd.

When I got to school some of the parents were outside in huddles. I kissed Pas goodbye and she ran into the classroom. I went over to talk to Tina, one of the German women I knew. She was short, blonde and worked for the same German company as Mel's husband.

'There's been trouble in the townships. Started in Soweto ... yesterday.'

'What sort of trouble?'

'I don't know, riots, they say it's spreading.'

'Oh dear! Maybe that's why!'

I told her about the patrol car, near our place, by the small entrance to Guguletu. This was worrying. I saw Melissa and asked her if she knew anything,

'Oh, it'll be fine,' she didn't seem bothered. 'They say it's all under control, most of the trouble's up near Jo'burg, in Soweto, not down here. We can pick up the Cape Times later, see what it says.'

We went upstairs, for our usual cup of tea and chat over a few cigarettes. Later, after school, I took Pas and Gabby for a walk on Clifton beach near Sea Point, as always, keeping a sharp look out for those long, blue tendrils of the Portuguese man-o-war jellyfish. I pointed at the red anemones and we tried to catch little, black catfish in the rock pools. We stopped for ice-cream on the way back and I dropped Gabby back at Brooksfield with chocolate ice cream round her mouth and all over her T-shirt. Lena opened the door and looked at Gabby.

'Ach! Yew face men – better git up the borthroom quick, so I can wash yew, before yew Ma gits home!'

As I pulled into the back yard that evening, I was thinking about something Mel had said when we were upstairs that day. TV had only just been introduced in South Africa, no one I knew had bothered to get one and we were all used to spending hours of leisure time reading, exchanging and passing on books between us.

'Mel, have you got any new books to read? I've read all mine.'

I was sitting on the brown leather sofa in the lounge, look-ing over at the low wooden bookcase on my left.

Mel laughed' 'Dahling don't look over there, that's were Werner keeps his 'Hitler' books.'

I looked at her puzzled, asking what she meant.

'Well his books about Hitler of course. They explain how it's all a 'British and American conspiracy that all those Jews were killed, that the numbers were... exaggerated...'

I was looking at her with shock. I was thinking, he can't seriously believe that? How can she put up with that? She caught my expression.

'No seriously, some of that crowd from the German club do believe that.'

She was dismissive and contemptuous, but also resigned. She shrugged, 'What can you do?' She lit another cigarette, throwing her head back and puffing the smoke into the air.

'But the Germans killed millions and millions in extermina-tion camps – it's not like there isn't the evidence, there's so much.'

Mel sighed,' I know, I know!' and changed the subject...

I was thinking about this conversation, as I walked in my front door. I'd glanced over at the Guguletu 'entrance' as we passed and the patrol car was still there. Pas was trotting behind me and Angel was dashing in the door first, as usual - straight to investigate her dog bowl. Werner's lack of social interest in Mel and her friends had always meant he was an ambiguous figure. Now this information... the more I heard, the less I wanted anything to do with him. What could I ever find to say to someone, who seriously believed what Mel had told me, enough to keep books on the subject, which backed up his distorted views?

My mother had told me about the concentration camps, how rumours had been heard during the war and ordinary people had refused to believe it and the horror felt by every-one at the end of the war, when the reality was far worse than the rumours. My father had told me a little about the Nuremberg trials.... I'd read books about it all. People who'd lived through it, rarely talked about it though. I shuddered. I wondered if it was a generational thing. Many of Werner's generation were born during the Second World War, perhaps it was a way of rejecting the collective post-war guilt on his generation of Germans, after all, I was thinking, they were also victims of Hitler's Germany and its aftermath. But still...

Now Angel was looking at me, tail pointing up eagerly, and eyes expectant. I took out the dog-food bag and put a handful of biscuits in her bowl. That would shut her up for a bit. She gulped them down fast and then looked round for more... sniffing round the floor in case she'd missed one.

Dave was up, yawning. He put the kettle on as I walked in. He'd been home a few days from his tour.

'It's so nice to be home.' He bent down to pat Angel. 'Hey girl, did you miss me?' Angel nuzzled his leg and then looked expectantly at her bowl.

'Never misses an opportunity for more food.' I laughed.

Pas climbed onto a chair and I handed her some play-dough I kept in the fridge. I sat down, thinking about the patrol car as I sipped my tea.

'There's been problems in Soweto, apparently.'

'What problems?'

Dave picked up a piece of Pas's play-dough and was rolling it into a pink snake with a cartoon-like face. She tried to grab it and he was holding it over her head, making it talk in a funny voice.

'No, no, no, you naughty girl, you just want to squeeze me. Storp it! Storp it!' repeating back to her, her favourite expression...'Storp it, storp it!'

Pas was giggling, 'No daddy! Give it...give it me.'

He was too distracted to have a proper conversation, so I started to prepare our lunch. The phone rang in the hall. I put down my chopping knife and went to answer it.

'Have you heard about the riots?' It was Di.

'I heard something this morning, they said it wasn't serious?'

'What are you talking about, of course it's serious!'

'The ones in Soweto?'

'It's terrible ... started in the schools.'

'What happened?'

'I don't know, something about speaking Afrikaans in the schools.'

'They speak Afrikaans all the time in schools anyway, don't they?'

'I suppose so, but the black kids don't want it in school anymore. Anyway what do I know? I'm not political.'

'I don't blame them, why should they have it in their bloody schools?'

There was a sharp intake of breath from Diana... what I was saying was dangerous, subversive even. The secret service often tapped people's phones.

'Look I don't think we should talk about it over the phone. I'm just saying, get the Cape Times tomorrow. They're saying it might spread to other townships, even here. The police have shot a young kid apparently...in Soweto. The kids are rioting and they've shot one of them.

'Shit, no...'

We all knew what the average South African policeman was like, it wouldn't take much to provoke them and they were trigger happy anyway. There was apprehension in her voice, an undertone like, perhaps this is it - the revolution, where the huge black majority turns on the white minority, like it might be imminent.

'The police will have Soweto sealed by now, won't they?' I frowned, my mind was racing.

'Yes, for sure.'

'But they'll crack down hard, they'll show no mercy,' I shuddered.

'It's true, you just don't know what'll happen next.' Di's voice was apprehensive.

There was silence for a moment, while scenes of mayhem raced around our heads. We felt helpless and sad for the kids in Soweto, as well as worried that the riots would spread to our side of South Africa.

'It's terrible, that little boy being shot. You should see the picture in the Cape Times. These are just children ... well, what can we do? Soweto's a long way off. They'll have clamped down hard. We all know that.'

'There's a patrol car, you know, near the end of our track, where that small side entrance to Guguletu is.'

'Oh, dear.'

'I'll get the Cape Times tomorrow, I tried to get it on the way back today, but the shop had sold out.'

Dave was standing, looking down the hall at me. Pas was trying to get his attention. He was still holding the snake up above his head.

'Daddy give me,' she was reaching up, trying to snatch it. He passed it to her. I could hear her talking to it and see her, beyond Dave, pushing it along the table, squashing it.

'Okay, I've got to go, I'm just going to tell Dave.'

'So ...?' Dave had heard snatches of the conversation. 'What's going on? Is this it? Do we need to pack our bags and run for it?'

'Don't be over dramatic.' I came back into the kitchen and started putting ham sandwiches on the table. 'I'll find out more tomorrow, when I get the Cape Times. It's in Soweto - a long way off.' I sounded calmer than I felt.

'And what's this about a patrol car ....?'

'Oh that, of course, you haven't been out yet have you?'

'Where exactly?'

I explained and he frowned.

'That's not good. I'm going in to Cape Town after lunch to meet up with some of the cast. Also this woman – Gillian Horowitz called me. She might have some work for me after Playboy finishes. I'm meeting up with her for an hour too. I'll have a look at the police car and ask what the others have heard when I get into town. Oh, look at the time, I better go.'

'Finish your sandwich.'

''No, I'll take it with me. Where's the car keys?'

'Here. But you've only just come back, I thought you'd be home this evening?'

'Look I'll be around for the next two weeks, I'm on holiday don't forget.' He grinned and gave me a hug, 'I'll be back soon, not going for long, just a couple of hours.'

'Well you're driving, so don't drink much!'

'Don't worry!' He bent down and kissed Pas, and swept out the door.

Next day, the patrol car was still there. Driving down the pot-holed main road on the way to Brookfield, I kept thinking about the situation. The white population was in the minority in South Africa and everyone had been nervous since the rumours started. Was this really the start of the uprising? Before I reached Brookfield, I stopped at a paper shop and bought the Cape Times. On the front page was a picture of a young man carrying a dead boy, with his sister running alongside crying. The front page article read:

'Two people have been killed in riots in Soweto, one white, one black. There has been looting and burning, as the riots continue. People have stoned offices and attacked and set light to vehicles. A thousand police went in armed with sten guns, FN rifles and machine pistols.'

Shit! I thought – a thousand armed men with all those . weapons – against school kids! After explaining that the strike began over compulsory Afrikaans in schools, it went on to say,

'It was reported that a policeman and four white women were injured. During the clash, a thirteen-year-old school-boy, Hector Pietersen, was shot dead. Soon after, two white officials of the West Rand Bantu administration were pulled from their cars and hacked to death.'

The article went on to say that the riots had spread to some neighbouring townships and that the motorway be-tween Jo'burg and Pretoria had been closed down. It said that in the UK hundreds had demonstrated outside the South African embassy.

I whistled to myself as I read it. This was serious; I won-dered how the Cape Times could get away with saying all that, under the strict censorship rules! No-one I knew had TV yet, and anyway there was only one channel so there was no point in watching all the government-controlled propa-ganda. What was going to happen? The police car, waiting near our track, must mean trouble might spread to Cape Town?

When I got to the school, I took Pas in and saw a few of the other parents, grouped outside, talking in low voices... Some like Mel, were blasé,

'The security forces have clamped down, it'll all be over quickly,' she repeated.

'But you saw the headlines?'

'Yis, ut's terrible I know. But what can we do about it? Nothing!' She flicked her slim wrist dismissively. Melissa was not that interested in politics, she was interested in the practicalities of everyday life. The school and her family took up all her time and attention. She had innovative ideas for teaching children and stimulating their minds, but outside of her world – if she couldn't change it, she dismissed it.

No one seemed to be talking about the situation too much. Was the hippopotamus being ignored again by everyone? Or was it anxiety that made it a closed subject? No one wanted their lives to change or be affected. No one wanted to think about the possibility that these events were going to have a major impact on them.

Since I'd been there, it had been difficult to have any discussion about the political situation in most of the circles in which I moved. Underneath, there was fear, people were nervous. In the Cape, which was largely English-origin South Africans and much more liberal, people felt suffocated by a government over which they felt they had no control.

We all knew that open talk might be dangerous, the Intelligence services might hear about any criticism of the regime. It was better to keep your head down and get on with your life. No one wanted to draw the attention of the secret police.

Diana rang again next day -

'Hi,' she was brisk, 'I've just been talking to this guy I know, just back from a spell in the army in South West (*the war in SW Africa [now Namibia]*). He's offered to show us how to use a gun, a handgun, he says he'll drive me over to your place - plenty of open bush for practice.'

'God, Di, a gun?'

'Well, we have to be prepared.'

For what exactly, I thought. For what.

A few days later, Dave went to Cape Town as rehearsals had begun on Richard III. He would be playing Cardinal Thomas Boucher, Archbishop of Canterbury, a small part - the Cardinal gives one short speech in Act III. He was quite happy as there were very few lines to learn and lots of time off from the rehearsals as he wasn't needed much. He was also meeting Henry Goodman for a chat about the next production at The Centre.

A silver saloon car pulled round the back of our bungalow and parked over by the chicken coop. Diana got out and introduced me to Jack, a wiry, dark-haired man of medium height. After a cup of tea and a chat, he explained that he'd finished a tour of duty recently, as a soldier in SW Africa against 'terrorists' there. I was highly suspicious of any war waged by the South African government, but I made no comment, it was unlikely that this guy's loyalties were anything less than pro-government.

Soon, we were outside the back door and he was pressing a grey metal revolver into my hand, standing behind me with both arms around me, holding the gun in my hands. The gun metal felt cold in my hands and I was trying to keep my hands steady. I didn't like his arms round me particularly, but he pointed across the yard.

'See that oil-drum over there?'

I looked to where he was pointing. The gun was aimed at the battered old oil drum, on the other side of the yard. I should be able to hit that, I thought.

'Okay, now you're going to fire at it, when I say 'fire!' Look straight down the barrel towards your target. Aim. Then fire. But first I want you to remember that this gun's got quite a kick. So hold it firmly.'

'Right,' I said nervously, 'So, I point over there.'

'Look down the sights, so you've got a straight line to the drum.'

I closed one eye, looked down the barrel and started to squeeze the trigger, trying to keep my hand steady. As he said 'Fire!' there was a sudden loud bang and both my arms holding the gun bounced up into the air above my head.

'Fucking hell!' I was stunned. I looked around, worried where the bullet had gone - nowhere near the oil-drum anyway.

'Have another go.' Jack un-cocked the gun – looking to see how many bullets were left. 'I'll show you how to hold it steadier next time.'

'Er, no thanks.' I didn't want his arms round me and the gun going off had scared me. 'Di why don't you go next?' I didn't like the thought of a handgun somehow. Guns were for killing.

'Oh shall I? I've never held a gun before, will it be all right Jack?'

I smiled to myself, Di was flirting, being a helpless female. He was standing behind her, his arms round her, holding her steady, as she tottered slightly on her high heels and giggled nervously. She managed after a couple of attempts to hit the oil drum, with his arms around her of course.

I refused to try again, deciding I wasn't cut out for guns. The idea of pointing one at a living person made me deeply uneasy. I thanked Jack for his help and he and Di drove off in his Mustang saloon. I never saw him again, so I guess another of Di's potential suitors bit the dust.

Over the next few weeks and months, we heard more occasionally about trouble in the townships. But as the news was heavily censored, after a short while the drama receded into the background and people got on with their lives. We had no idea at the time of the scale of the unrest, due to the blanket censorship.

We talked sometimes to Peter or Steve and British friends like Robert or Pam, our few coloured or black friends, but not anyone else. Everyone was careful about who they talked to. There was however, an underlying tension, an anxiety - we all became watchful.

Meanwhile there were occasional stories from Rhodesia about white famers being attacked and their wives and daughters being raped. Some of these attacks were crossing the border, across the Limpopo River into the Northern Rand in South Africa. It was worrying, how far would it spread?

Chapter 24: The Garden Route

Sunbird

The tiny bird hovers, not much bigger
than a bumblebee,
rainbow reflecting wings,

a blur of movement, long curved beak
digs deep into the nectar
of the pink, trumpet-like flower.

Waking early to stand at the window,
I looked out at the tropical garden
of the motel room in the Tsitsikama forest.

And there in an instant
frozen in my mind's time
a brief exquisite moment.

The radio turned on speaks excitedly
of the Entebbe raid
and Israel's triumph.

World events so far away
for in that moment all that existed
was me, the watcher and the bird and flower.

By Anna Meryt 1985

* * *

If we'd had any knowledge of the extent of the riots and
discontent that had spread across the Western Cape, maybe
we'd never have undertaken the journey that followed. News
censorship was so total that all we heard was a few minor
rumours, isolated newspaper reports and plenty of propa-
ganda.

* * *

'So, the cast is getting there by bus?' My tone was delib-
erately neutral, an idea beginning to form in my head. Dave
looked at me sharply.

'Yeah, the Garden Route's amazing, stunning. I've only seen bits of it on my other tours.'

'Hmm ... yes, I've been thinking...'

'Uh oh, here it comes.' He was grinning, the gap between his two front teeth always made him look roguish.

'What if we drove to Grahamstown? You could drive us there, I'd drive back.'

'It's a bloody long way. What about Pas?'

'She can come can't she? She's no trouble on car journeys.'

'Well you'd have a very long drive back on your own. Are you sure you could do that? I suppose we could stop overnight to break the journey...' Dave was getting interested.

'I don't know though, girlfriends and wives may not be allowed.'

'... and we could stay a night or two with you in Grahamstown perhaps?' I ignored the last remark. 'At least it would give us a little more time together before you go off again. Besides, I'd get to see the Garden Route that way, why should you have all the fun?'

'Hmmm. Be nice to have you with me on the journey. I'll check with the director tomorrow about bringing wives to Grahamstown, I can't see why it'd be a problem. I'll get a map so we can work out the best route.'

On the following day, the director gave the go-ahead for us to travel separately from the cast. He 'saw no reason why not.' The next few weeks were spent planning, pouring over the map, working out the best route - we'd stick to the coast where possible.

We became more and more excited about the trip. For me, it alleviated my fear of being left alone for weeks, gave me something to look forward to. Of course there was that long drive back on my own with Pas. I didn't want to think about that too much. There were no motorways then. It was a 500 mile journey on uncertain roads over some rough terrain.

* * *

We were up at 6 a.m. on the morning of departure. We planned to start by heading towards the mountains, across the wine-growing valleys of Paarl and on to Somerset West. Then we'd come back to the coast via Hermanus. We'd go as far as possible in daylight and look for a bed and breakfast when it was getting dark.

* * *

A cool mist hung over everything like layers of cotton wool, flattening out the hills. As we got further from Cape Town towards the wine valleys of Paarl, the sun was beginning to burn away the mist, but only on the tops of the hills. The old blue beetle would crest a hill into bright sunlight and the view to the horizon was of peaks poking out through the thick white haze. Each hill was covered in green - winter in the Cape is the 'green season' due to the frequent rain, and swathes of yellow wild flowers were interspersed with pink proteus and 'red hot pokers' - cactus plants with tall red flowers. The air smelt clean and fresh and there was little traffic. For a while it was like a switchback ride. Gradually the sun burned away more mist, until it was all gone. It rose high, in a deep blue sky and by 11 am the air was hot and still and we were all getting thirsty. We'd left the wine valleys behind now and had climbed onto a flat plateau which stretched ahead for miles. Occasionally, it broke into a deep cut slashed across the plateau and we'd drive across a strutted wooden bridge with huge rocky drops on either side. The scenery was spectacular.

In the distance, like a mirage, we saw a roadside stall and a hand-painted sign 'Fresh Pineapple Juice.' We pulled to a halt, in a cloud of dust and I jumped out. A tall handsome black woman, wearing a turban-like head wrap and a yellow and orange printed cloth tied above her bust, stood under a small rickety wooden shelter. It was hot, very hot. There was no other shade around except under the small shelter. I asked her how much and she said '10 cents'. I bought three tall glasses of crushed pineapple and ice. We all got out of the car, stretched and lolled about in the heat, quenching our thirst. It was utterly delicious. We thanked her - 'Danke, Danke.' She spoke no English - out here in the rural hinterland of the Eastern Cape, there was no call for English. Then we set off again quickly in a trail of dust, it was too hot to hang around.

By late afternoon, we'd reached Hermanus. We couldn't stop though, as we wanted to get as far as possible by dark. Now billowing grey clouds had pulled across the sun, covering the blue sky although the temperature still felt hot and humid. As we drove past Hermanus town, through the trees along the long coastal road we glimpsed the ocean - a vast sweeping bay where whales come to spawn and great slate-grey rollers were in constant motion under the darkening sky.

We pressed on, the road took us left now away from the sea, heading for Swellendam before curling back to the coast and Mossel Bay. We skirted George and then there was Knysna. As we came over the top of the hill the sun came out again and the scene in front of us made me catch my breath, a huge lagoon, like a vast lake, lay at the bottom of the hill in a beautiful bowl-shaped valley full of trees and greenery, dotted with houses around the water's edge. I studied the maps and it appeared that a small gap in the high rocky crags on the other side of the lagoon, let in the seas from the Indian Ocean beyond.

The road we were on wound down the hillside and then straight out over a long, narrow, flat bridge across the lagoon, before it rose up a steep hillside. We so wanted to stop and look, the blue-again sky was reflected in the calm lake on either side of us as we crossed the bridge, it was stunning, but time was short. We passed Plettenberg Bay and then the road wound away from the coast through a forested area. We began to see road signs for the Tsitsikamma Forest.

'Look Pas,' Dave pointed to an elephant sketch on a warning sign.

'Elephants! We might see elephants.' We looked and looked all around, but saw no elephants. The road gradually climbed deeper into the forest and the trees got slowly denser. Suddenly a sign said 'Tsitsikamma motel 5 km'. We had a small amount of money to stay somewhere and wondered if we could afford it.

By now dusk was falling rapidly and there were long shadows on the road, the tall trees dimming the fading light. A sign for the motel pointed down a narrow track off the main road. We drove down through the trees and suddenly the track opened onto a large grassy clearing. There was a long low-roofed L-shaped building, with wooden struts and white plaster walls, surrounded by flower beds full of colour and large bushes of deep pink bougainvillea.

A tall thin man with an Afrikaans accent came out and greeted us. His manner was cheerful and friendly, the price was okay, manageable. He showed us where to drive, past the main building to a single-storey row of wooden cottage-like buildings. He beckoned us to follow him, took out some keys and unlocked one of them, we parked outside. Inside was a comfortable living room with a kitchen alcove, a bed-room and a bathroom.   We'd brought tea, milk, bread, cheese, eggs and tomatoes from home. After cooking our-selves cheese and tomato omelettes with hunks of bread, and a mug of tea, we put together the cot for Pas, laid her in it and just before we went to sleep, I set the alarm clock radio beside me to wake us at 6.30 a.m.

I woke with a start. A newscaster was saying something about the plane hijacking that had been going on in Uganda since the week before:

'On the 27th June, an Air France *plane with 248 passengers was hijacked by Palestinian terrorists and flown to Entebbe, near Kampala, the capital of Uganda'.*

Dave had been particularly interested, as he had lived in Kampala with his father and brother for over two years in the early sixties, before being sent to a boarding school in Wales.

'The hijackers have been threatening to kill the hostages if their prisoner release demands aren't met. The Ugandan military were planning a rescue operation.'

[Dave had been deeply sceptical about such a mission, fearing it would result in a massacre].

The newsman carried on, '…in the early hours of today, the 4th of July, the Israeli Defence Forces performed a daring rescue operation. Our information is that all the hostages were saved. The hijackers were all killed or wounded in the operation.'

'Wow, that's amazing,' I said yawning, 'They rescued *all* the hostages. That's great news.' I turned off the radio, got up, strolled to the window and opened the curtains. Dave was just surfacing,

'What happened?' He was sitting on the edge of the bed, stretching. I told him the story again and he shook his head. 'I thought for sure, that if the Ugandan military were involved, the hostages would all die.' Dave had seen the activities of the Ugandan military at first hand, dead bodies on trucks covered with banana leaves.

'Well it was the Israeli military. They're so bloody efficient at what they do, thank goodness the hostages were saved.' I changed the subject. 'Just come and look out of this window, the garden is absolutely beautiful. Oh! Oh! Oh! I don't believe it, the smallest bird you ever saw is just outside the window, sticking its beak in a flower.'

Dave came up behind me and looked over my head.

'That's a hummingbird, I think – a little bigger than a bumblebee isn't it?' Look at its curved beak, so it can dip right into the flower and get the nectar. We used to get them in our garden in Kampala. Look Pas, come and see.' She had come running over talking excitedly.

'Daddy, daddy, pick me up, I wan see likl bird.' He bent down and lifted her up and pointed to the bird.

'Shhhh!' I said, 'It'll fly away if you make a noise. Look its wings go so fast they seem like a blur.'

We all stood there watching and whoosh suddenly it was gone in the flit of an eye. I turned and went over to the tiny kitchen to make us some toast and tea. Dave slung on his jeans and began packing up

After Tsitsikamma, we drove on, sticking to the coastal road through Port Elizabeth (PE), a largish town, past empty beaches – a thin strip of white sand fringing the dark blue ocean for mile after mile. We stopped the car at one point along this stretch, for some lunch. We'd bought fresh bread, cold ham, cheese and tomatoes along the way. We sat looking at the constant breakers of the Indian Ocean washing into the shore. The road now wound away from the coast and after an hour and a half, we arrived in Grahamstown.

Grahamstown was an old colonial town, built at a time when ox-drawn wagons were the main means of transport.

The streets of this small town were wide, wide enough to accommodate two wagons passing each other. We found our accommodation – a room in a low wooden building facing this street.

That night, Dave went to meet all the other actors for a few beers while I put Pas to bed. The show would be opening the day after tomorrow - as the Archbishop is only in a few scenes, there were not too many lines, so he was fairly relaxed about the show. The main rehearsals had all been done in Cape Town.

Next day the three of us went for a drive down towards Port Alfred, which I could see on the map was on the mouth of an estuary leading out to the ocean. We stopped at a little shop and I saw a simple but beautiful watercolour of storks, in front of a distant seascape. It was just a few Rand so we bought it. We had a picnic sitting on the shore and then drove back. One more night together I thought to myself trying not to be mournful.

Next morning, we packed up the car again and Dave stood outside the room waving us goodbye. He was looking forward to the opening night and some fun nights out with the cast. I waved with a heavy heart, not looking forward to the long drive back alone - it had taken about 11 hours to get there. I knew we'd have to stop for a night on the way. Pas was quite happy on the back seat with Big Doll, chatting to herself, she didn't seem to notice my mood.

The long drive home was exhausting. I stopped briefly after Knysna, near the Wilderness National Park close to another forest and got out of the car, then lay on my back staring up through the tall pines at the rays of sun piercing the dark treetops and filtering thinly onto the forest floor. Pas was glad to get out and run around, exploring around me while I dozed for 20 minutes.

Afterwards, we carried on to the town in Mossel Bay where I found a small hotel and booked us in. It was dark by the time we checked in and I couldn't see much of the town, although I could smell the sea air. Our small single room looked onto a tiny plain courtyard and I was too tired to go out exploring by then. I put up Pas's cot in the small space next to my bed and held her hand until she fell asleep.

I lay down feeling very alone, wondering how I would get through the next few weeks without Dave. As I lay there I prayed to whatever god was out there for help. Suddenly it seemed that I was surrounded by a safe warm glow and a feeling that we'd be taken care of somehow. I fell into a deep sleep.

Settlers Monument Theatre, Grahamstown, 7th July 1976
and Nico Malan Theatre, Cape Town 13th Aug 1976

Chapter 25: A pig farmer, a rifle, an incident

Pas and I made it home and she went back to nursery. Life carried on and for the next few weeks, until Dave's return, I kept myself busy, taking her to school, stopping off to chat to Mel sometimes and doing chores when we got home in the afternoon. Di drove out to visit me occasionally and one day, she asked if she could come and stay for a few weeks. She was no longer living with Jane in Mowbray but had been sharing with another girl in Cape Town for a while. Her flatmate had moved to Johannesburg and she couldn't afford the apartment on her own. She didn't mind sharing with Pas and I was delighted to have the company when she was around – she was often at work or busy with her social life. Pas continued to play with Markus most afternoons.

Dave came home a few weeks later, his CAPAB contract now ended. A director called Gillian Horowitz had booked him for an impro show that was touring schools around Cape Town and they would be doing dramatized scenes from exam set books. He was fitting this around radio plays with Springbok radio to make sure enough money was coming in for us to survive.

On a warm sunny day in late August, I decided to walk to the pig farm down the road. I was worried about all the rumours and thought it might be an idea to get to know our nearest neighbour. What if Dave wasn't home or was away and something happened? Dave was still in bed, but was meeting Gillian later for a rehearsal. I'd dropped Pas at nursery and Mel had suggested leaving her with Lena after school to play with Gabby for the afternoon. She was going out to a 'business' lunch.

A dusty yellow track led about two kilometres through bush and scrub. It was a pleasant day and I was wearing the usual t-shirt, shorts and flip flops. The sun was warm on my face and a blue haze shimmered across the bush to the horizon. A weaver bird flew past with a piece of grass in its beak. Winter was nearly over and spring was starting early, signalled by the Cape daisies springing up amongst the cactus. There was a small disused quarry over to the left – I had walked over before with Pas and seen the weaver's big dome-shaped nests clustered along the sides of the quarry.

Each nest was intricately woven from pieces of dry brown grasses.

As I got closer to the farm, the over-powering smell of pig manure got stronger, a familiar one - on a bad day if the breeze was in the wrong direction, the smell would waft over our bungalow and hang there all day. I strolled into the yard outside the main house and a great barking was followed by 4 dogs the size of small horses lolloping over towards me – Rhodesian Ridgebacks and a Rottweiler – luckily I'm not afraid of dogs as I grew up around them. I stood quite still and waited for them to smell me ...the farmer came striding out to meet me, alerted by their barking, calling them to heel.

'Hi, I live over there with my husband and baby.' I pointed back along the track. 'We rent our place from Mr Schmidt.'

'Ach, men,' he made a face. 'Him!' His meaningful look spoke volumes. We both knew what he meant. Mr Schmidt was well known in the area for being eccentric, tight fisted and penny pinching to the extreme. I asked him about the farm, how many pigs he had and so forth. He took me on a tour of the huge concrete buildings, with corrugated roofs. About fifty small pens inside the first building contained mother pigs and their litters. The huge sows were separated from their piglets by a metal bar, which meant the area they had to move around in was tiny – barely twice their own size, hardly room to turn round. I asked him why they were kept separate and he explained,

'The sows roll over in their sleep onto the piglets if they're in together, so we used to lose a lot. Now they can get to the teats and come out again.'

I looked at the sow in the pen next to us and felt appalled by her narrow confines. Her eyes were brown, intelligent and sad, she was looking at me in what felt like a hopeless way. I resolved (again) to become a vegetarian, how could I continue to be complicit in this cruel way of life? I'd miss bacon though, I thought, and then felt guilty and moved away from her. I said nothing to the farmer - what was the point of upsetting our nearest neighbour.

We started talking about the riots and rumours and I told him about the guy who had come round to teach me to use a handgun and what had happened. He frowned. 'What you need's a roifle men, a hend gun's no use.'

I wasn't too sure about that so said that we couldn't afford one. I asked what he thought we should do in the event of trouble, there were so many rumours going around.

'Yew wanna git over here quick as yew can. I've got some roifles here. And the dogs of course. I'll tell you what, yew can borrow one of mah two-twos if you loike. Ah'll go get one, but it's just a loan, roit?'

I frowned thinking about the handgun, but maybe a rifle was different. He went back into the farmhouse and when he came out, he pushed it into my hands. I had tried rifles before in my teens – an older cousin had an air-gun he'd let me try. I knew I had a good eye and could hit a target. This rifle was altogether different though, bigger, heavier, a serious weapon. He took out a box and gave me a handful of bullets – they were an inch and a half long and brass. I wasn't too sure about taking it but he was insistent so I thanked him and went off down the road, carrying the heavy gun gingerly.

I showed it to Dave, who was very excited.

'And he's just letting us borrow it? Wow!'

We loaded it, as the farmer had shown me, so we could try it out. I took careful aim at the oil drum on the other side of our yard, watching out for the kickback this time. BANG! It went off and the oil drum leapt into the air and fell with a clatter. The sound echoed across the yard and bird and cricket sounds fell silent for a moment. A smell like sulphur lifted into my nostrils. Dave walked over to the oil drum and called me over.

'Come and look at this.'

I walked over and stared at a hole the size of my fist on two sides of the drum.

'Bloody hell! Think what it would do to a human being,' I stared at it.

Dave then tried it a few times for practise. But as we only had a few bullets, we decided to conserve them. I wrapped the gun up in an old sheet and put it on top of the wardrobe, out of reach of kids. I hoped I would never have to use it, but we were all nervous of the way current events were unfolding. I also found a small red hat box there and decided to put our passports, some money and a change of clothes for Pas in it, so that if we had to leave in a great hurry, we'd have a few essentials. I mentally rehearsed picking up Pas, the hat box and the gun and running down the track to the pig farm ... on my own, if Dave was away. It would not be easy, Pas was heavy now.

It was time to fetch her from school, I dropped Dave in town for his meeting with Gillian and drove to Brooksfield to collect her from Lena, preoccupied with thinking about the escape plan.

Two nights later, I thought the moment had come. That afternoon, Dawn had come to tell me what had happened. She and Jakub had turned onto our track from the road, in the bakkie. As they were driving up, three black men had jumped out in front of the truck and waved at them to stop. Instead of stopping, Jakub had put his foot flat on the accelerator and driven hard towards them, the men had leapt out of the way at the last minute, shouting. Dawn came round to warn me about it a bit later.

'Look men, we y'ave to go out in a whoile agin, we gotta maike a living, ay? D'yew thunk yew'll be awl roit? If yew loike I'll stay with yew?'

'Well, Dave'll be back in about an hour ... and I have got the gun.'

'OK, if you're sure, men?'

I wasn't at all sure, but didn't want to stop them from making money. They had Markus wrapped up behind the front seats, sleeping. Di was still with us but she'd gone away for a couple of days. It wouldn't be long until Dave came home, a couple of hours at most.

I was tucking Pas into bed when I heard their truck pull off again. As soon as she was asleep, I went to the wardrobe in our room, pulled down the rifle and unwrapped it. I put two bullets in the barrel then laid it on the kitchen table, as I made myself some tea. Having done that, I took it into the sitting room, put it by my feet and propped myself up on the sofa with a book.

Then it started ... the dogs, Angel and Max (Dawn and Jakub's Alsatian) started barking in the yard, not just ordinary barking, but going-mad frantic barking. I picked up the rifle and turned on the outside lights so the concrete yard was lit up. Dawn and Jakub's place had exterior lights on too. The darkness outside the lit-up area was absolute. I lifted the gun to my shoulder and marched to the centre of the pool of light, so I'd be clearly visible.

'Who's there?' I asked, 'I've got a gun and I'll shoot. Get off my land.'

I held the gun up against my shoulder and pointed it, as I walked around within the light. Adrenalin made me alert to every sound and hyper-aware of my surroundings. I could hear little else but the dogs barking ferociously in the outer darkness. Suddenly Angel shot into the light and stood beside me growling, her lips curled over her teeth. Max was still barking in the distance. Again I said it,

'Who's there, I've got a gun and I'll shoot.' I listened - there was no response, no sound except the not too distant barking outside my vision.

High above it was a clear moonless night, the sky crowded with stars. The night air was warm enough still, to walk about in a T-shirt. I felt sharply awake, as I peered into the darkness and moved to the edge of the light. I wondered what I would do if suddenly someone stepped into the light. I thought of pointing the gun at their head or their chest. What if they ran at me with a machete or some other weapon? All at once I knew that if someone appeared, I could not shoot them. My gun-waving act was total bravado, I could not shoot another human being, not even to save my life and my child's life. Everyone always thinks they can, but in that moment I knew I could not press the trigger, with the gun pointed at someone. The thought made me feel physically ill. I could bluff, but in the end they could walk up to me and take the gun from my hand.

Luckily I was not put to the test. Max returned to the yard, panting and looking excited. The two dogs circled me, sniffed each other and then flopped down at my feet, both having stopped barking. Whoever was out there, must have decided not to challenge the mad woman with the gun and left the area. Either that or they had moved far enough away for the dogs to no longer see or smell them. What if they circled around and came back? I stood for a while still holding up the gun-that-I-could-not-shoot and looked round glaring. Then, lowering the gun I walked quickly back into the bungalow, locking the door behind me. I went to check that the door on the other side was locked too. All the curtains were pulled tight shut. Pas was still asleep in her bed. I put the rifle down carefully by my feet and flopping down on the sofa, picked up my book again.

My hands began to shake as the adrenalin subsided. I tried to concentrate on the book, checking my watch regularly, but Dave had phoned earlier – he was going for a drink with his co-actors after the rehearsals. He would not be back for another hour. The tension in my body did not abate, until I heard the sound of a vehicle coming up the track to the yard. I lifted a corner of the curtain carefully, until I could see our old, blue beetle's headlights as it pulled up outside the front door. Then I ran out with relief, hugged Dave and told him what had happened. He came in looking worried and poured himself a glass of wine. After taking a large swig, he walked in to the sitting room, put down his glass and picked up the gun from the floor.

'Be careful,' I said, 'it's loaded.'

He uncocked the barrel and checked the bullets, then clicked it back.

'I'm going out for a look round.' I looked at him apprehensively.

'Be careful then, I couldn't see anything, but the dogs went absolutely mad, there must have been someone out there. If you see any mad machete wielding guys....'

'I'll shoot 'em.' He winked at me.

Suddenly, I started to smile, Dave was into his favourite fantasy dream, where he was a cowboy, riding into town for a shoot-out, saving the girl and becoming the hero.

He strode out the front door, raising the gun to shoulder height, while I stood in the doorway watching – this tall skinny guy, with blue eyes and blonde hair flopping in his eyes, wearing a pink-stripy T-shirt, not exactly the big butch hero type. Angel and Max followed at his heels. He walked outside the lit-up area, in a big circle round the house and then came back.

'Nothing!' he put the gun down carefully on the kitchen table. 'Can't see a thing out there. If there was someone out there...'

'The dogs would be barking.' I handed him his glass of wine.

'Well anyway, if there was, they could see me, hunkering down with mah gun, walking round.' He drew an imaginary gun from a holster, cocked it, squatted down and fired from his two fingers. Then he blew the gun-smoke away from the barrel and winked.

'Yeh OK, Mr Lone Ranger.' I was smiling, the tension was broken and we both started laughing.

The strain of that night took its toll though. I began to think about whether this was the right place to be, what with the riots and the current uncertainty. I was out here in the 'bundhu', as my mother used to call it – on my own with a small child every night.

Chapter 26: A scorpion's tale

On a day off from his schools tour, Dave had met up with Henry Goodman, who'd directed him in Son of Man. Henry had been asked by Jo Dunstan at The Centre to direct Waiting for Godot, by Samuel Beckett, a strange play with two main characters and another who brings in a slave (Lucky) attached to a rope. Lucky doesn't speak until Act Two when he gives a soliloquy. It was due to open in October and rehearsals would start at the end of September. He offered Dave the part of Lucky. Dave was pleased as although he didn't have many lines, the character is on stage a great deal and is a central part. The play itself is world famous and much studied and theorised about. The salary was important too as the tour of schools would be finishing by the time this play started.

* * *

One morning, just before Dave's rehearsals for Godot were due to start, I rose early. It was mid-September and spring was well underway - the sky was blue and the sun warm. It felt like it was going to get hot later, summer was coming. Pas got up, wandered in to the kitchen and sat at the table and I gave her some cornflakes and milk. I washed up last night's dishes, then made myself a cup of tea and strolled out into the back yard wearing an old pink T shirt, faded blue shorts and flip flops. Angel was slumped in front of the stable next to the house with one eye open, watching me. I had an uninterrupted view over miles of scrubland from my back door. Di was back with us for a few weeks and had split up from whichever boyfriend it was, so wanted some TLC. It was good to have her company now that Dave was going to be out every day until well into the evening. There were always arrays of beautiful flowers about the place when she was around.   She was still asleep, as was Dave – the day before, he'd had a busy day performing at a school 50 miles away and then been up late working on his sci-fi story.

Across the yard, I noticed the pile of sand we'd bought last summer for Pas and Markus to play in. Up-turned on it was the two-ring rubber paddling pool I'd got for her the year before, as well as buckets and spades. I could fill it up in the yard, I thought, looking up at the blue sky. That would keep the kids busy later on when it got hot enough. I sniffed the air as I strolled over to take a look and could smell the warm, dry air drifting across from the bush and the frying boereworst and onions from next door.

Next door's truck was parked outside their place, in the wide, concrete yard and our old blue VW beetle was beside it. I could hear Dawn yelling something at Jakub in Afrikaans as I walked past, as well as the distant sound of Pas singing to Big Doll, as she tried to feed her cornflakes – I groaned to myself, there was probably milk and sugar everywhere by now.

The pile of sand had dirt and twigs all over it - I'd have to clean it up. The paddling pool was looking a bit grubby and flat too, still it could be scrubbed out and pumped up then I'd fill it with buckets of warm water. I yanked it up and stepped backwards into the sand.

That's when I felt it – a searing pain in my right foot which shot up the back of my leg. I dropped the pool and looked back to where my foot had been – there it was, a pink scorpion about 3 inches long with its tail arched high – I'd trod on it with my bare flip-flopped feet and I'd been stung in my right heel. In that moment, I knew for sure I only had a short time to live, unless I got an antidote. The nearest medical centre was seven miles away – I'd never make it in time. My brain seized in panic and then suddenly I was racing across the yard, running through the kitchen and into the bedroom in two leaps. Dave was fast asleep on the double bed. He would normally sleep for another couple of hours before getting up slowly, doing a few chores and then driving off to whichever school they were performing in. I screamed loudly -

'Dave, Dave, I've been stung by a scorpion and I've got 10 minutes to live! Help! Help!' I was sobbing hysterically by now…

My first screams made Dave sit bolt upright in bed. He looked at me dazed, like he was dreaming…

'Get up,' I screamed 'Do something! I've only got ten minutes to live!'

He looked at me stupidly, 'What do you mean, ten minutes to live? What? How?'

'I've been stung by a scorpion,' I screamed again. 'I trod on it by the pool,' his questions were making me even more hysterical...

'Get up! Drive me to the medical centre!'

'But it's 7 miles away. That's more than ten minutes!'

We looked at each other. 'What else can we do, get me there now.' I was sobbing. He leapt out of bed. 'Go start the car,' he was talking loudly. I ran outside and saw Jakub in his pick-up truck, Dawn was standing by. I screamed to Jakub, my words staccato, big gasping breaths in between -

'Jakub ... been stung by a scorpion – have to get to the med-centre fast!' The words were punctuated by large sobs. Jakub was not a man who wasted words.

'Git in the truck!' He was already revving it up, 'Ah'll drive yew theh.'

'Yeh,' Dawn, caught on to my urgency fast. 'He's a really fawst droiver, he'll get yew theh in munuts.'

Dave was rushing from the house in his shorts, pulling on his shirt. Di was close behind him roused by all the yelling.

'Dave, Jakub's gonna take me, he can drive fast.' I was still sobbing and tying a tight rag of cloth as a tourniquet round the top of my calf – I was thinking - mustn't let the poison spread up my leg, if it gets to my heart I'll die - the pain felt like it was burning up my leg from my foot into my ankle.

Dave said 'OK, get going, I'll phone the med centre.'

Di was fussing over Pas, who was getting upset, calling 'Mummy! Mummy! Me come too!'

'It's OK.' Di said smiling down at her 'We'll go and make some cakes shall we?' She grabbed Pas's hand, 'You stay here with me ... Mum's got to rush, she'll be back soon.' Dave interrupted, his face grim, 'I'll let them know you're coming.'

I jumped in the truck, waving goodbye to Pas, putting on a false smile to reassure her, as Jakub 'burnt rubber'. 'See you later Pas', I shouted just before the truck leapt down the track skimming over the bumps, with dust flying in clouds behind us. I was thinking - will I ever see her again? I was too caught up in the drama of it all, wondering if I was going to live, to cry.

The truck raced from our track onto the main road and zig-zagged round the potholes. Jakub had his foot flat on the pedal all the way to the Med centre, where he pulled into the car park skidding to a halt, gravel spurting from the tyres, by the front entrance. It had taken about 15 minutes, which was fast. I leapt out and ran for the double doors. By now, I didn't know how long I'd got – I was already well into injury time and my minutes were running out.

Jakub had leapt out of the truck and was right behind me as I ran in and pressed the button for the lift – the doc was on the fourth floor.

Let me take a quick moment to describe that med centre – this was not the NHS, it was for paying guests only. GPs charged a good fee for each visit - plus the not inconsiderable cost of the prescription. Dave and I rarely went to the doctor therefore. This med centre was modern, had plush red carpets, smartly-dressed reception staff, smart red and white couches in the waiting room and you got seen promptly. It had all the mod cons of that time and the latest diagnostic equipment. It was built on several floors with rooms for consultants on one floor, in-patients on the lower floors.

Here was I in the soft hissing lift with Jakub – he looked like poor white trash in his old dusty khaki shorts and vest top and 50s style short back and sides haircut. I was in a scraggy old pink vest top and blue shorts - I looked the same. The lift doors swished open at the fourth floor and we rushed over to the smart, wide reception desk. The receptionist with her beautifully manicured pink nails looked up smiling, she was typing at the other end of the long counter.

'Did my husband call, I been stung by a scorpion, the doc's expecting me, I need antidote fast?' I nodded to the doctor's rooms behind her.

'Take a seat over there', she drawled, indicating the waiting area.

I was shocked by her casual attitude, didn't she realise I was about to die? I tried again, this time I raised my voice a few notches.

'Look, I'VE BEEN STUNG BY A SCORPION, I'LL DIE WITHOUT THE ANTIDOTE, CAN YOU PLEASE GET THE DOC STRAIGHT AWAY, ITS URGENT AND I'M NOT SITTING AND WAITING ANYWHERE!'

The doc must have heard me, since he came out of his room quickly. He looked me up and down, taking in my faded threadbare clothes, my dishevelled appearance and lastly the old rag tourniquet tied around my thigh. He was a man in his late 30s, about my height, freckle-faced and ginger haired with a long fringe flopping across one eye. He was wearing a white coat.

He laughed. 'Take that thing off your leg.'

I was shocked, 'it's to stop the poison spreading.'

He looked at me unfazed. 'Look, take it off. A scorp sting's no big deal, not much worse than a bee sting!'

'What! But I thought I was going to die, haven't you got some antidote?'

'You don't need antidote,' he was frowning hard, trying not to laugh I could see, '…you need antihistamine, just in case you have an allergic reaction – step into my surgery and I'll give you an injection!'

I undid the 'tourniquet' sheepishly, feeling very foolish. Well how was I to know? Everything I'd ever heard told me that a scorpion sting was fatal. The doc told me to lie face down on the couch and pull my shorts down – he quickly stuck a needle in my bare backside and then 2 seconds later he said 'Get up, you'll be fine now, you can go home.'

I looked at him, stunned. 'That's it? You're not giving me anything else? Just sending me home?'

'Yep, that's it.' He was grinning at my disbelief, 'Should be no ill effects. How does it feel now?'

Well, I thought to myself, now I come to think about it, the pain's nearly gone and I can't feel anything. In fact, it had been gone for some time, but I'd attributed it to numbness creeping up my leg. Actually I was feeling fine, now I knew I wasn't going to die.

'Um… actually,' I was looking up at him and then down at my leg, reluctant to let go of the drama completely, running my hand along the leg and squeezing and poking it ....slowly, 'I suppose it feels OK', I said reluctantly.

He smiled. 'You see? Go home then – just settle up with my receptionist on the way out!' Brisk!

No, this definitely wasn't the NHS, I thought as I walked out of his room. I stepped over to the receptionist and asked for the bill, searching around in my bag for my cheque book. It was definitely improving, I thought to myself.... I felt OK. I'm going to live. I'm going to see Pas and Dave again.

'Come on Jakub. Take me home please.'

When I got back, everyone rushed into the yard and I had to tell the whole story over and over, I was feeling a little foolish about all the drama by then. Di put her arm round me, 'I was sure you'd be all right. Come in and I'll make you a nice cup of tea.' I couldn't stop smiling and Dave was grinning, looking very relieved. He had to get ready to drive to Cape Town to meet Henry and now he could relax and get on with the show. We'd all had a big shake-up.

Dawn wasn't one for smiling much - she came out and looked at Jakub enquiringly.

'Thanks, Jakub.' I was thinking about him and the axe - he had semi-redeemed himself now. 'You got me there so fast, I can't believe how fast you drove. You saved me, well nearly.'

After Dave had driven off, Di made us some lunch and then we both cleaned up the paddling pool, (being very careful to look out for scorpions and boboyani). We filled it up with buckets and sat drinking tea, watching Pas and Markus jumping about naked in the water, splashing each other.

It was good to be alive.

* * *

Life is full of ups and downs isn't it? And in our life the dramas were gathering pace. Soon I had something else to worry about – Pas!

A few weeks after the scorpion incident, Pas woke up again in the middle of the night with another earache. She'd been getting quite a few ear infections and each time we'd be doing what we could to relieve the pain, until we could get her to the doctor. Over the preceding months, we'd tried hot water bottles, a sock full of salt warmed up in the oven and Calpol to try and ease the pain. It was distressing for all of us.

Next day, I took her to the doctor and again he put her on antibiotics. I knew she'd be fine for a while, but the cycle would start again. We kept her off school for a few days but I knew there'd be more antibiotics eventually. I asked the doctor what to do and he decided to refer her to Groote Schuur to see the ENT specialist. He said the condition was not uncommon for children her age.

Another thing happened too, which eventually turned out to be related. One morning, I was brushing her hair and to my horror, a large chunk of her hair came off on the brush. The next day the same thing happened. Again I took her to the doctor, but he didn't know the cause and suggested a trichologist (hair specialist). I rang up to make an appointment.

'... and how much is a consultation?' I was nervous as our budget was very, very tight.

'That'll be twelve rand (about £6).' Oh dear, I thought, that's quite a lot. But I suppose we'll have to find the money somehow.

I took Pas along a week later and he examined her head carefully. He talked generally about what could cause hair-loss or 'alopecia', as he called it.

'Has she had any sort of trauma or shock?' I thought about the Jakub/Dawn incident, but Pas knew nothing about it, she'd slept through it all. What about the scorpion sting? Nah! It's me who should have bloody alo- bloody-whatsit, I thought.

He was writing out a prescription – for a tube of cream, some kind of steroid cream.

'You part the hair lahk so and rub in the cream lahk so.' He was parting her hair to demonstrate. Pascale was quiet, she kept her eyes on me and held my hand, but as he talked to me over her head, she more or less ignored him. I was thinking – cream? In her hair? Greasy, greasy! It doesn't make sense. It doesn't explain why... why is she losing her hair? I don't think he had a clue. Twelve Rand to tell me that!

Pas was chatting as we came out, making up for the silence inside there.

'Mummy, what dat man doing my hair. He was pulling my hair Mummy. Not like him.' We got back in the car and she found Big Doll on the back seat. Clearly it was time for dolly to get a change of clothes and a talking to. She seemed to have dismissed the hair guy from her mind as irrelevant and didn't seem bothered about the hair loss, not as bothered as I was.

'Mmmm ...' I was still thinking about what he'd said and the cost ...

'It's coz some of your hair came out last week, he gave me some cream to make it better?'

I think I attempted to put the cream on once, but she looked a complete fright, her hair all greasy. How could she go to nursery school looking like that? I then spent hours washing it all out. No! There had to be another solution.

Chapter 27: Wynberg incident, decisions

In the following weeks, we heard bits of information, either from the Cape Times or through rumour. The government was clamping down everywhere, tightening censorship laws, banning more books. The Cape Times reported arrests of journalists and activists white and black. Tensions were high. It wasn't until many years later that I found out the extent to which the riots and unrest had spread to the Cape. We had very little idea what was happening while there, apart from the rumours, as censorship was so absolute. So we got on with our daily lives.

The patrol car near the end of our road, stayed there for about three weeks. Everyone was somewhat nervous, but we tried to maintain our routines. You couldn't talk about it too openly, as critical comments might go to the secret police Those who had money furthered their plans of escape to Australia or Canada, talking to contacts about work abroad and getting money out of the country to start up again. After the incident with the rifle, I was now thinking seriously about moving back into the suburbs.

Meanwhile, Dave's rehearsals for 'Waiting for Godot' had begun. The show would open on October 21st. A recently graduated drama student called Alan Leas was playing the second lead, an interesting chap who was also writing a play and was trying to get funding to put it on. Dave's part was not too taxing - he was to be led around stage with a rope round his neck, looking hopeless and drooling a lot.

Jo Dunstan was over-seeing the production, although Henry was directing (as well as playing the lead). The great thing about working for Jo (apart from the fact we both liked her) was that the productions were in the cathedral. As always, the shows could have mixed-race audiences and casts, the churches being largely exempt from temporal law and therefore able to bypass the apartheid laws to an extent. Dave was not really interested in religion, he could probably be described as an agnostic. My religious beliefs were moving away from Catholicism towards more universal beliefs, which a few years later drew me towards Buddhism. We'd both been brought up in different branches of Christianity – although Dave's family's adherence had been rather more loose and vague than mine. This was probably because his father, a professor of physics, had travelled and lived abroad so much and Dave was sent back to Wales to his aunts and boarding school. The story in Waiting for Godot could only barely be recognised as having any religious theme. Jo was stretching it a little with that play.

* * *

In the last week of rehearsal, they were doing a final run-through, dress rehearsal on the Saturday - a matinee, and the opening night would follow a few hours later. I was going to bring Pas to see the show, mainly because I couldn't get a babysitter. The quickest route into Cape Town by car was through the townships of Wynberg and Manenberg, coloured townships which under normal circumstances were quite safe. Most townships were generally out-of-bounds for whites, except in the daytime. However on that day, although we had heard a few rumours of some unrest spreading, we were running late and decided to take the risk. Pascale was in the back of the car, playing with Big Doll. Dave and I were in the front, he was driving, as always.

On entering the outskirts of Wynberg it seemed at first that everything was normal. On both sides of the road were the typical small low brick houses. Usually, there were plenty of people walking down the road and no one took any notice of us. Today as we drove further along we noticed there were very few people around and those that were, stopped to stare at us. Up ahead at a crossroads, we saw something wasn't right, we could see black smoke.

Cape Coloured people did not usually join in with the protests or aspirations of the black tribal population. They were more likely to side with the whites. But the negotiations of their leaders with the government for more representation were constantly stalling. Everyone knew that the apartheid government was just playing them along, keeping them from real power but also keeping them on their side.

We were approaching the black smoke quite quickly and there seemed to be groups of young men to the right of it. Some of them were gesticulating, with short angry movements

Oh Shit!' Dave had his foot on the brake pedal.

'What is it?' I was trying to see where the smoke was coming from.

'Look ...up ahead! Shit! Shit!'

He slowed the car right down. I could see now – large objects in the middle of the road – smoke seemed to be coming from these objects...

'What is it? What are they doing?'

'Burning tyres!' Dave said half under his breath. 'Now what? Shall I turn round? Go back?'

I could smell it now, that strong acrid smell of burning rubber! The youths didn't seem to have seen us, yet. What would they do when they noticed a car approaching with white occupants? Some white people had been murdered up in Soweto when the riots started. But that had been a few months ago in black townships only. Surely it was all calming down now, the police – using their usual brutal tactics had brought it all under control, hadn't they?

'No, it's too late to turn round ... I'm going to keep driving. I'm going through.'

As he spoke, I felt the surge from the engine as he put his foot flat on the accelerator. The small VW engine gathered itself together and then shot forward.

I felt a moment of panic then squashed it – I had my child to deal with. I turned round to Pas immediately and said,

'Pas get down under the seat. Now!' I pulled her down into the gap between the back and front seats and told her to lie quietly there. I swept Big Doll onto the floor next to her and she hugged her close as I grabbed a blanket off the back seat and covered her over. She'd done what I asked at once, her almond-shaped eyes wide. I guess she heard the urgency in my tone. My hand slid under the blanket and held her small hand.

As I turned to face the front we were screeching round the burning tyres and racing down the road. The startled youths that were gathered there barely had time to react. I looked back and saw them in a cloud of dust looking down the road after us, too late to prevent our forward passage. One had started running after us, but it was too late, he gave up. They were waving their arms about and pointing in our direction.

Would we encounter any more trouble on the way out of the township? We held our breath as the car sped down the wide road past tin shacks and a liquor store with more groups of young men standing around. We were going too fast for us to see a reaction, but the expressions on their faces seemed hostile. There were no more road blocks of any sort along our route.

After about a mile, we pulled out of Wynberg and back onto the main road to Cape Town and breathed again. I pulled Pas onto the front seat with me and hugged her.

'Phew, I think we better avoid the townships from now on and go the long way round.' Dave was looking at my tense face.

My heart was still thumping in my chest and I took a few large breaths of air to steady myself. 'That was a bloody narrow escape!'

Dave had slowed down now. 'What the hell was going on there? I thought the coloured townships were okay? That was scary.'

Then he looked down at Pas. Her face was pale and her eyes big. She had picked up the atmosphere of fear. He changed the subject with an effort,

'So, you're going to see Daddy in a play. We'll sit at the front and you have to be very good and very quiet and not call out to Daddy, OK?'

'See Daddy play! See Daddy play!" She was waving her arms about, already forgetting what had happened. I told her that Daddy was playing a very silly man called Lucky, who did stupid things, but he was only pretending. I hugged her close, we'd all had a bad fright.

We parked near St George's and Dave went to the dressing-rooms at the back of the cathedral to get changed. Pas and I walked to our front row seats. Jo was standing by the podium, greeting people as they walked in. She looked at me sharply.

'Are you OK? You look a bit pale?'

I told her briefly about our journey and she was concerned, but not surprised.

'It's not good to drive through the townships with this unrest. We don't know half of what's going on. Geoffrey hears
about it from his parishioners... some terrible things are happening.'

Then she was called away before she could say more, she
had a show to run.

Di came in – I saw her at the back and waved her forward
to come and sit with us. She'd moved from our place now
and was sharing a flat with a girlfriend, in Cape Town somewhere.

I looked up at the magnificent high ceilings and stained
glass windows and porticos of the cathedral, remembering
when Dave had played Jesus on the cross above the podium. I would have to keep a close eye on Pas, so she didn't
yell out when Dave appeared – with his character being led
around with a rope around his neck, looking dejected, it might
upset her. I needn't have worried - when Dave first appeared
in the story, Pas looked at me, her eyes shining and whispered excitedly.

'Look Mummy … it Daddy!'

I put my finger to my lips and she sat still, squirming in her
seat, but managed to remain quiet.

The show went on without incident, although after a short
while her attention span dropped and she crept onto my lap
and fell asleep.

Afterwards I walked, with the sleepy Pas holding my hand,
down the dusty corridors at the back of the cathedral to the
changing rooms near the vestry. The men were in one largish
room. We waited outside the door until they'd finished show-
ering and changing then went in.

As it was a matinee the cast had to hang around for the
evening show, which usually meant a quick dash to the nearest bar for a drink and snack. We chatted to them while Dave
finished changing. Henry, as usual was entertaining us with
funny stories, he and Dave competed to get the most laughs.

As the first live performance was a few hours later, Dave
left his make-up on for the evening show but changed into
casual clothes. Afterwards there would be a cast celebra-
tion, with drinks in a bar round the corner.

Pas and I were going home and as we were taking the car, Dave would come later by taxi. Dave didn't talk openly about our difficult journey as some of the cast were Cape Coloured and lived in Manenberg and Wynberg. He told me quietly that he might ask them later about the situation, it was a sensitive issue. We talked briefly in the corridor as I was leaving, about my route home.

'Just be careful and stick to the main roads this time – you'll be fine.'

* * *

As I was putting Pas to bed that night, I thought about the events of the last few weeks and months. We had moved to the bush, hoping to lead a rural life. There'd be open air, lots of space, we'd grow vegetables, keep chickens and geese, it would be an outdoor life for Pas - she'd be able to run around in the fresh air with few restrictions. Everything we'd tried had gone wrong. There'd been the incident with the rifle and the dogs barking. I was feeling isolated too, miles from friends – I'd tackle it with Dave that evening when he got in.

When he arrived, it was late – of course the cast party meant there'd been a lot of drinking. Steve had turned up to see the show and a few other people we knew. Dave was buzzing with alcohol and adrenaline and striding up and down the lounge still in performance mode.

Eventually he sat on the sofa and got out his cigarette papers, licked four to join them together, split a cigarette down the middle and put the tobacco in. Then he went out to the stable next door, to his hidden stash and came back with a small bag of grass, which he sprinkled liberally on top of the tobacco.

'Pete got me this grass - excellent stuff!' He looked around for a piece of cardboard for the roach. I handed him a piece torn from the top of the cornflake packet. He finished rolling his giant joint, lit the end a few times, blew it till it was red, took a deep drag and sat back on the sofa, relaxing from the tension of the day at last.

'Pas and I really enjoyed the show, did you see her? She fell asleep after a bit – at least she was quiet. It seemed to go well anyway? You were fab of course! Although all that drooling was a bit yuk.'

He laughed, 'Well yes, but it's in the script so ... I got my lines muddled in the soliloquy, had to improvise – it nearly threw Henry.'

He took another large drag of the joint and offered it to me, but I shook my head – I'd never get anything done next day if I did. Dope had that effect on me - I'd be in a dreamy state for days if I smoked it.

'I never noticed.' I smiled, 'It all went smoothly, I thought'.

'Oh you didn't notice that bit where Alan nearly dropped the cup?' I didn't dare look at Henry, my shoulders were heaving!'

'Ah, yes' I said 'I noticed a slight pause, but I'm sure the audience didn't'.

He was so full of talking about the show that I decided not to broach the subject of us moving until the following day after breakfast. Besides it would be Sunday so we could relax as there was no show on.

* * *

We all woke up quite late and I made us a big breakfast – fried eggs, tomatoes, baked beans, mushrooms and toast, (no bacon as by then we'd been trying to be vegetarian for about two months). As we were finishing up I said ...

'There's been so many problems here, the ground's hard and dry, we were going to grow our own veg, but it's so difficult to dig. Then there's the boboyani...'

Dave, stretched across the table for the last bit of toast,

'... remember the one that attacked my fork – and the scorps too. I keep turning them up every time I dig the garden.'

I reminded him when we'd got Big Cat to deal with the scorpions.

'Fat lot of use he was! Won't go out in the bush you bloody drip, will you?' He was poking Big Cat, who was curled up on a chair.

'Who'd have thought with all those miles of bush outside, we'd have to keep a litter tray indoors for the bloody cat!' He prodded the cat again, who of course knew that we were talking about him. Big Cat yawned, stretched, stalked to the door and began to wash very thoroughly.

Dave stood up, stacked the plates in the sink and put the kettle on for the washing up. I reminded him about the snake he'd had to kill – an eight foot snake curled up on our land, just past the garden, somewhere where Pas might have wandered.

'I chopped its head off with a spade, took ages, horrible! I'm not sure it was dangerous either.' He was pouring hot water on the dishes.

'A shame, but we couldn't risk it,' I sipped my tea and felt sad. I hated killing anything – until we had the infestation, I couldn't even bear to kill a cockroach or a spider, they had to be caught and taken outside and let free away from the house. I shuddered, but knew it had been too risky to leave the snake there.

'Then there was the geese,' he sighed. 'Those bloody geese - that bastard knocked me flat!' He finished the dishes and sat down.

'Never saw them again.' I shrugged and we laughed thinking about Dave flat on his back and the geese flying over his head and off into the bush.

'Then Max swallowed all the chicks, whole!' Dave was getting in to the flow.

'Horrible! Not a feather left, so he must have. Weird!'

I got out the orange juice from the fridge and poured him a small glass. 'And then there's the water problem, that bill was such a shock, I don't know how we scraped the money together. There's so much water wasted from those pipes.'

We'd complained to Mr Schmidt, but he'd stubbornly denied any responsibility.

'We can't afford another bill like the last one,' I was wiping the crumbs from the table. '...and there's the riots, police at the end of our track and having to have a gun. I don't like it, it's too much. You're off working all the time and I'm stuck here on my own every night.'

'You think we should move back to the suburbs?'

'Yes! I think it's the only answer, what do you think?'

I lit the gas under the kettle and made us some Rooibos tea, watching the water go deep red as the hot water was poured over the leaves. I took mine and stood by the open door, looking out at Pas and Marcus playing in the back yard.

'It'd be a lot easier for me to get into Cape Town and back and Jo Dunstan says we're putting on Noah next. Henry'll be playing Noah and she's playing Noah's wife. She's deciding on a part for me.' Dave was thoughtful now. 'What about that mixed area we heard of near Rondebosch?'

Discussions with Dave were always easy, we generally agreed on big decisions. If we were going to argue it would be about petty things, but those arguments didn't last long. The only thing we had bigger rows about was the subject of his alcohol consumption – because when he did drink, it would usually be a lot. I was never able to drink much, I couldn't hold it, my head would spin and I'd feel dizzy after 1-2 glasses of wine. Dave didn't drink so much at home – a couple of beers generally, but when there was a social occasion to go to ... he would cane it and then later on, he might say things to people, things he'd never say when sober.

So, (I thought), our country 'idyll' is coming to a close. I felt sad that it hadn't worked out, but relieved too. Country life was too isolated for me.

'When do you think we should move?' Dave sipped his tea. 'We can go quickly don't you think?'

'As soon as we can find somewhere to move to, shouldn't take long! We can give Mr Schmidt a fortnight's notice. I'll get the papers tomorrow and start looking.'

Hopefully (I was thinking) by the time we move, Godot would be nearly at the end of its run and then Dave'll be in rehearsals for a few weeks. He would be nearer town, I'll be nearer my friends and Pas can have other kids round to play.

I felt a great surge of relief now that we'd made the decision.

* * *

Before I could start packing though, the appointment with the ENT specialist at Groote Schuur hospital came up for Pas - we'd waited for months. She'd now had five or six courses of antibiotics for her ear infections. We didn't have to pay to go to Groote Schuur, as there was a three tier system there. Third class, free treatment for the 'non-white' poor, second-class, free treatment for poorer whites (that was us), and first class paying treatment for the well off.

The day came and Pas and I sat in the waiting room. Dave couldn't come as he was in rehearsals. A young doctor eventually called us through. I was never able to bear seeing my child in pain. It upset me a lot. This young man said he would need to take a blood sample, to test her blood. He took her small plump arm and then tried to find a vein, the needle pierced her skin in a couple of places, then quickly was removed as Pas started to howl and no blood was going in the tube. He was squeezing her arm in various places from wrist to shoulder looking for a vein, without success. Then he switched to the other arm.

'You have to hold her firmly,' he instructed. I was holding her arm out tightly. Meanwhile as her cries got louder and louder, the tears were pouring down my face too. Still no luck. I was holding her firmly and the needle was puncturing her arm in various places.

Pas started wriggling and shouting in Afrikaans...

'Ek vil huis to gaan! Ek vil huis to gaan!' over and over. This was somewhat embarrassing, as I had no idea what she was saying and had to ask the doctor to translate.

'She's saying 'I want to go home,' he was frowning and peering at her neck.

'I can't find a vein in her arms so I'm going to try a different location.' I looked at him apprehensively.

'Where?'

'Her neck, you can usually find a vein in the neck quite easily.'

I looked at Pas's tear stained face, her howls had subsided to quiet sobbing now. She was sitting on my lap and I had my arms round her. Her neck I thought, her neck....oh no, no, no. He took her from me and was holding her tight as he was examining her neck. I thought of a needle going in her little neck, she would be utterly traumatised. She was now howling loudly again.

'No! You're not going to do that.' I gathered her up from him, my face set. 'She's had enough for today.'

I took her home and made a big fuss of her ... I think I was more traumatised than her as she seemed to forget it quickly, soon playing outside with Markus and chatting in Afrikaans to him. I watched them sadly, for a while – her days with Markus and the outdoors were soon to end.

* * *

In the next two weeks I found a pleasant two-bedroom bungalow in a mixed-race suburb near Rondebosch, called Harefield Village. Although it was scheduled to become a 'white's only' area under the Group Areas Act, the removals of our neighbours had been delayed. Next-door they were Indian and the neighbourhood was a mixture of Indian and Cape Coloured people as well as white English-speaking South Africans.

On the moving day, Dave had started rehearsals for Noah and so, although he'd helped pack up all our stuff in an assortment of old boxes the night before, he was not around when the bakkie turned up. The driver loaded all the boxes in the open-backed truck, Pas and I climbed into the cab next to him and drove off depositing us and belongings at our new home in Harefield Village.

Our departure from Mr Schmidt's place was quick and quiet, we were determined not to pay the next huge water bill. We also delayed paying the last month's rent so the deposit would cover it. He was not pleased when he found out we'd gone so quickly and later rung up demanding the money for the water bill, which we refused to pay.

Dawn and Jakub had come out to wave goodbye before we drove off. I was fond of Dawn and Pas was going to miss Markus, but I was quite glad to get away from Jakub – the mad axe-man, even though he was quiet and shy as long as he was sober.

Big Cat settled himself by the wall of the small front garden of our new home on a branch of the pomegranate tree. At last he used the outdoors, no longer needing a litter tray. He seemed happy and contented, now there were lots of houses, fences and walls around. Clearly wide open spaces did not suit him, not a bit - maybe that included all of us.

Dave in Waiting for Godot

Chapter 28   Harefield village, the local kids

When Ah wayke up

In the morning loyt

Ah put on mah blue jeans an' ah'm all royt

Ah put mah blue jeans on

Ah put mah ol' blue jeans on ...

Thomas was the first to arrive, when we moved in to our new place. We had chosen this Cape Town suburb not only because it was one of the last few remaining mixed-race areas, but it was also within easy reach of the theatres and centre of Cape Town and all the lovely beaches around. It was the next suburb to Mowbray where we'd lived before moving to Philippi, so I knew the area quite well. I chatted to my Indian neighbours – yes they would have to move sometime they said, but the removal policy seemed to have slowed down, for the moment.

Thomas just turned up at my garden gate one day. The house was a typical South African old style bungalow with low roof and a tiny front stoep. In the small front garden, walled on three sides, the already-mentioned pomegranate tree was home to some praying mantis - those weird stick-like insects who swivel their heads 180 degrees to look at you and you look back and get a weird sense that you are being closely observed. No other insect I've known ever looks directly at humans. They live on smaller insects like aphids, so are good for the garden.

'Hello medem! How'r yew?' This little boy with a cheeky grin had appeared at the front garden gate, looking over the top bar with difficulty. He was about 7 or 8 years old, short curly hair, light brown skin and a face filled with energy and life. He bounded through the gate and up to my door and shook my hand as if he'd known me for years. Through the doorway he spotted Pascale – he waved to her and she looked at him with interest.

'What's her name?'

'Pascale.'

'What?' he said, so I said it slowly, 'But we call her 'Pas' for short.'

'Oh OK! Hi, Pas!' He was waving – his grin was totally infectious – she was grinning straight back at him.

'Would you like to come in?' I asked rather unnecessarily as he was already edging his way in. He looked around at this new environment. He gazed with interest at the fridge and the bread on the bread board.

'Oh!' I said 'You hungry? Would you like a cheese sandwich?' He nodded hard and then turned his attention back to the room. I started cutting the bread, thick slices and took out the cheese from the fridge. Wholemeal bread was sold here cheaper than white bread - for the 'non-whites' - to improve their nutrition or so Peter had told us.

'What's your name?'

'Thomas, medem.'

'And where do you live?'

'Harefield village – other side,' he waved vaguely behind him.

That was as far as I got with my questions. He on the other hand had not finished with me. Thomas fired off a rapid series of questions - When did we move here? What was my name? Where did we come from?

'Inglan d-ey? Wairs thet?'

'A long way from here across the ocean.'

'Yis I year'd of Inglend....What's ut loik ther?'

'Well....... that's a big question, it's cold for a start. And it rains quite a lot.'

'Ut rayns a lot here to.'

'But you have short winters – they last about 3 months and usually it only rains for a month or so and not every day. We get long winters, sometimes it's cold for 7 or 8 or even 9 months of a year.'

'D'yew git snow? Ah yerd about snow – Ah sor a pucture once.'

'Sometimes ...' I was cutting slices from the cheese block and putting them on the bread 'But in London, where I come from, it doesn't snow much.'

He picked up a ball and started throwing it to Pas - she was running around trying to catch it and shrieking with delight. I told Thomas to sit down and handed him the sandwich on a plate.

'So wair's your husb'nd?' His voice was thick with bread and cheese.

'At the theatre.'

'What's his werk?'

'He's an actor.'

He fell silent for a few seconds, considering this....

'What duz en ektor do then?'

'He gets up on a stage and plays parts in a show and people come to watch.'

'Do they pay?'

'Yes they do.'

'So he's rich roit? Lots of muny?'

I laughed – 'No he's not rich, actors don't get a lot of money, unless they go to Hollywood. He just about gets enough to feed us and pay the rent here.'

He looked dubious – after all, didn't everyone know all the whites were rich - was in that look.

He moved on to the next topic like lightening.

'So how old is Pas?'

'She's three.'

I interrupted his next question by shoving another sandwich into his hand.

'Eat that will you.' I poured him a glass of juice. 'Now' I said, trying to regain control of the situation, 'Pascale's going to bed in a minute, so then you must go. Do your parents know where you are?'

He looked puzzled by the question,

'Ah dunno,' he shrugged and raised his hands palm up.

'Well they might be worried about you, it's not safe for a boy to be out so late in the dark (it was now about 9 pm).'

'They don't mahnd.'

'Well next time tell them where you're going, OK?'

'Ken Ah cum beck toomorro?'

I sighed, 'Yes I suppose so. But you must tell your Mum and Dad, OK?'

'But ah'm awt every naht, they niver ask.'

'Well just tell them or you can't come, all right?'

'OK medem.'

'And don't call me madam, call me Anna.'

'OK medem – tomorrow oi'll brung ma frin Jake...'

'Oh will you.' My eyebrows raised.

He had eaten the sandwiches and drunk the juice in no time and just to demonstrate his energy levels, he did a back flip and a somersault across the small living room, narrowly avoiding a jug of juice, which I managed to grab in time. Pascale clapped her hands in delight and Thomas went to the door, grinning at the applause.

'Ah'll see yew tomorrow then.'

I laughed, 'OK, bye now.'

Thomas became a regular visitor after that – he would turn up at any time between 8 and 11 pm. I discovered that he had 4 brothers and 2 sisters and that they all slept in one large bed together. He was out wandering the neighbourhood streets until late every night, totally unsupervised.

Soon he began to bring other friends too. The girls would sit and play with Pas for hours, so I never minded. I would put out sandwiches and juice on the table under the pomegranate tree in our small front garden and they would sing songs and chat to her and ask me an endless stream of questions. They were full of life and laughter and company for Pascale, she loved them all.

The girls all learnt a current pop song and they would stand in line and perform it for me and Pas and the boys:

'When I wake up (stretching their arms)

in the morning loit (miming the sun)

ah put on ma bloo jins end ah'm all roit (miming pulling on jeans)

ah put mah bloo jins on (strutting)

ah put mah ole bloo jins on

Yew and me (pointing)

go mot-rr boik riding (miming getting on a motor-bike)

in the sun (pointing up) and the moon and the rain (pattering fingers)

ah got money in ma pocket (turning and patting their backsides)

Toiger in mah tenk (rubbing tummies)

End ah'm on the road agen (back on the bikes)

When I wake up ...

Pas and I loved to see them performing the whole song – we laughed all the way through at all the gestures and facial expressions and tried to copy and keep up with the hand movements.

Most of them came in the late afternoon or early evening. Thomas, however, often came late and on his own and always of course with a stream of questions. He was endlessly bright and full of curiosity about everything. Sometimes when Dave came back from the theatre at 11 pm, Thomas was still there, demonstrating his cartwheels and keeping up a running commentary.

After a while his energy would get too much for me or for Dave.

'Ok Thomas, time to go home.'

'Ach no men, uts erly.'

It was no use arguing with him.

'Bye Thomas.'

One of us would stand by the door, holding it open.

'O-kay, O-kay, boi medem, boi mester, See yew tmorro yeh?'

We'd groan inwardly sometimes, as he'd worn us out,

'We'll see Thomas, all right we'll see'.

* * *

Thomas's activities served as light relief against the political situation. Many of us were worried as more news or rumours filtered through here and there about continuing unrest in the townships. We were getting the Cape Times regularly as our only source of trustworthy news. They reported when the lone voice of Helen Suzman MP challenged the constant excesses of the government policies and the police's brutal behaviour.

Dave and I talked in low whispers about it with Pete, when he called to see us. 'There's going to be a bloodbath. What did you say Pete? There's fifty million blacks and about fifty thousand whites?'

'Ja, that's right Dave.' He shrugged and smiled. No one wanted to think about what might happen.

A regular small column would appear on the front page of the paper that this or that 'Bantu' arrested for questioning had unaccountably 'jumped' from a window in the police building (interrogation centre?). Everyone knew what that meant, we knew they hadn't 'jumped.' Dave made dark jokes about all those plate glass windows and so many men being taken up lots of stairs in these tall police centres and seizing the opportunity to escape their tormentors. I felt both angry and helpless when I read about it. I didn't know what I could do.

'You'd think the police would know by now,' he cracked, 'wouldn't you? To take them in the lift?'

* * *

'Noah' had now opened at St George's. The play had been written by a French playwright - Andre Obey, and was translated from the French. Jo Dunstan played Noah's wife and Dave played the part of Ham, Noah's eldest son, always at his father Noah's side, a rational, sceptical, realist who scoffed at his father's doomsday predictions about a great flood and simple faith in God.

It was a role he enjoyed and it was a strong cast. Backstage there was plenty of funny antics, Henry, Dave and Allan shared a dressing room. Of course I went to the final dress rehearsal with Robert, our mad hatter friend who, as usual made me laugh with his camp observations and droll commentary.

'Dahling, what's the name of that one (pointing to one of the actors), mmm ... he's nice.'

'He's straight, Robert!'

'Well, he could be turned you know.'

'Married, with two kids, Robert.'

'That's what I mean, they're the easiest.'

'Oh, Robert! You're incorrigible!'

'I know dahling, I know!'

Dave liked me to go to the last dress rehearsal as I'd give him detailed notes the next day.

'The first scene was good, quite pacey, but Scene Two - it slowed down a bit too much. Then that bit in Scene Three with Henry, you're getting pissed off with him talking about a flood – maybe a bit more anger in your tone would give it more punch!'

He'd be nodding and memorising what I'd said. Quite often he felt he hadn't been given enough feedback by the director.

Dave and Henry in Noah

The production was a great success - the reviews for Noah came out in early December 1976 and of course focused on Henry, but Dave had a good mention too.

Chapter 29   Pas, Mel and Dieter

Apartheid was the background to everything and the events of the last few months were pushing the whole situation more and more into the foreground of our lives. But sometimes we had to focus on the domestic events of our lives and these were now gathering pace. Firstly we had to deal with the next event around our daughter, which really turned out to be partly of our own making, our own lack of knowledge.

In November, we'd seen someone more senior at Groote Schuur, and he decided Pascale needed grommets (tiny plastic tubes) in her ears, to drain them. He explained that they would be put there under anaesthetic and that they would stay in her ears for a few months and eventually fall out on their own.

We went to the hospital a few weeks after Christmas and I put her on the bed in the hospital gown. After a while, a nurse and an orderly came into the room. I was asked to put her on the trolley. I had explained in simple terms, a little of what would happen. Now she lay on the trolley looking at my face and I kept smiling and smiling and stroking her face.

'Ooh look Pas, this is a special trolley and you're going to have a ride on it. Then the man's going to make your ears better, so you won't wake up with earache any more, that's good isn't it? Ooh look we're coming to this special room.'

The anaesthetist called me aside and told me that I could not go with her into the operating room, but that he would bring out the gas canister and we would see if she would breathe some before she went in to the room. He had a good way with children, unlike most of the doctors there, who hadn't got a clue.

He brought over the gas and air and showed her the mask and explained a little about it - a big rubbery looking thing.

'Oh you're such a brave little girl, aren't you?' He was showing her the mask. 'Now I'm going to put this funny thing here on the trolley, next to you...'

'No take way,' said Pas pushing it,

'It's only going to be there for a very short time, just a minute and then I'll take it away, promise.' He smiled warmly at her. Meanwhile he'd turned up the gas flow.

'Wat that smell, Mummy?'

'It's coming from that thing,' I said, 'It does smell funny doesn't it ...' I pushed it a little closer to her face.

'Have a smell,' I bent down smiling at her, 'Phew it's a funny smell isn't it?'

Her eyelids were beginning to droop as the gas began to work and soon the guy was able to put it closer and she was out.

Afterwards they took her to the children's ward to recover from the anaesthetic and then kept her there for a few hours. She quite enjoyed being in the ward with the other children, once she'd come round. She was reluctant to leave when I came to get her, but I took her home and she was quite bouncy again.

'Mummy look, look painted pitcha for you, in hopital – that's you an that's Daddy an that's Angel'...on the page a series of squiggles and blobs.

'Well that's fantastic, we'll show Daddy when we get home and put it on the fridge.'

However, all these illnesses and antibiotics still worried me. I decided to read up about nutrition over the next few weeks, In the local bookstore, I discovered a series of popular nutrition books by an American writer called Adele Davis. I bought one called 'Let's Have Healthy Children' which gave information about how different illnesses were the result of different nutritional deficiencies and how to correct diet and vitamin intake. From reading this book, I realised that there was a possible connection between Pas's illnesses and lack of protein. Dave and I had stopped eating meat a few months before. Children have high protein needs for growth and the build-up of a strong immune system. We'd been totally ignorant of how to manage a vegetarian diet - protein sources like eggs, cheese, nuts and beans should have been included in every meal. What had recently happened at a local supermarket should have given us a clue.

'Where's Pas?' said Dave, suddenly looking round. She was nowhere in sight.

We spread out and searched the store and suddenly I spotted her. Her nose was pressed to the glass front of the meat counter, looking at the raw meat. When I rushed over to grab her, she was reluctant to come.

'What dat Mummy?'

'It's meat darling.'

'Me want some meat.'

'No darling, we don't eat meat,' I'd pulled her away.

After her operation, we went back to eating meat and a carefully managed diet. I only bought wholemeal bread and we had eggs, cheese or meat with either salads or cooked fresh vegetables at every meal. Vegetables and fruit were so fresh and cheap in the Cape after all – a large sack of naartjies (tangerines) cost 99c for example. I bought her some vitamins, in particular Vitamin B5 (Calcium Pantothenate), which according to Adele was essential for boosting the immune system and crushed them in her food. After a few months of this diet and the vitamins, Pas's hair stopped falling out and was re-growing. She had no further problems with her ears and hardly even had a head cold for the rest of her childhood. So much for the trichologist, I thought later.

Once Pas had made a full recovery from her little operation, we resumed our visits to Mel, so she could play with Gabby. My day would usually involve taking her in the morning to Brookfield nursery school and in the afternoon, I often saw Mel and sometimes spent the afternoon with her.

Whenever I went to see Mel, Werner was at work. Every evening, he seemed to go to the German club, straight from work. It was becoming obvious that he and Mel saw little of each other and led separate lives. It also became clear, after a while, that she was going to see Dieter regularly and occasionally he would call by. Mel was a very attractive, vivacious woman with many friends. She had another social group she'd met at the German club, which included Dieter and some German women, who she often spent time with either at her place or she'd be at one of their homes.

Dieter was a gentle giant, 6 foot 4 inches tall, built like a bear, with huge shoulders and arms, large hands and feet. You could imagine him lifting tree trunks with his bare hands. He had a sun-streaked, mop of blond hair and looked fierce, until his face broke into smiles and big guffaws of laughter. He had twinkling blue eyes and a very droll, dead-pan sense of humour, which I connected with - from our first meeting I was captivated. I could see why Mel was attracted to him. In his company, she was always smiling and laughing – he was sociable and friendly, unlike Werner in every way.

Sometimes Mel talked about him when we were alone and gave clues about how the relationship was developing. She was always quite dry and matter of fact when referring to Werner. The relationship with Dieter was kept very much under wraps from her family – her teenage daughter Noelle, aged 15 then and her son Errol, aged 11, saw him as a friend and surrogate uncle figure. He usually came to visit with one or other of the German women, rarely alone.

On one occasion, when I was visiting, Dieter called by. He invited myself and Dave to a barbecue at his house in Table View. Dave was busy with Noah, so it had to be a Sunday, the only day he was free. The two German women – Sally and Heidi were there with Mel and a tall German called Kurt. We all sat round Dieter's swimming pool in the sun, sipping cocktails and eating barbecued boereworst and chicken and other meats. Dieter showed me round his house –

'I built it myself you know', he was telling me – I looked around – the main living room was large and had a big square pit, down slated steps into the middle of the room, with a huge copper chimney above – the sort of room that would be lovely in a freezing Bavarian winter, with a big log fire in the 3 foot square grate below the copper chimney. The logs were there ready, but as it was summer and over 80 degrees outside, it seemed somewhat incongruous. However, he was clearly proud of all the work he'd put in,

'So when do you light the fire Dieter? Surely it'd be too hot here, even in the winter?'

'Oh ze winters' can get cold here sometimes, you know,' he was poking the great chunks of tree trunk, with an outsize brass poker. 'One day, I'll light ze fire and you'll see.' His blue eyes twinkled at me.

It seemed an alarming prospect, and I strolled back out to the pool to see Gabby and Pas in the pool with their water wings on, screaming and splashing. Mel and I lay on the sun-beds, in our bikinis with the others, getting brown and sipping juice. I smiled to myself, thinking about Dieter and his Bavarian fire pit in the heat of Africa.

Meanwhile, the men were going through frosted bottles of German beers which Dieter pulled out of his fridge by the handful and the wine was flowing amongst the women. That's when I saw it and screamed. On the wall to the left of the pool a black thing scurried sideways – it looked like a tarantula – big, black and hairy and my heart practically

stopped with fright. Pas and Gabby were in the pool splashing and oblivious.

Dieter walked calmly inside, got a large whisky glass and a piece of cardboard. He and Kurt approached it and I screamed again as it ran sideways to get away from them. Mel told me to cover my eyes and she'd tell me when they caught it. Quickly Dieter got the glass over it, scooped it off the wall and took it out to the street and dropped it some-where. He strolled back in and sat down as if nothing had happened glancing at me laughing – 'Often ve get zees here, ze boboyani...' It was so much bigger than the ones we'd seen at the farm, I was horrified. I kept looking at the wall to make sure another one didn't appear.

My spider phobia was not as bad as it had been in Eng-land, it was often challenged by the insect life here in Africa

- by the time we left South Africa it had all but disappeared. British spiders were of little consequence by comparison

Dave n Dahlia Margalit (Ham and Naomi) in Noah

Chapter 30: Climbing Table Mountain

By now we had several groups of friends – Mel's group was one of them and that included several of the other parents from Brooksfield. However a few months before, I'd had a letter from my cousin Alana, who was in her early 20s, she was in Malawi, after leaving art school and having qualified as a textile designer, she had taken a job there, being interested in African traditional patterns and designs. After 6 months in Malawi, she wanted to come to Cape Town and work there for a textile design company. She wanted to incorporate some of the traditional African prints into her own innovative ideas. Could she come and stay with us for a few weeks until she found her own place? I was delighted to have a family member arrive, I missed my family a great deal, my brothers and sister and parents. Although I didn't know Alana well, we had a shared family history and had often been together in family gatherings as children, although she had been younger than the rest of us.

When she arrived, she told us stories about Malawi and what a beautiful country it was – she compared it to Wales – green and rolling hills. Pascale loved her and Alana (who was not a bit fat) called herself the 'fat auntie' and it became the running joke. I was very slim and medium height and Dave of course was a slim 6 foot 3 inches, Alana was about 5 foot 4 inches with medium length dark hair, and was a little rounder than us , but no way 'fat'. She was always very self-depreciating and self-critical. We all quickly became very fond of her.

It was lovely to see her and after a while she made new friends and moved out. Some of her friends became ours too. One evening, we were all chatting over a glass of wine, about Table Mountain. Patsy, a friend of Alana's from Ireland was one of them. She had come over from the UK to Cape Town on the QEII liner. She was apparently renowned on the voyage for having drunk the ship's mate under the table. Dave and Patsy were often in competition at parties for the prodigious amounts they drank, although I never saw Patsy get to a state where she was more than swaying slightly. She was tall and slim, had a bob of brown curly hair and a strong handsome face. Her boyfriend was now Nigel, a stocky man in his late twenties of Afrikaans origin, with short hair and a receding hairline, He was quite reserved, pleasant and seemed very down to earth and sensible. A stabilising influence on the rather wild Patsy!

Nigel had one other great passion in life, besides Patsy and that was mountain climbing. He went climbing every weekend when he could and if he disappeared, Patsy knew that he'd gone climbing and she might not see him for a few days. The hallway of her flat, after they had moved in together, was an obstacle course of ropes, boots, tents, picks etc.

Dave was saying 'We should go up Table Mountain, we've been here all this time and never been up,' which launched us in to a long discussion about how people who live in a city never go and visit its sights and monuments.

I steered it back, 'I'd love to go up Table Mountain though. We could get the cable car I suppose? But someone told me that there are ways you can walk up and it's not too hard?

'I know them,' Nigel looked eager, 'I could take you...'

We both turned and looked at Nigel. 'You know the walking route up Table Mountain? Are you sure, just walking up, no climbing involved?' I looked at him suspiciously....

'Yes ... yes, over on the west side, there's a path up...If you want to go I can take you.......'

I looked at Dave and then nodded. 'That'd be great!'

We made a date for a weekend a few weeks further on and I felt exhilarated at the thought of the nice stroll, seeing the view and then a fantastic view of Cape Town from the top of the mountain.

A few weeks later, there we were on the lower slopes, getting out of Nigel's old green Landrover. It was parked on a scrubby rocky area, high up, overlooking the suburbs we'd come from. Below was the dual carriageway – this skirted the mountain, past Mowbray, Observatory and round the mountain to Green Point, Sea Point and beyond.

I looked around for the pathway we were going to follow, the one gradually meandering up the lower slopes, but couldn't see it... maybe it was round the corner. Nigel would be leading the way..... I looked towards the mountain – a fairly sheer rock face towered over us and then in craggy steps above that, the rocks disappeared into the distance. Nigel, meanwhile, was opening up the back of the jeep and pulling out loops of rope and metal things like large square curtain rings. Dave and I looked at each other – I frowned, Dave shrugged....

'Er Nigel..... We are WALKING up aren't we?'

'Mmmm... Well, there's a bit of climbing,' his voice was casual, 'but don't worry, it's all easy stuff and you'll be roped to me anyway, quite safe!'

I looked at Dave and he grinned, he was up for the adventure ... 'Well, lead on McDuff!' I sighed and trudged behind, thinking Oh God, what have we let ourselves in for...

Nigel led us to a vertical funnel shaped crevice, cutting straight up into the rock face. 'This bit's dead easy,' Nigel had positioned himself at the base, 'you put your back on one side, like so and your feet on the other like this and you push and slide until you get to the top – simple!. You go first, Anna, then Dave and I'll come last'

'Aren't you supposed to go first and drop the rope down?'

'No we won't need the rope for this bit – it's easy enough!'

I looked up, it was about 20-30 foot high, but it didn't seem too hard, plenty of hand-holds on the way. I put myself in position, braced my back and started – not bad, this was going to be quite easy really; soon I would be at the top. I began to feel just a little smug; I'd always been quite sure-footed and had put many guys to shame, clambering over rocks along the Welsh coast. Nigel's right, I thought. Not too hard!

My foot slipped and I quickly pushed the other one above it, hard into a cleft. My back was pressed against a lumpy piece of rock. Phew, I looked down – it was about 15 feet to the bottom, my head spun and I quickly turned my eyes away and looked up. I was more than half way. Taking a deep breath I moved up – hand, foot, hand, foot, carefully until finally I clambered out of the crevice and onto a ledge about 4 foot square.

The view was great – I could see across to the harbour and the docks and across the bay to Table View. Looking to either side of me though, there was no sign of any paths or easy walks. In fact the rock face became more sheer – he couldn't be expecting us to go up that way.... could he? A vein in my forehead started throbbing and I began to feel a little anxious. How long was this walk going to take? We'd told my friend who was looking after Pas, that we'd be a few hours. Also the sunny day was turning cloudy and the wind was beginning to gust and whistle through the crevices around me. It was spring turning to summer, but the weather had been unusually unsettled and cool.

Dave's head popped up through the top of the crevice and then his long arms and legs were clambering out – he looked like a giant spider, all limbs everywhere. Then Nigel was up too, on the ledge, and he began unlooping coils of rope and pulling out the metal curtain ring things –

'What are those for?' I asked.

'Oh they're karabiners to attach you to the rope so you don't fall. OK put these harnesses on' – he pulled some old blue tangled webbing from his rucksack. 'You step in like so, and click it in front like this – then we take a karabiner and click it on to your harness and then the rope.'

'But Nigel you aren't expecting us to climb that next bit are you – it looks really hard, I don't know if I ...'

Nigel spoke quickly, as he glanced up at the rock face. 'Oh, nothing to worry about, all easy stuff. Did I mention that Pete's coming too?'

'Who's Pete?'

'Another climber, friend of mine, very experienced! I'll go first and he'll go last.'

'When's he coming then?' I looked round. 'And what about the next bit – it looks quite hard, where's the easy walk bit?'

'Yes, well, it's really not hard this way! I'll go first and then throw the rope down, Pete will come after you two – it's actually a lot easier than it looks – you just got to feel around for holds with your finger-tips – there's plenty of them up there and you'll be attached to the rope – quite safe.'

'OK then,' I said reluctantly, not wanting to appear a wimp. Soon a tall, gangly bloke with long messy black hair appeared through the crevice – he reminded me of a crow or raven, beaky nose, beady, dreamy black eyes.

'Hi, nice day for a little walk!' he smiled brightly.

He was striding about the ledge, bouncing around like Tigger, my heart lurched as he stood right on the edge, balancing like someone poised to jump, looking down as if the drop was a couple of inches. Clearly he either had nerves of steel, no fear of heights whatever or was barking mad with a total reckless disregard for his own safety. I began to suspect the latter explanation after a while. I kept my back to the mountain, well away from the edge.

He sat down cross-legged and fished in the pockets of his old green wax coat. He brought out a crumpled cigarette, a packet of extra-long cigarette papers and a brown paper bag. He and Nigel briefly conferred, while Pete was skinning up – rolling a big fat joint. First the cigarette was split along its length and teased onto the long paper, which he held between thumb and forefingers. Then grass and bits from the brown paper bag were sprinkled on and mixed in and it was carefully rolled. A small piece of cardboard was torn from the cigarette paper's packet and rolled small. This was put in the end – the roach (filter). He licked the glue strip, stuck it down and twisted the end. Then patting his pockets, he found a lighter and shielding it from the wind, lit the twisted end and puffed hard, until the lit end glowed red and a smell like smoky bonfires wafted about. He handed it to Nigel, Dave had a big smirk on his face and when Nigel passed it to him, he took a couple of long deep draws. I took a brief puff – I needed a clear head. Besides, my head was beginning to throb slightly, a sign that a migraine was coming on.

'Right then.' Nigel got up, 'I'm going first with the rope and then I'll chuck the end down to you. Clip it on to your harness, like this (demonstrating) with your karabiner (handing us some). Pete will hold the rope at the bottom of the slope and come up last. You'll be fine, the next bit's a piece of cake, really!'

Suddenly Nigel was gone, as I watched, crawling up the rock face ahead of us with the rope looped over his shoulder. We were left with Pete who was looking down over the ledge, hopping from one foot to the other. He moved to the rock face:

'Ok find yourself finger holds like this one,' his finger-tips were in a small crevice and he was pulling himself up '... and then find a toe hold like this,' he was jamming the toes of his boot onto a half-inch deep rocky edge, '...and then push up!' He smiled, as if to say 'You see! Any idiot could do it!' And then he leapt lightly back onto the ledge, like a mountain goat.

Nigel called from the top and threw down the end of the rope. Pete caught it neatly and attached it to Dave's harness. 'If you slip, don't worry, you can't fall far.' (That's reassuring, I thought)

'Well', I was talking to myself as much as Pete, 'Nigel went up quite quick, so it can't be that bad – he wouldn't take us if it was too difficult, would he?'

Dave glanced at me, 'I s'pose not,' his tone was doubtful ...then, 'OK here I go!' He started up the flat stretch of rock ahead of us. He seemed to be having difficulty in places to find a crack or tiny crevice to put his finger tips or the toe of his boots into, but because of his long limbs he could stretch far.

Nigel was lying on his belly above us, leaning over the ledge, calling out encouragement, and keeping the rope taut –

'OK, Dave, that's it, now look to your left and stretch your arm up, a bit further, a bit further, that's it, can you feel it now? OK, push your leg up until you find a toehold.'

Dave's foot kept slipping off, ' ... stretch out a bit more, yes that's it, push the tip of your shoe into that crack, that's it, now push up, good, good, well done, well done...nearly there.'

Soon it was my turn and I was in the same position, flat against the rock, arms and legs wide, holding on grimly and scanning ahead of me for finger and toe holds, holding down panic and NOT looking down.

'Ja, that's it now, put three fingertips together and jam them into that crevice to the right of your head, as hard as you can, see! Gives you a better grip.' A glimpse of the drop below bounced into my brain and scrambled my thoughts. Spread out as I was, arms and legs wide, cheek pressed to the rock, I could not see another place in reach to put my finger tips. I looked down and across for my next toehold, there was none. I was stuck. Panic surged up through my body and into my throat and then my ears were ringing. My breath was coming in tight gasps. 'Nigel,' I croaked,' I'm stuck, what shall I do? I can't move!'

'It's fine,' Nigel was cheery, matter-of-fact... 'Just stretch out your right hand!' Tentatively, slowly, I crept my hand across the rock face...

'Now feel around – with your finger-tips, down a bit,' I looked – there was a crack, barely enough to put my finger nail in, 'No further on a bit, that's it, that's it, OK push your fingers in and grip.' I did as told, my finger-tips barely went in, the tiny cleft felt flimsy and unsafe, not strong enough to hold my weight. I took a deep breath and pushed down the panic again.

'Now, which foot have you got your weight on – left? OK, bend your right knee and move it up, see if your foot can find something to catch on.' He was peering down at me from fifteen foot above – 'OK, good, good, Ja, found something?'

My foot snagged on a piece of crevice narrower than a cigarette paper sideways.

'Now! Push up slowly with your foot and pull with your fingertips and reach your left hand. Ja! Ja, until your fingers find a grip, that's it, good, Ja, well done.'

My frantic fingers found a tiny bit of edge and I breathed out. Phew, I'd been holding my breath, hard. I looked towards my feet; yes there was another toehold to the left. Slowly, up, up I went inch by inch. Dave was looking over too now.

'Come on girl, you can do it, nearly there,' he was smiling and reaching his long arm down to grab my hand and then he was pulling me over in a final heave. I lay there gasping with relief and getting my breath back.

Soon Pete came bounding up the rock and bounced onto the narrow ledge, where we were all squeezed together. Clearly for him it was a breeze.

'Ja,' Nigel was saying. 'That was quite a difficult slope, only the more advanced climbers at the mountain club will tackle that bit.'

I looked at him with disbelief. 'But Nigel you said that bit was going to be easy?'

'Well yes, but you wouldn't have tried otherwise and you managed fine. It gets easier from now on.'

As I was getting my breath back I began to be aware of my surroundings more – where on earth was he taking us next – the ledge was about 3 feet wide. And up above our heads, there was a huge jutting bulbous piece of rock – there was nowhere to go – except maybe sideways – for quite a long way, more fingertip and toe holds – oh no, no, no. Was that what we had to do next? It was worse than that.

Pete meanwhile was doing something alarming – he was going above us onto this rock, which jutted out over our heads, clinging to it with his back hanging down above us and then as he came to the edge of the overhanging lump, pushing himself round and suddenly disappearing over and up and out of sight. There was NO WAY Nigel could be wanting us to do that, NO WAY!

Nigel was saying to Dave, 'Yes that last bit was a bit tricky, but the next bit is fine!'

I followed his gaze – he was looking where Pete went - Oh No! Oh No! I CAN'T.....he looked down and our eyes met. 'It's much easier than it looks,' he smiled broadly. You'll be roped to Pete at the top and me down below. It's fine.'

I looked at the overhang and felt sick, no, no, ... I looked over at him but he was standing below the overhang, whistling cheerfully to himself and looking up, he called up to Pete: 'OK mate, chuck it down...'

A long coil of nylon rope snaked down from the invisible Pete. Nigel gave it a good hard tug, until it was taut.

'So I'll hang on to this end and Pete has secured the other – all you have to do is climb up and over. You can't fall, you're attached to the rope with the karabiners, if you slip, just hang on, we'll talk you through...'

Panic was beginning to constrict my chest and my breathing, but I squashed it down hard. I couldn't afford to lose it now. There was no choice, we couldn't go back and it seemed the only way forward was up. The wind was beginning to tug us and howl around our feet and it was getting colder.

I thought of Pascale, she liked it at Jenny's house; Sara was her best friend (apart from Gabby). What she liked best was that they had a dog, a Maltese poodle and she loved to play with the poodle. We'd already been gone three hours; it was not going to be the 2-3 hours Jenny was expecting. She *probably* wouldn't mind and Pas would be quite happy there, but how long were we going to be?

'Er Nigel, when we get to the top.......'

'Oh you'll love it... the view... stunning!'

'Yes, you said, but will we be able to get the cable car down?'

'Well that's on the other side of the table top, but yes, it should be OK, it should be still running...'

'Why what time does it run to?

'About 5 ish I think, maybe 6?

'What time is it now?'

'Just after 3... plenty of time!'

'So, we can get home quite quick then?'

'Oh yes, that won't take long!'

I couldn't stop now, the sooner we got on with it the sooner I'd be back to Pas. My head was throbbing but I walked over to the rock face, clipped my karabiner onto the rope that Nigel had thrown down and stretched up my hands, looking for fingertip holds. Behind me Dave was calling encouragement, but I knew he was scared too, his voice was tense. Pete was cavorting about above, doing his impression of a mountain goat again.

Somehow, I made it to the edge of the overhang, and then, with lots of encouragement from Nigel and Dave, over the top to the ledge above, Dave followed, then Nigel.

'Phew!' said Nigel cheerfully. 'That was pretty good. That was an F1 slope. A lot of climbers at the mountain club wouldn't have tackled that one.'

Dave and I looked at each other in disbelief, but said nothing. What was the point now?

'Anyway, it's easy from now on! No really.' He was pulling out more karabiners from his rucksack, 'I mean it this time!'

We'd heard that before, but by now were so weary, we just wanted to focus on getting there, standing on top of the mountain. Then we could get the cable car and go home.

'Just wait until you get to the top!' Nigel was jovial. 'The view is so great; it makes it all worth it. You can see for miles and miles.' I thought, I don't care about the fucking view, I just want to get home and lie down.

My head was seriously aching by now, developing into one of the migraines that I suffered from, at that time. I didn't even look at Nigel, just grimly turned to the mountain, to get the next bit over with.

Three or four more slopes followed, I don't remember, it's a blur. Once, we 'traversed' sideways across to another wedge or funnel bit. I froze again on that one unable to find a hold, but was talked out of it by Nigel and got moving again. Dave slipped on another slope, lost his foothold and went upside down. As he was joined by karabiner to the harness and rope he was OK. Luckily, Pete had secured the rope to a rock above when it happened. It gave Dave a shock, but Nigel talked him through it, so he could right himself again.

Finally, wearily, I climbed over the last rock and on to the craggy top of the mountain, Dave and Pete behind.

'You see!' Nigel beamed enthusiastically. 'Just look at that!' spreading his arms expansively. I looked at him wearily, but with burning resentment.

I would like to say how I shared his enthusiasm for the beauty of the view. But all I could think was - Fuck the view, I don't give a shit what it looks like, how can I get home quickly and lie down on my bed with lots of pain killers?

'Oh yes, lovely, where's the cable car?' I was gritting my teeth.

'Well!' Nigel, glanced at Pete. It was now after 4.30 pm and big black clouds raced above our heads, the wind howled in our ears. 'I hope the cable car's still running. Sometimes they close it when it's windy.'

No, I thought, No they can't, they can't. Panic was rising in my chest, but I stayed silent and looked at Nigel, my eyes dull with exhaustion and pain from the migraine.

'What do we do then?' asked Dave.

Nigel frowned looking across at the darkening sky. 'Well, we'd have to belay down on the ropes, back to the Land Rover shouldn't take too long! '

I looked at Dave and he turned to Nigel, 'Where's the cable car station?'

'Over there,' he was pointing to the far distant side of the Table top.

'OK, let's get over there shall we?' We started in the direction, stumbling tiredly over the rocky surface. Until Pete said 'I'll go and you lot wait here, it's quicker – I'll find out if it's running.'

I sat down on a rock with a sigh of relief. I could have a rest. If we walked all the way over there and then had to walk all the way back again before 'belaying' down the mountain, I didn't know if I could make it.

Dave put his arm round me, 'You ok?' 'No,' I snapped. 'Got a migraine.'

'Oh shit. Well let's hope the cable car's....,' he broke off as Pete was returning ... Nigel walked to meet him and they stood some way off, talking low, the wind howled around us and we stared at them anxiously.

'Er, well, sorry folks, cable car's off, shut. Too windy. What we'll do is belay down, no problem. It won't take too long - back to the car, about an hour...or so. Nigel at last looked sheepish...

I felt complete shock, then numb. I felt like shaking Nigel. And Pete. There must be a mistake; surely it couldn't be off, I craned my neck to see if I could see it in the distance...

Nigel and Pete walked back to the edge we had so recently climbed over and stood looking over, this way and that, for the best route down. Then they were nodding to each other and Nigel went to some large boulders, unlooping the rope from his shoulder.

Nigel was to wait at the top, the rope tied over the boulder and then Pete went over the edge, scrambling down like a monkey on speed.

'OK! you two ready?' asked Nigel, giving us basic instructions on 'belaying', how to use feet and hands, how we'd be always attached to the rope and how Pete would lead, with us following. Then Nigel would bring the rope down for the next bit.

By now it was after 5 o clock and we all knew that darkness was only an hour away. In fact, the shadows were already long on the ground and the light quality was fading like the dimmer switch was slowly turning towards zero.

By the time, we finally got to Nigel's car, scrambling and exhausted, it was dark and we were stumbling to find our way and where to put hands and feet without tripping over and breaking a leg or a wrist or worse. We were forced to find our utmost reserves of concentration to get there, mine through a miasma of throbbing migraine. By the time we got into the back of the Landover again, I was white and shaking and nauseous. Dave had long since stopped cracking jokes and was silent and pale. Nigel drove us to pick up Pascale, Dave apologised to Jenny and we took Pas home. Dave put her to bed, as I had by then collapsed on my bed with some heavy painkillers. I stayed there for 3 days. Our Sunday 'stroll' up the mountain had turned into a nightmare. I didn't speak to Nigel for weeks, but because Patsy was our friend it all blew over. Dave had to get up early the next day to go to rehearsals. Luckily for him, he had a constitution like an ox.

Jane ,Patsy, Alana and Herman

Chapter 31: Surprise news, and Constance

Constance and Victoria

When I'd recovered from the 'stroll' up the mountain, I thought at least I can always say I climbed it, when I go back to London. Even if it was a god-awful experience, we did it.

Over the next few weeks, life carried on as normal. Every day I took Pas to Brooksfield School in the mornings. When I went to fetch her, I continued to go to the kitchen or the lounge of Mel's house, which was attached to the school which was an annexe at the back. Or sometimes if Mel was really busy she'd say – come back later. If I went to the kitchen to wait for her, Lena, Melissa's nanny/maid was usually there. One day I said,

'Lena, what happened to your two front teeth?'

I had noticed that many Cape Coloured women, had a gap where their two front teeth should be.

'Ach men, they got pulled out...'

'But why?'

She just smiled, secretively, but I wanted to find out. 'Do the men like you with no front teeth?'

She had her back to me at the sink and her head down, she was nodding.

'But why?'

She turned and picked up the drying cloth. She had a big smirk on her face and I looked at her, frowning, then suddenly light began to dawn.... I frowned -

'Oh God! No! You're joking! Is that the reason I see all these coloured girls with no front teeth? That's terrible.' Lena was laughing at my shocked expression, when Melissa came in. We grabbed a cup of tea and went upstairs to the lounge and lit a cigarette.

'So what was so funny?' She asked.

I told her. 'Oh yis,' she laughed. 'Ut's very common here, you know?'

Melissa went to the cabinet and got a bottle of wine.

'It's a shame, but what can you do?' she took out two glasses, 'Let's have some wine shall we?'

Our regular pattern was one glass for me which I'd sip slowly, Mel would have several but really I preferred tea. Pas and Melissa's daughter, Gabby, would be playing in Gabby's room down the hall. Lena would bring them a sandwich and some juice.

I told her about the migraine on Table Mountain and she looked sympathetic. We both suffered badly from cluster migraines, sometimes they would go on for days. We shared info about the best painkillers. Melissa went to see a specialist and one day, after she had the results she told me...

'He found a tumour – just here?' She pointed to the base of her skull.'

I gasped and put my hand to my mouth in shock. 'It's small – don't worry it's not malignant.'

'But can they remove it?'

'No, they don't think they can operate, it's in an awkward position. It's what seems to be causing my migraines.'

'How're you feeling today?'

'Not too bad. How about you?'

'It was bad this morning, I had to take two Doloxene before I could get up?'

'Two?'

'I know, but it was really bad, I feel OK now, a bit dopey though.'

'Yis, those Doloxene knock you out for sure, but they the only thing that works with mah migraine.'

That was one thing we both agreed on – they worked, but after a long while, I also noticed they were affecting my memory – I had holes in my memory from all that time of taking Doloxene. Sometimes, I couldn't remember what I'd done for days before.

I was about to ask Mel more about the tumour, although it was non-malignant and she was laughing it off, I was worried for her. Then I heard the sound of Werner's key in the lock, which was the signal for us both to jump up. Werner was particularly unsociable when he came in from work.

'Right,' Melissa picked up the glasses and put them on the sideboard. 'I'll see you tomorrow at school?'

We heard Werner coming up the stairs to the lounge.

'Don't say a word to Werner about this,' she whispered quickly, pointing to the back of her head... 'I'll tell him when I'm ready.'

Werner walked in to the room.

'Hi, Werner!' I said 'Wie gehts?'

'Ok,' He said shortly, going over to the drinks cabinet and pouring himself a whisky. Mel gave me a look and I widened my eyes at her,

'Well I'm just going, see you soon!'

I gathered up Pas (protesting) from Gabby's room and took her out.

'No, baby, we have to go, Gabby's going to have her supper now – we have to go home too.'

* * *

'Noah' ran until mid-January and the actors just had two days off for Christmas, which of course was hot and sunny as it was mid-summer. We had a barbecue and Alana came too, with her new boyfriend, as well as Di. Steve said he'd drop by with the boys later on. Dave did the chicken and boereworst sausage on the braai and I cooked - in the kitchen in my bikini - the roast potatoes and vegetables, butternut squash instead of swede, carrots and salad, instead of brussel sprouts, washed down with cold beers and iced squash. I'd also made a Christmas pudding with coins in it, because it wouldn't seem like a real Christmas dinner otherwise.

On Boxing Day, we packed up all the left-overs for a picnic and drove to Haut Bay, where we found a place near the dunes. Pas had her bucket and spade and was soon making sand-castles with some of the other kids on the beach. It was so hot, we had to have frequent swims to cool off or lie under our sun umbrella, to keep cool

Dave making a braai at Hout Bay

Dave enjoyed the short break from performing and it was great having a nice family day-out. He'd been working almost non-stop the whole year, after all the struggles to get work in the UK he was very pleased to have so much acting work. It was great to have a few days respite though – for both of us and to forget, for a few days, the tensions we were all living with.

* * *

A few weeks later, a new surprise awaited me - I went to the doctor – a familiar symptom had appeared – my breasts were very sore. The doctor asked me some questions, tested my urine and it turned out I was about 8 weeks pregnant. On the one hand I was delighted, we'd been trying for another baby for two years and had all but forgotten it could happen. As a result, I was not expecting or prepared for this and as I'd had a few bouts of migraine over the last couple of weeks, had taken Doloxene, those powerful painkillers– might this affect the developing baby? I pushed the thought to the back of my mind.

* * *

A week later, Dave was out doing a radio play that morning, Pas was at nursery and Mel had told me to leave her after school, so she could play with Gabby for an hour or two – Lena could look after them. There was a knock on the front door. We had a five-foot high stone wall and gate separating our small front garden from the lane. Big Cat was on his customary perch, lying out on a large vertical branch of the pomegranate tree. The front door was split into a stable door, the top part was open. I saw a tall fine-featured black woman, in a faded print dress, holding the hand of a toddler.

'Hello,' I smiled, 'Can I help?'

'I was wondering if you needed a maid, medem.'

After the dramas and disasters around Katrina, I was wary of a replacement. Actually though, due to the progressing pregnancy, my energy levels were low and I needed to rest a lot. Some extra help with housework might be welcome.

I looked her over - she held her head up proudly, her eyes were clear and intelligent, her back was straight. Her toddler looked up at me with big brown shining eyes.

'Please medem, (her voice was polite, but firm, she was not looking for sympathy) I need the werk…'

'What's your name?'

'Constance, medem.'

'And what about your little girl?'

'She'll be with me.' She spoke flatly, a statement not a request.

'What's her name?'

'Victoria.'

'Well I could only afford once a week.'

'Why not twice, medem?' She smiled briefly.

'No,' my voice was firm. 'It can only be once - for three hours.' I was thinking, how will we afford that?

'How much do you want for three hours?'

She said a figure, it was reasonable,

'OK that's fine, when can you start?'

'Today! Medem, I can start today.' I looked at her for a moment.......there was an urgency in her voice.

'OK then, and please don't call me madam, my name is Anna.'

'Yes, medem.'

From then on Constance came every week without fail and was totally reliable. I had to demonstrate how to clean the surfaces, using spray polish, but when she had been shown something once, she picked it up quickly. She always brought Victoria with her. She was quiet and reserved and gave little away about her situation.

Eventually, I found out that she lived in one of the informal shanty areas up the main road towards Langa (one of the black townships).

Peter dropped by later for a visit and while I made him some Rooibos, I asked him a few questions. I wanted to know what kind of situation she might be living in...

'Her kid's father must be working on a farm nearby. The men have to stay in bachelor accommodation because of the pass laws. 'Wives can't join them – most of them are supposed to live in the 'homelands' like Swaziland or Lesotho.'

'Why? Why can't they join their men?'

'The government created the 'bantu' homelands – up in the North East - the land is poor and there are large numbers of blacks from different tribes living there. Any who don't come from there have to be registered there anyway. The government pretends these lands are 'separate countries' but they're not really. It's just a way of keeping the blacks separate and under control and reducing the ratio of blacks to whites.'

'But they're still South African yes?'

'No, now they're citizens of Lesotho and Swaziland.'

'So, the government took away their South African citizenship? But then they have their own leaders now, right?'

'Well, if you count leaders with no power, of countries totally dependent on South Africa. There's very high unemployment rates and poor soil, the only way for people to survive is for the men to come to South Africa to work. But their wives aren't supposed to come too....not allowed to under the Pass Laws.'

'But they go home at weekends don't they?'

Peter laughed drily.

'Their contracts are for a year at a time. Far as I know they can go home to their wives once a year only, for 2 weeks. They live too far away to go more often anyway.'

'Once a year?' I whispered, staring at Peter in shock, 'Once a year, that's terrible, so they get to see their kids once a year, their poor wives are pregnant and giving birth on their own?'

He smiled faintly, 'Well lots of the men find second 'wives' here and start new families. Some women follow their men from their 'homelands' and live illegally in those tiny shacks in the squatter camps you see on the road out to Langa and Guguletu.'

I thought about that a lot, every time Constance came to clean for me. Her little girl – Victoria would play quietly, following her Mum around, if Pas was there I'd sit them down at the table together and give them crayons and colouring books or home-made play-dough.

After a while it became apparent that Constance too was pregnant, so sometimes I would drive her back along the long, straight, pot-holed road towards Langa. She would point to a place at the roadside to drop her off and then quickly disappear. If you looked far into the scrubby bush I could see some of the tiny shacks that people lived in, with corrugated tin roofs – about the size of a garden shed in Britain. I was glad to have her though, a rest from the heavier housework was well needed, as I got tired very quickly now.

* * *

Noah came to an end in January and Dave was soon in to his next venture – Henry had been talking to him about it, while they were doing Noah. He wanted to form a new group called 'The Roundabout Theatre Company'. It was an innovative idea – they would do a lunch–time show. Dave came home after 'Noah' one night and told me all about it. It sounded terrifying to me.

'Henry wants the show to be totally improvised, no script.'

'Sounds ... scary!'

'Yes and no – it'll be fun!'

'But how will you know what to do, who plays what?'

'Well, Henry wants us to talk to the audience and get them to give us the story, or the characters – then we'll improvise and see where it goes ...'

'But Dave, that'll be a mess, no one will know what they're doing?'

'Maybe! Maybe not ... it's risky,' he was grinning, his wicked grin. Dave liked 'risky', he liked the adrenalin rush of being on the edge. He was relishing the opportunity.

They called the show 'I'm Ready for you Miss Jones,' a drama to be loosely based on office life.

Dave Henry, Allan and some new young actresses who'd been in Cape Town University drama department with Allan (a cast of seven), would stand on stage and interact with the audience. The Cape Argus (Jan 20th 1977) who sent a reporter to their dress rehearsal, said

' ... *an approach to drama radically new to Cape Town receives its first exposure tomorrow at St George's Cathedral hall... and ...It makes for astonishing viewing, much of it hilariously funny. . . the cast all agreed the process was initially terrifying.'*

He added, the company have been trained to take on any character, climb into any situation ... it offers the audience the chance to play Boss, turning their favourite fantasies into visible reality. It is going to be part of the Cape Town Festival and travel the city from the centre to the townships ...'

I went to see it in Cape Town one day and sat in the front row. The audience was quiet at first, not being used to being asked to participate in providing the storyline – one of the girls sat at a typewriter, the other actors took up position in the 'office' set and Dave came to the front with a clipboard, encouraging the audience to shout out. 'What's happening? What's the next bit? Is she having an affair with the boss?'
Someone called out,

'It's five o'clock and the boss comes in and dictates a long letter and says it has to go out tonight?'

'The boss tells her to go make him a coffee.'

'The boss's son comes in and starts flirting with her.'

'The boss wants her to come on a weekend conference.'

'The boss is a bully and shouts at everyone about deadlines.'

The actors took their cue and starting taking the suggestions to outrageous lengths ... the boss (Henry) flirting and putting his hand on her knee. The boss's wife walks in and the scene deteriorates into farce, the audience is laughing and Dave's whipping them up to more and more ridiculous suggestions. It's scrappy, farcical and funny and a great show, the audience depart buzzing with conversation and smiles back to their offices.

I waited at the back for Dave to come out, telling him how great the show was of course and we drove back to Rondebosch to pick up Pas from Brooksfield and get home. He was buzzing with adrenalin and couldn't stop talking about the show.

'Henry and I kept pushing it to see how outrageous we could get.'

'Yeh I know that scene where he puts his hand up the girl's thigh.'

'I nearly corpsed, yesterday it was her boobs, hands everywhere. But it's the audience – they egg you on to do something outrageous!'

A̲R̲T̲S̲ *and entertainment*

Following the audiences' wishes

A new approach

■ THE Roundabout Theatre, from left, Alan Swerdlow, Michelle Fine, Shirley Johnston, David Janes, Meryl Hendler and Allan Leas, giving an impression of being in a braking bus.

* * *

The next day, I drove Pas to school and came home feeling really tired. I put it down to the pregnancy – I was now ten weeks and it was still hot summer weather. I cleaned up the flat and was feeling so tired, I lay on the bed.

That's when they started - shooting pains in my back and a slight show of blood. Dave got home from the show an hour later. He rang Mel and asked her to keep Pas there with Gabby for a few hours, then took me up to Groote Schuur hospital.

They put me in a cubicle. Dave went to get us some tea from a machine. Pain now started in earnest. A big bustling blonde Afrikaans midwife came in... I started crying

'What is it, what's happening? Am I losing the baby?'

'Well dear, lots of pregnancies end at this stage. Perhaps it's for the best, eh?'

'What do you mean,' I sobbed, 'it's for the best?'

'Well dear,' her tone was soothing, 'Sometimes something's wrong with the foetus. It's nature's way, isn't it?'

'Something wrong with my baby?' I focused in on that part of her sentence and froze. *No! No, it couldn't be true.* My mind raced, I didn't want to lose my baby. *But what about that Doloxene? Suppose she was right? Suppose the drug had caused some damage?*

She left the cubicle, 'Ah'll be back in a munute dear.' Dave arrived with the tea and as soon as I saw him, I began to sob uncontrollably. He put the tea down and stroked my face. I didn't tell him what the nurse had said, I didn't want him to worry too. 'I just don't want to lose the baby.' I blew my nose with the tissue he handed me... 'You're not going to lose the baby, you'll be fine.' He stroked my back and put his arm round me.

Gradually I calmed down and the pains seemed to have stopped. The nurse came back. 'Yew look a but better,' she said, 'Let's see how we go for a but.' She took my blood pressure, 'Seems OK.' She took the sleeve off my arm.

'Uf this carries on yew can go home.' I looked at her and thought to myself, yes now you're sending me home after telling me there's something wrong with my baby. Suddenly, I felt angry – at her at myself and at the hospital. I wanted to go home... she left the room.

'Dave, what time is it?'

'Half five.'

'We should go – you have to be at the theatre.'

'No, it's OK. I've finished for today – Miss Jones is a lunch time remember.

'Well I want to go home now. I feel OK, I want to get Pas and go home. I'll rest at home.'

'Are you quite sure?' Dave knew me well enough that once I said I was OK, then I was impatient to go. I hated having to wait for hospital bureaucracy. I HATED hospitals. I'd been in and out of hospitals frequently in my late teens due to kidney problems and had ended up having a big operation. As soon as I was feeling better I was out. No stopping me.

'Yes, I want to go home now please.' I was out of bed and getting my clothes from the cupboard next to it.'

'OK darling, I'll tell them we're leaving now.'

The nurse came to see me with a doctor. 'You seem to have made your mind up to go, dear. We can't stop you. I think we'll put you on a series of hormone injections, to make sure there's no further problems. We'll arrange for a nurse to come over twice a week, to give you injections, OK?' The doctor was looking at my notes on the clipboard, frowning slightly.

I questioned him about the injections, but if the doc felt they were necessary and would help keep the baby, I supposed it was all right. He said they were quite high dosage.

I've often wondered since about the validity of this procedure. Was I being experimented on and what were the long term effects? But at that time I was just relieved that they were doing something to ensure my pregnancy stabilised.

We went home, collecting Pas from Mel's on the way. On the surface at least everything seemed to be fine. Except the words of that nurse kept popping into my head. 'Something wrong with the baby.' I'd push them out, but then later they'd pop back in. Now I couldn't take so much as an aspirin if I had a headache.

Twice a week for the next four weeks a nurse dropped by and gave me an injection. They'd told me to rest but the problem was, I'm not someone who can sit down while there are things to be done. I had Constance to do the heavy housework which was great, she was very strong, but still there was shopping, cooking, washing and taking Pas to school, fetching Dave from Cape Town, trips to the beach to organise – visits to friends - I didn't lead a quiet life. I was lucky though, that I didn't suffer from morning-sickness. I'd read books about nutrition so I took folic acid (lack of it can cause birth defects), B6 (to prevent oedema or swollen ankles) and a multivitamin. Mostly I felt quite well, although tired in the afternoons. I hoped that all this would counteract my forebodings, but sometimes hope is not enough is it?

Chapter 32: Pets

Big Cat loved it at Harefield village, he had hated it out in Philippi, with all those miles of bush and wide open spaces. He was happy in the cottage and most happy taking up position as sentinel in the front garden on a large branch of the pomegranate tree. As for killing scorpions or any other insects or small vermin about, Big Cat was just a big girl's blouse.

One evening I was sitting in the front room reading – Dave was doing a show. I heard a frantic high pitched mewing. I looked around - Big Cat was curled up on the settle, purring softly. I opened the front door – at first I thought it was from our stoep, but then I realised it was coming from further away. I walked on to the road, looking around in the dark trying to trace the sound, which then stopped suddenly. I shrugged and was just about to go back in when it started again. I was sure it was coming from next door's stoep, so I went up their front step and looked around the porch. In the farthest darkest corner were 2 bright yellow eyes and as I approached sharp little teeth and flat back ears were spitting and hissing at me. Slowly I put my hand to the back of its neck and scratched gently, quickly withdrawing my hand from a nasty nip at one stage. Gradually I managed to pick up the tiny bundle and hold it close to my t-shirt. I knocked on my neighbour's door - the Indian occupant – a small middle-aged man, came and looked at me briefly. I smiled and said

'Oh, hi.'

'Yus' he said, 'Ken ah hilp you?'

'Well, I live next door – just over there and I heard a kitten mewing. I just found it on your stoep and wondered if it's yours or you know who it belongs to?'

He glanced at the kitten without interest, 'No ah doan know, I he-ard some mewing a few tahmes round here in the lahs few days, but ah didn't know where ut cayme from. There's so many wild kets round here, isn't ut?'

'OK well I'm going to take it home with me, it might be hungry.'

'Shame, eh! Ut's fine by me,' he shrugged.

'So if it belongs to anyone, you can tell them I've got it, yes?'

'Ah don't think ut belongs to anyone. Uts from one of those wald kets, for sure. The mother lef it or got killed or something, who knows?'

I took her into the kitchen and put down a saucer of milk and a little minced cat food. She was clearly starving as she wolfed the lot down very fast. After a while, Big Cat uncurled himself from his nice snooze on my bed down the hall and came in to investigate the strange mewing sounds. He went to give the intruder the once over, sniffing around– but from a distance – he sensed her wild spirit. Just as well, as the little black thing puffed out all her fur, hunched her back, splayed her claws and hissed and spat at the monster intruder on *her* territory!

For the next day or so, she hid after eating, in the darkest corner – usually under the settee and sometimes had to be coaxed out with bits of meat. Pas, of course, had a way with animals. They were always attracted to her and never threatened by her - soon Pas was tickling her under the chin, stroking her fur or carrying her over her shoulder and the little spitting minx adored her. Pas decided to name her Blackie and after a few days she got used to Big Cat and curled up next to his stomach to sleep or jumped and hopped and pounced around him, annoying him with her antics. Luckily, although she got the occasional pat from his big paws when she pushed it too far, he had an easy-going nature. She behaved as if the place was her territory and she was in charge of it, stalking around, exploring every corner, guarding the doorway. She tolerated Dave and I, as food providers, but spat or hissed if we tried to boss her around or tell her what to do. She knew she was in charge – we just needed reminding occasionally.

And so cat number two joined our household. Angel, our bull terrier, came to investigate on that first evening, putting her face just a bit too close and leapt back yowling as she got a slash across the nose for her interest. She kept a safe distance after that.

At the back, we had a yard about 30 foot square, concreted over, with a 6 foot wooden fence. On the right-hand side, was a small brick building about 12 x 8 foot, with 2 steps leading up to its door, which was opposite our backdoor. This was obviously intended for 'the maid' to live in, except we had no maid, we couldn't afford such luxuries. As it was generally warm or hot, the back door was always open.

When we first moved in, I continued to do all our washing in the bath, but after a while Dave got hold of an old top-loading washing machine, with a wooden mangle on top - oh the luxury. Then I would hang out the washing in the yard on a long washing line, for a fast dry in the African sun. Now with the pregnancy advancing, the twin tub was a godsend – no more bending over the bath and scrubbing with Sunlight soap. Angel and the cats would follow me out to the yard and Angel would curl up in some sunny spot, basking in the sun or if it was too hot, find a bit of shade to lie in.

We soon had a problem however - Angel came in to season and as we couldn't afford vets bills to put her on the Pill or get her sterilised, we thought we could keep her safe from other dogs for a week or two by keeping her in the yard. However we reckoned without the resourcefulness of the other dogs in the neighbourhood.

One day, Dave went out to find a Dachshund had crawled up a drainpipe leading into the yard from outside and was attempting to mount the larger and taller Angel. Another day, I glanced out the kitchen window while washing up, to see a large Alsatian leaping over the fence. I ran out yelling and banging pots and it jumped straight out again, clearing the six-foot fence in one leap.

The result became all too obvious as the weeks passed and Angel got fatter and developed teats. We were not overjoyed with this news, but naively thought she would have one or two pups and we'd find them homes with our friends. A dog pregnancy lasts about 8 weeks, which is really fast. When I was about 10 weeks pregnant and hardly showing, Angel was waddling around looking fat and panting in the heat. She would find the shadiest spot in the back yard, under a scraggy tree and flop there every day. I'd bring her out a big bowl of water and put it near her. We explained it all to Pas, now aged three and a half. She was really excited for weeks leading up to the birth.

'Mummy, when's Angel's puppies coming? Will it be today?'

'I don't think so baby, not today. Maybe next week.'

The next day, the same question and the next. My answer was always the same,

'No not today.' Until one day I looked out and Angel had got up from her shady spot under the tree and, just in time, I saw her lumbering up the steps and into the outbuilding, the 'maid's' room. There was nothing much in there, just a few bags of clothes and pieces of wood and a concrete floor.

Hmmm ... I thought to myself, is she going to have the pups in there? I rushed out the back door and up the steps and found her lying panting on a piece of cardboard in the corner. She was turning herself round and round trying to get comfortable and her eyes looked glazed. I ran back to the house and got an old blanket, a bucket of warm water and a cloth. I called out to Pas,

'Pas! Angel's having her pups! Come quick. I hope Daddy gets home soon.'

Pas followed me up the steps all excited, 'Puppies, Mummy, puppies coming!'

At last it was happening. This was going to be an education for Pas, she was going to find out about giving birth and how it really happens.

'Okay you need to stand over there at the back,' I said. Angel was whining loudly and I didn't think it was a good idea for either of us to get too close. This was something she had to do on her own and we couldn't interfere. Suddenly the whining got intense and she was squatting and then out slithered the first puppy, covered in a slimy membrane. Angel turned round and was biting and licking the membrane off. The little thing started wriggling and squirming, so I knew it was all right. I stayed back and suddenly she was squatting again and yowling and another came out and then another. I glanced round at Pas, her eyes were like saucers and her mouth was an O.

I looked back and saw that one of the puppies was not moving, it was smaller than the others and the membrane was still covering its face. I quickly brought over the cloth and the bucket and tore the membrane off its face and started to massage its tiny body. Pas had come running over and put her hand out to touch the tiny face and suddenly it stirred and was moving. I dipped my cloth in the bucket and wiped off the blood and membrane. It was a tiny replica of Angel, white all over, except for a black patch over one eye and two black paws. Its tiny tail was moving feebly. I lifted it to its feet and it wobbled uncertainly, its head appearing too heavy to hold up.

Dave appeared in the doorway, just in time to see Angel give birth to puppies 6, 7, 8 and 9. Nine puppies, she'd had nine puppies. I kept counting, yes there were nine. Oh my God, what the hell were we going to do with nine puppies? I went round each one wiping their faces with the cloth, as Angel lay on her side panting with exhaustion. Dave was grinning from ear to ear and he had picked up Pas and they were pointing at each one. The puppies were crawling towards Angels' teats, and finding them, clambering over each other with their blind eyes, already suckling. The little one was at the back and couldn't reach, didn't have the strength. Dave brought Pas over and helped her bring the little mouth onto a teat.

Angel, Pas, Sarah and pups

It must have been a Monday, as luckily Dave was not at the theatre that day. He'd been to teach his impro class to a group of teenagers in a local school. I fetched a bowl of water and put it next to Angel and went back in as darkness was falling, to cook supper. It was time for Pas to go to bed also and leave Angel in peace for a while. Pas was so excited, it was going to be impossible to get her to bed. We went in the kitchen and I poured a large glass of wine for me and Dave and a glass of juice for Pas. I was exhausted and kept thinking, nine pups. Oh God. Nine.

Angel, the pups and Big Cat

After six weeks, we'd found homes for three of the puppies. We were getting desperate. What were we going to do with the other six? As a last resort, we checked out a pet shop in Claremont. The owner said yes he would take them, but we looked and saw that other puppies he had were kept in cages in the shop. The thought of Angel's puppies being put in those cages broke my heart. But it was beginning to seem like there was no other choice.

In the end, events forced a rapid decision - I came home after nearly losing the baby, in a severely weakened state. I would have to rest, if I was to keep this baby. The puppies would have to go.

We arranged for Pas to go and play with a friend for the afternoon. Then we put them in a box and Dave took them to the pet shop. He told me afterwards how the guy had put them all in a cage together, we just hoped that they'd quickly find new families. When Pas came home, she was upset that they were all gone, but we told her that they had all gone to new mummies and daddies to take care of them. After she'd gone to bed, I kept crying and thinking of ways to rescue them from the pet shop.

When I dropped off Pas at school the next day, Mel called me to come up to the lounge for a chat. I was glad to get out of the heat, to her cool living room with windows open and plenty of breeze coming through. It was February now – late summer in Cape Town. I told her about Angel and how Dave had taken them to the pet shop, but Mel was a pragmatist, unsentimental about animals and was matter-of-fact about it.

'Well, you couldn't keep them could you?' She was lighting a long cigarette and puffing slowly.

'I don't know how we could have fed that many dogs much longer,' I sniffed. My eyes were red from crying the night before. I took a cigarette out and lit it, although I was smoking far less now, only a couple each day. Mel blew out a long curl of smoke.

'Nine pups is just too much, you did what you had to do, hey?' She changed the subject.

'I'm going to change the timetable around. I'll have several different teachers doing half hour sessions with the children - different subjects every half hour. You know Thomas' mother – Alison, yis? Well, she's a music teacher – she's going to do music with triangles and small instruments, Becky's going to do a maths session, she used to teach it before the baby - I'll pay them of course.'

'Sounds great, lots of variety – the kids'll love it.'

'I want them to do drama too.... it's great for confidence, don't you think? Well, I thought of Dave of course – do you think he'd be interested? I'd want him to come in 1 or 2 mornings a week ...'

I could see that Mel wanted to help us out with a bit of extra cash, as well as revamping the curriculum at her school. Dave was busy now doing radio-plays once a week for Cape Town radio, teaching impro to teenagers – all of which contributed to our income. And the lunchtime impro show with Henry was running for a few more weeks, although he was looking round for what would be next.

'It sounds great Mel, I wonder how Dave will cope with nursery age children? Do you think he'll be OK?'

Mel stubbed out her cigarette firmly – 'I think he'll be fabulous,' she smiled. 'Just ask him for me.'

A week or so later, Dave did his first class with the nursery kids at Brooksfield. He told me all about it later - he decided, before walking in the door for the first time that they might be intimidated by his height, he was 6 foot 3 ... so he went in the door on his hands and knees – the kids loved it and soon he was taking different groups one morning a week. He'd discovered a new talent - for teaching small children. In March, he started rehearsals for another production, directed by Henry, put on at various Cape Town venues – Lovers (and Losers). It opened in April.

The weeks passed and my belly was expanding very slowly, autumn slipped into winter and it got colder. I took to wearing a large loose jumper, my jean's zip was held together with a big safety pin. Even at six months, most people didn't notice that I was pregnant - very different to my pregnancy with Pas, where I'd rapidly put on weight – then I'd gone from my usual eight stone to ten and a half and it was obvious quite early, that I was pregnant.

Dave had been telling me the night before, about how Allan Leas, who was doing the impro show with him and Henry was excited about a play he'd written, called 'Forms', based on the testimony of Bertolt Brecht in the hearings of The House Committee on Un-American activities. These hearings were really a creeping anti-communist paranoia that had swept America and were intended to unearth communism in all American institutions. Although the hearings started in 1938, they carried on until it was abolished in the mid-1970s. People were encouraged to inform on their former colleagues and associates and even famous Hollywood actors were put under scrutiny. Brecht's interrogation took place in late October 1947.

Allan had asked Dave, a few weeks before, to direct it with him as soon as funding came through, as well as play the part of the Defence Attorney. Of course, the play would be a hooded critique of the Afrikaans government and its apartheid policies and the 'mock' trials of black leaders, like Nelson Mandela, in the Rivonia trials of the 1960s.

Dave heard that Allan had got funding - it was an exciting project and anything that criticised the apartheid regime, however obliquely, was something Dave wanted to be involved in. If all went well it would open at the end of May 1977.

The Space *presents*
The
Roundabout Theatre Co.
in
" LOVERS "
by brian friel .
" *a spectacular success*
on Broadway "
directed by
HENRY GOODMAN
the co. that brought you
" *the sparkling wit* " *of*
I'm Ready For You . . . .
. . . Miss Jones
now !! at The Space .
Mon-Fri. 1. 05 DAILY

Lovers' was coming to an end at the beginning of May. Rehearsals would start for 'Forms' at the same time and Dave was really pleased to be taking part in such an innovative production.

Forms - a thinly disguised criticism of apartheid.

Meanwhile, for me life went on as usual, taking Pas to Brooksfield, meeting up with friends, I had to take it easy though as the pregnancy progressed. Driving to the theatre or to the school was often through heavy rain now - that winter was a bad one, lots of gale force winds, rain going on for days - perhaps that weather was a portent of what was to come.

Chapter 33: Mummy's Baby

One day, when I went to collect Pas from school, Melissa said –'I have to go and visit a friend of mine down the road...'

'Do you want me to go home or wait here?'

'No, you can come wuth, if you like, Hilda's getting on a bit, but she'd enjoy meeting you.'

'I'll get Pas.'

'No leave the girls with Lena, they'll be fine, I just drop by to see her occasionally, she lives on her own since her husband died.'

Hilda's house was cosy and old fashioned. The front room had dark sofas with white lacy squares on the backs and arms. On the mahogany sideboard, were black and white photos, in silver frames. Shiny shelves held lots of glass ornaments – I was glad we hadn't brought the girls. I was now nearly 6 months pregnant and was wearing my same old loose jumper over jeans.

Melissa and I sat down while Hilda brought in tea in a teapot, covered with a woollen tea-cosy. She handed me a china cup with a saucer and I sipped my tea, while she and Melissa started chatting. Hilda had grey hair pulled back tightly in a knot. She was wearing a brown skirt and fluffy slippers. She looked me over, smiled and said to Melissa, 'Who's this then?'

Melissa, who was wearing her usual pink slacks and frilly pink top said, 'Meet my friend Anna, Anna meet Hilda.' I smiled shyly.

'Her daughter goes to my school.'

'She looks too young to have kids.' Hilda raised her eyebrows.

'I'm twenty-six,' I said firmly, being used to this reaction.

'I thought you were about eighteen.' She looked surprised.

'And she's expecting another – you're six months now isn't it Anna?'

'No! 'She looked amazed. 'Where are you hiding it?'

I pulled my jumper flat against my stomach, but had to admit there wasn't much of a bump.

'I was much bigger by now with my first,' I said.

Hilda shook her head in disbelief, 'Well I can't believe you're six months gone.'

Melissa and she chatted for a while and then we said goodbye and went back to Brookfield. I was surprised that Mel had a friend like Hilda, she was always so busy rushing about and Hilda didn't seem her type. When I asked her about it she said Hilda reminded her of her grandmother and she didn't have many visitors. So she went there once a week if she could.

I was relieved to get back, as I wanted Mel to tell me the latest instalment about Dieter. Today, she poured us a glass of wine and leaned back on the dark brown sofa, puffing her cigarette. I knew something was going on with him, but she still wasn't giving much away. Sometimes, it felt like she looked at me as if I was a small child and she was the much older sister, like she was looking at me now, weighing up how much I would understand. She seemed so much older and wiser and more experienced than my twenty six year old self, after all Werner was her second husband. She'd had a lot of life experience it seemed to me. Looking back, it seems funny to think that she was only 32.

'How's Werner? Things still difficult with him?'

She exhaled slowly, 'Still can't communicate with the rest of the human race, what can I say?' Her tone was dry. 'How is Dave getting on in the new play?'

'Oh, that's 'Forms' – opened last week, he's got a good part. I told her a little about it. Seems like now he doesn't have to search for work anymore. Everything he's been in for the last 6 months – directors contacted him, he didn't really have to look. He's got acting work lined up to Christmas and offers for next year coming in too!'

'How exciting, we'll have to all go along and see it. He's been great with the kids here too – they all love him. Oh by the way, I'm going out just now. I'm meeting Dieter for lunch.' She sounded casual, but her eyes were sparkling.

I stood up. 'Are you now?' I smiled at her, 'Well don't do anything too naughty, will you?' I was glad for her really, she looked so attractive with her frilly pink blouse and shoulder length auburn hair. Werner spent so little time with her – she deserved a bit of appreciation.

We both laughed and I went off to do my shopping. When I came back to collect Pas, Mel wasn't there anymore. I smiled to myself on the drive home.

Once I got home, I'd be handing the car keys to Dave, he had to get to his workshop for teenagers that afternoon. I wondered how Mel was getting on with her 'lunch'. She'd be sure to be back in time for Werner's return.

* * *

In June 1977, it was the day of my monthly ante-natal check-up at Groote Schuur hospital. I was 26 weeks pregnant. Pascale, then 3, was supposed to go to nursery school that morning and so I got up, and got her ready to go. Dave had already left as he was doing a play for the Cape Town radio station that morning; he had been picked up by one of the other actors early.

As we were about to leave, to drive to the nursery, Pas said, 'Where you going Mummy?'

'To the hospital – they want to listen to the baby in Mummy's tummy.'

'Oh!' she said, 'Me come.'

'No darling, you have to go to school.'

'No, no, no, want come wid you to hoptal'.

I thought about it for a minute. She had a determined look and was going to make a fuss if she didn't come. It would be fine, I thought, she could have a day off for a change. Pas was as immovable as a rock once she had made up her mind.

I said OK and she broke into a big smile and threw her tiny arms round me, 'Me come wid you.'

We got in the beetle and drove to Groote Schuur hospital. Hospitals in South Africa then had a three-tier service. Most white people (and some well off black and coloured people – in separate areas of course) had private treatment with the best possible care. If you couldn't afford that you could get basic hospital care, which was free, no frills (although all GP consultations had to be paid for). Most black and coloured people had third class free treatment at the hospital, with long queues, crowded wards etc. Although there was many dedicated health care staff working in that environment, many people received care that was barely adequate, due to sheer numbers.

For Dave and me, private gynaecology treatment although it might have been nice, was not an option. Besides we were used to the National Health Service in the UK and the kind of treatment I got didn't seem that much different.

After a short while in the waiting room, the midwife called me in and I lay down on the bed while she got out her stethoscope and a trumpet like metal thing. She pressed it to my bulging stomach, to listen for the baby's heartbeat.

We had been to a party the week before and I had had two glasses of wine. I had many times pushed to the back of my mind, the words of the nurse who, after the near miscarriage, had told me 'there must be something wrong with the baby'. I had been to a few parties since then (we had an active social life). At some subconscious level, I was in denial about the pregnancy. Yet as the weeks passed, inevitably a bond had started to build up between me and the baby. Pas had often asked questions about the baby 'in Mummy's tummy'. Dave and I had decided to name the baby Merlyn, after the Welsh magician, if it was a boy or Jesse if it was a girl. The latter was a version of the name of Dave's aunt – Auntie Jessie in Swansea, whom he adored, who was one of the funniest story tellers I have ever met.

Pas was chatting away to me, when I became aware that the midwife was trying the trumpet in all different places on my stomach – 'Could you lie on your side?' She was helping me to turn, so she could try it on my sides and back. Then she returned me to my back and tried low down on my stomach again. I looked at her face sharply, she was frowning. 'What is it? What's wrong?' The expression on her face was concentrated, unsmiling.

'Er, I'm just going to get the doctor to come and listen, I'm just having a bit of difficulty, finding the heartbeat.' She shot off through the doorway before I could ask any more questions. A slight feeling of panic began in my head, but I pushed it down. The doctor would find the heartbeat for sure.

I began to review the last few days – had I felt the baby moving. Not for a few days actually, that fluttering feeling, was it longer? A week?

She came back. 'We're sending you to ultra sound, they'll be able to find it better than I can, don't worry, I'm sure it'll be fine.'

I hate it when they say that, medical people – don't worry, as if you can switch it off, when their body language and tone of voice is setting off a siren call in your head.

In the cubicle, I was putting on my white gown with ties on, my fingers fumbling. I was telling myself it was alright, the ultra sound would find the heartbeat...the baby was probably lying in a difficult position. Pascale was outside in the waiting room, playing with a colouring book and crayons I'd brought her, chatting to the nurses. They called me in and I lay down on the padded reclining chair. They squirted KY jelly on my stomach and then pushed the instrument around all over my belly. Back and forth, I was looking between the face of the radiologist and the black and white squiggles on the screen. There was a long silence of concentration as she rolled the instrument all over my belly. Then suddenly she stopped and removed the instrument from my belly and looked at me, as she took a cloth and began wiping the gel from my belly.

'I'm afraid this baby's gone, dear!'

'What?' I felt like I was dreaming, 'What do you mean 'gone'.'

'There's no heartbeat.'

I looked at her without comprehension, her eyes were full of pity, but she was matter of fact.

'What does that mean? Why can't you find it? No, it can't be, try again ...'

'I'm afraid not, there's no heartbeat, this baby's .....not survived.....I'm sorry...it's dead.'

It was as if there was an explosion in my head at that moment. After a while I found myself back in the waiting room fully dressed again. The midwife was handing me a cup of tea and urging me to drink it – it was sweet. She left me alone, saying she'd be back in a minute, she was sorry, very sorry. Pas was there next to me, staring intently at my face,

'Mummy mummy what wrong, why you crying?'

'It's the baby Pas, the baby....'

She was patting my belly

'Mummy's baby there.'

'Yes, but the baby's dead now Pas, Mummy's baby's dead.'

The midwife came back in and Pas ran up to her, 'Mummy crying, Mummy's baby dead.' The midwife stopped and looked at her, then walked over to me and asked 'Is there someone you can phone?' Dave will be in the studio, I thought, so I should phone Melissa, she'll know what to do.

'It's best if you go home, get some rest and come back tomorrow, then we'll have to induce you.' Another explosion of shock went off in my head. I was trying to grasp the words.

'What? Induce me?'

'Yes, we'll have to induce labour. You must come back tomorrow.'

It started to sink in, they were sending me home with a dead baby in my belly and telling me to come back the next day. Then they'd make me go through labour and give birth to a dead baby.....no, no, this was a nightmare. It could not be happening.

'Why can't you induce me now?'

'No,' she said firmly, 'We have to get a bed organised in the labour ward – it must wait until tomorrow. Now, who would you like to call?' She was helping me to my feet, 'The phone's over there.'

I called Melissa and told her. There was a stunned silence; I asked if I should come over there.

'Yes come here now, can you drive?'

'Yes I suppose so, can you call Dave for me? He's at the radio station.'

'Yes fine, I'll see you in a little while, I'm so sorry...'

Pas was trying to show me a picture she'd drawn of a house and a cat, wanting me to look. I was nodding dumbly, gathering up her things, putting them in my bag. The nurse was hovering over me.

'Be back here at 7 am tomorrow, we'll see you then.'

I just wanted to get away, escape to someone who could reassure me, someone familiar. But the thought of having to wait a whole night and then come back to be induced was exploding in my head. I staggered, righted myself and then grabbed Pas's hand and started walking fast out of the door, down the corridors, out to the car park.

I must have got in the car and driven to Melissa's house, but I remembered nothing of that later. Lena answered the door and said nothing as she looked at my face, just ushered me into the lounge. Pas went up to her and said, 'Lena, Lena, Mummy's baby's dead, Mummy's baby's dead.' Lena hushed her and took her off, to play with Gabby.

After a while, Melissa walked in and took both my hands in hers. She started asking questions and I replied in mono-syllables to her about what had happened and that I had to be back there next morning. Dave had another radio play next day and I wondered if he could come. Melissa said not to worry as she would come with me.

Dave must have arrived and taken me and Pas home at some point – I don't remember. I lay down with the worst migraine I'd ever had.

'Are you all right, Anna? Anna, speak to me.' Dave's anx-ious face hovered over me. I looked at him – his voice was a long way off and I was tired, so tired. He kept trying to get me to answer, but my tongue was immobile - it was too much effort. Then he was sitting me up to give me a Doloxene. I soon fell into a deep, drugged sleep.

I awoke at 5 a.m. and struggled to remember what was happening, something ....terrible... oh yes. I looked at my belly with the dead baby inside and felt the tears pouring down my face. Dave woke next to me and jumped up,' I'll make tea.' He put my hands around the cup and handed me a wad of tissues – 'Can you speak now?'

'Yes.' I whispered

'Oh good (with relief) I've got a radio play this morning but I'll ring and cancel it.'

But I insisted he go, we couldn't afford to lose the money anyway. Melissa had said she'd come to the hospital for the beginning. He tried to insist, but I reminded him that the show must go on.

'Well let me talk to Melissa first.'

'I'll be fine with her until you get there.'

'She told me that last night – she said to ring her at 6 this morning and let her know.'

I was in the car with Melissa, driving to the hospital. I was very frightened. When we got there we were greeted by a hard faced Afrikaans ward sister.

'And who is this,' she asked looking at Melissa. My eyes flicked to Melissa and back to the nurse.

'She's my sister,' I said quickly

'Only husbands allowed in the labour ward, no other friend's or relatives'.

'My husband can't be here now, he's coming later. My sister is staying with me until then.'

She shook her head and her mouth went in to a firm line

'No that's not permitted,' she said, 'We had a lady last week, whose husband was away in South West fighting SWAPO (all white males over 21 had to serve 2 years call up). She wanted to bring her mother in, but it was not permitted.'

Melissa was beginning to back down. 'Well, shall I wait for you outside? You'll be OK, they'll look after you...' but I was desperate. I could not do this alone.

'No!' I raised my voice, 'Either she comes in or I'm not doing it, I won't go in there.'

'Well I'll have to call the doctor, but he won't allow it.' Her voice was firm.

In the end, Melissa was allowed in. She held my hand while they laid me down in my white gown on the stretcher and put a needle into my arm - the induction drip. I was so relieved she was there. The contractions began slowly and then Melissa was called out – Dave had arrived and she had to leave before he could come in.

It was cold, so cold in that room. The room was sharply white, white walls, neon strip lights. It made it feel even colder. The doctor came in occasionally to check how it was progressing. I asked the doctor 'Why is it so cold?' I was starting to shiver; my feet were hurting with cold.

'It's the air conditioning.'

'Can you turn it off, please - my feet are freezing.'

'No, sorry, we can't turn it off, we've tried, and it's stuck.'

'But I'm so cold...'

He took my pulse as my teeth had started chattering.

Dave asked, 'Isn't there a blanket or something? Look at her!'

The doctor strode out of the room and a midwife came bustling in with pillow cases which were tied to my ankles, covering my feet. The doctor said that he was going to give me something. He carried a glass phial, which was inserted into the needle taped to my arm and whoosh! A warm glow swept from my feet to the top of my head.

I was feeling euphoric, detached, dreamy and asked him what he had given me.

'Morphine.' He was fiddling with the tubes as he spoke. Then he walked out leaving the midwife.

An hour or so later, I felt something warm between my legs, it felt like I'd wet myself – I called out to the midwife who was walking out the door of the room...apologetically.

She strolled over and lifted my white gown and looked. Her face froze, and then she ran to the door and called for assistance. She came back in with a metal trolley, picked up a stainless steel kidney shaped dish, scooped something in and covered it with a white cloth. She looked at me, 'It's the baby. It's come out, do you want to see?' My heart constricted and I thought I might collapse with shock if I looked at the baby. I started to sob. I looked at Dave, his eyes were wet too, 'No, no, I can't,' I sobbed.

The nurse turned and carrying the dish, walked quickly from the room. Dave put his arms round me and we both cried and held each other. When she returned I asked,

'Was the baby a boy or a girl?'

'Girl,' she said briefly.

We cried again for our little Jesse who would never grow up with us. Never play with Pascale.

The midwife delivered the afterbirth and cleaned me up. Soon I was wheeled to a side room, which opened on to the post-natal ward. I was still crying. I could hear the nurses bustling amongst the new mothers, babies wailing. Dave had been sent home and anyway had to pick up Pas from Mel's. Eventually I cried myself into an exhausted sleep. I woke up next day, crying again as the trauma and grief and loss came crashing back into my mind. A nurse kept coming in to check on me. She was a plump blonde English speaking South African and each time she came in she took my pulse and my temperature, her eyes on my face, as I sobbed quietly. She tried to engage me in conversation, but I was in a black dark place of grief and despair.

'So is your husband coming in today?' she asked brightly.

I shook my head, not knowing, nothing mattered.

At that moment Dave walked in, holding flowers awkwardly, not knowing where to put them. She took them from him and went in search of a vase. He stayed for a while dumbly holding my hand; there was nothing to be said. We cried together and after a while he left. He had to pick up Pas from Mel's.

Later in the afternoon, the same nurse came in again. I was still crying, crying like I was never going to stop, great sobs wracking my body. She picked up my wrist to take my pulse.

'How long are you going to keep on crying?'

I stared at her dumbly. I didn't think this grief was ever going to end.

'You have to stop,' she was taking my pulse again, 'You can't go on like this, you have to stop. What about your other child? And your husband? You have to stop.'

I looked at her through red, watering eyes. She was right, I knew - I did have to stop. But how? I would have to push it down somehow, close off the grief, put a lid on it. I had to start functioning again and move forward, somehow.

She left the room and after a while I sat up, found some tissues, dried my eyes and blew my nose.

Next day, a physiotherapist came in, saying brightly,

'I'm getting all the new Mums on the ward together to do some gentle stretching exercises, start getting those stomach muscles working again, in about half an hour. What did you have by the way?'

'Girl!'

'Oh lovely, so where's the baby – nurse taken her so you can have a rest?' I sighed, 'No my baby was born dead.'

Her smile froze. 'Oh, er...oh dear, my, oh I'm so sorry, how could I be such an idiot. Why didn't someone tell me? Perhaps I can come and give you a few stretching exercises on your own...if you like?'

Dave came at visiting hour that evening. 'I want to go home,' was all I could say.

Chapter 34: The Aftermath

After I came out of hospital, everything had changed. The shock went deep. In our place in Harefield village I walked around in a daze. I sat and stared into space. Situations where other people were around I avoided. I didn't want to talk about what had happened or deal with their sympathy. My days were spent on basic household chores, washing, cooking, cleaning in robot fashion. I got Pas up in the morning and took her to school. When the nurse at the hospital had told me to stop crying, I took it to heart. The box was sealed, the key hidden away and that lid would not be lifted again until many years later.

Dave started doing some of the cooking, curries became his specialty but he was worried about my vacant listlessness. Di and Steve and Peter called sometimes for supper and I would smile and chat, but my mind was far away in a numbed out world. I lost weight, food was of little interest to me. The winter weather reflected my mood, it was cool and cloudy, sometimes raining for several days. I wore a loose jumper indoors and a light raincoat on the few occasions I went out somewhere. Two years on from our arrival in Cape Town and in winter we did not bother to go to the beach, even on sunny days it was not warm enough.

One night Mel came round, maybe Dave had rung her.

'You need to get out of the house more,' she lit one of her long cigarettes.

'Yes,' I smiled, her lively vivacious presence always cheered me.

'I have a proposition for you... How about you come to Brooksfield and teach?'

I stared at her; that was ridiculous. What could I teach? I had no skills or experience teaching small children.

'I think you could teach crafts.' She had seen me painting patterns on stones and on an ostrich egg. Dave had brought it back from an ostrich farm in Oudtshorn which he'd visited on his last tour. I enjoyed drawing and making things.

'I don't know, what would I do?'

'Oh, painting and making simple things – as long as the kids go home with something, it keeps the parents happy.'

'But...'

'No buts,' she stubbed out her cigarette. 'Come on, you'll be wonderful, you'll be doing me a favour. Do an hour or two a few days a week and I'll pay you...'

* * *

Two weeks after losing the baby, there I was sitting in a class of four to five year olds, with paper, card, scissors and paint. As the weeks passed, I became too busy to think and gradually emerged from my numbed-out, far-away place. I began to feel like I was back in the world again.

Dave too was now very busy. He was often running drama classes for various teenage groups a couple of afternoons during the week and teaching drama to the kids at Brooksfield several mornings a week, as well as being in demand for radio plays regularly on Cape Town radio. He'd just started rehearsals for the part of 'The Devil' in The Fall and Redemption of Man' – he was back at St Georges with Jo Dunstan. Ironic to be playing the Devil there this time, after playing Jesus a year before.

Jo and her husband Geoffrey – the vicar at the Cathedral, asked us over for a braai in their garden around this time. It would be my first social event since losing the baby. We all sat round a big wooden table in their beautiful garden, which was attached to the vicarage. There were about 10 of us, including some of the other actors Dave had worked with in 'Jesus' and 'Noah'. I was sitting beside Geoffrey, who was chatting to everyone and being the perfect host. Pas was playing on the lawn with a couple of bigger kids. When I had arrived, Jo had taken both my hands.

'How are you, my dear? So sorry to hear about...'

'Yes,' I'd interrupted nervously, not wanting her to dwell on it, 'I'm much better thanks' and we'd left it at that.

Dave was cracking jokes and making everyone laugh in his usual way. Geoffrey was watching Pas running around, playing tag with the other kids. Then he turned to me and asked in a voice that carried clearly to the whole table -

'... and when are you two going to have another one, eh?'

It was as if everyone froze at once around the table, including me. I stared at him in shock for a moment and saw

Jo glaring at him across the table and watched light dawn in his eyes. Quickly, to cover his look of panic, I answered,

'It won't be for a while, as I've just lost one.' There was no easy way to put it. I felt sorry for him, as he was clearly devastated by his own memory lapse.

'I'm so sorry, so sorry,' he kept saying.

'It's okay, I'm fine,' I kept replying, wishing he would shut up and stop apologising.

After that, everyone started talking and being busy. Geoffrey kept fussing over me, trying to make amends, could he get me a drink, a piece of cake? Catching Dave's eyes in a momentary break in his story telling, I indicated that I wanted to go. It was not too far from sunset by then. We shook hands with Geoffrey and Jo, his farewells were effusive and we left. It had been an ordeal I was glad had ended. Dave had been drinking so I was on driving duty. Pas was in the back of the car and I was looking forward to getting home. I started the engine and Dave said suddenly,

'Let's go and watch the sunset from the beach.'

I said I was tired, but he was insistent, 'Come on it'll be great – look its turning pink already – it's not far to Sea Point – we can just park and walk across the pavement to the beach there. It won't take long. Remember we went once when we first moved here – it was fantastic!'

'See the sea! See the sea!' chanted Pas in the back.

It had been beautiful, I remembered. Maybe seeing the beauty of the sunset and breathing the sea air would clear my head, ground me again, as I had felt myself flitting away at the party - the strain of making small talk, facing sympathetic looks. Then dealing with Geoffrey's gaffe and trying to put him back at ease.

'OK, OK!' I gave in and turned the car towards Green Point, drove down the busy high street and in to Sea Point. Then we turned right at a side turning and parked on the roadside. We got out and walked past a tall building with a pavement café on to a small grassy area beside the beach.

There it was in front of us, the Atlantic Ocean. This was not like looking out to sea in the UK - small seas there, never too far across to land. This was different, vast - the ocean.

The sun always set rapidly in South Africa, regular as clock-work, starting soon after 6 pm darkness fell like a black-out curtain being dropped. By 7 pm the sun would be gone; darkness would have descended.

When we arrived, the sun was turning from pink to blood red and going down fast. A few wispy clouds ranging from grey-blue to black, deepest indigo to orange, were streaked across the face of the sun. A vast area of colour - mauves and reds was reflected on the surface of the ocean, an ocean that had turned from cobalt blue to black within minutes. We stood in awe of the most spectacular sunset we had ever witnessed as the colours deepened and darkened. Quickly the sun was falling below the distant charcoal smudged edge of the horizon, now it was half gone and now three quarters. A last spectacular burst of oranges, purples and reds sizzled across the black sky and it was gone.

I turned to Dave, 'I'll always remember this. When we leave I'll always remember it.' The beauty all around us, that's what I'll miss if we leave I thought, the beauty of Africa.

Afterwards it seemed that by speaking the words out loud – 'When we leave,' I had broken an unspoken taboo. I had opened the possibility, brought it to the surface. Back home in Harefield village, homesickness came in waves, the kind I'd felt in the first six months of our arrival, the kind I thought had gone. I wanted to see my family again; I missed them all.

I had written to my parents, after leaving hospital, to break the news.

Dear Mum and Dad.....

My mum had rung to let me know that she had sent a baby clothes parcel.

'I sent it a couple of weeks ago, I suppose you'll have to give it away.'

To my relief, the parcel never arrived. A card with my grandmother's writing on the envelope did arrive though - flowers on the outside, then lots of writing on the inside. As I read it, I sat down heavily and lit a cigarette. She was telling me that she knew what it was like, that before she'd had her four children she'd given birth to a still-born child at full term, born with the cord around its neck. My grandfather a doctor at Guy's hospital, who'd been a doctor in the First World War trenches, was away in Scotland at the time. A family secret, I was sure that none of her adult children knew about. Next time I phoned my mother, I told her. She made little comment. 'Good Lord,' was all she had to say. She was not one to dwell on emotions or the past. I felt a bond with my grandmother - she alone, out of all my family, had some inkling of what it was like.

Now, a few weeks later, the impact of it all was bringing questions about remaining in South Africa to the surface. The riots, the apartheid, losing the baby and a feeling that this was not our country. The feeling that things, bad enough at the beginning were getting out of hand. It was all building up.

A few days later, Peter called round late one evening. He was between his monthly injections for his schizophrenia and was relatively alert. He hated the early phase after the injection when he'd be all dopey.

Dave had just got back from the theatre, he brought in his black mask with horns and laid it on the kitchen table – he'd promised Pas he would show it to her - she'd see it in the morning. He was playing several parts including the Devil - lots of lines and appearances on stage. The play was described, on the posters that had gone up, as '*a selection and translation of assorted mystery plays in verse*'. It was a quick whip through the main themes of the Bible, from the creation myths through to the life of Jesus. The small parts were taken by amateurs and the main parts by actors, as in all the plays at St George's. Many of Dave's old mates were in it playing assorted parts – Henry Goodman, Gillian Horwitz, Allan Leas and Ethwyn Grant (who went on to Dave's next play with him). They were having a ball, camping it up and pulling each-others legs constantly. Who would 'corpse' who on stage was a running joke?

He was high with that adrenalin surge that comes to actors after a performance, full of the news of that night's show:

'Good audience tonight! You could have heard a pin drop, big applause at the end. I nearly dried half way through though, I was staring hard at Henry – he had to say his line twice and then it suddenly came back, thank God! Then in the second half, Ethwyn knocked the bottle over on the table. I didn't look at the others, I nearly went!'

I waited until he'd had a couple of glasses of wine, rolled himself a joint and calmed down. Then I talked about my thoughts on our future in South Africa; that I was homesick and sick of the censorship and the restrictions on who we saw, who we mixed with.

'Last year, Tommy came round and I was going to the swimming pool in Rondebosch. He wanted to come too and then I realised it was whites only. It was so difficult.'

'You should have taken him then.' Dave snorted.

'Ha! That would have caused a stir.' Peter laughed.

'Precisely,' I said, 'I thought about it....but I just couldn't face it. What if he'd been asked to leave? It would have been embarrassing for him and for me. How would I explain it to Pas? No, I had to tell him, sorry, wish I could take you but I just can't.'

'What did he say?'

'Well, not a lot really, what could he say? He knows the score. I gave him some food and we chatted for a while. Then he left and I just felt guilty.'

I passed a mug of Rooibos too Pete and sat down with mine.

'It's not just one thing. What about segregated beaches? Everyone keeps pretending it's not happening, like it's all going to stay as it is, like it's all normal. And what about Pas? Is she going to carry on in schools for 'whites only'? Do we want that for our daughter?'

'Anyway,' Peter changed the subject, 'What's this talk about leaving?'

I sighed and said I didn't know, that I was just feeling homesick and tired of everything.

Dave sipped his beer. 'The thing is I'm getting good parts now. Directors are getting to know me... hearing about me. They're contacting me to see if I'm free for later in the year. For next year too. I reckon there's work there for the next 6 months at least. How can I leave now?'

I felt mean for bringing it up, talked about how much he'd achieved since we got there, everything he'd set out to achieve. He'd made a name for himself, his confidence as an actor had built up. But the situation in South Africa wasn't improving. The riots had been followed by security clamp-downs everywhere. It was difficult to meet up with the few coloured or black friends we'd been able to make.

I talked about living in one of the last mixed race areas left in Cape Town. But how long was it going to last? Mr Patel next door had recently told me that he'd heard they'd all be moving to the new coloured township on Mitchell's Plain in the next six months.

'Ach!' Peter was contemptuous. 'The Group Areas Act strikes again. Soon it'll be whites only round here too, once they've finished building at Mitchell's Plain. They did the same thing to District Six in Cape Town a few years ago. Remember I told you about it? Have you ever been down there?'

'No, I never did go down there, not sure where it is exactly?'

'Past the centre of Cape Town – not far from St George's. It used to be great, Indians, coloureds, Malays, some blacks and whites – anyone could live there - fantastic, everyone got along fine! Then they decided it was going to be 'whites only' and knocked it all down. Thousands of people had to move. Ach, it was terrible man.' He shook his head sadly.

What would happen when Harefield Village became 'whites only', I wondered. All the kids that came to play with Pas would be moved too. We didn't want Pas growing up in a whites-only area as well as going to a whites-only school.

Dave sighed, 'I know, I know. We'll have to think about it.'

Peter looked sad. 'You can't leave, we have to finish 'Goldfields' Dave.'

I knew he was worried about losing his friends if we left. I also knew he'd met someone - a new girlfriend and they were getting serious. I told him he'd be all right now he had her to spend time with.

Dave smiled. 'Come on then Peter. I'm still buzzing from the show. Let's work on 'Goldfields' for a bit.'

I yawned, it was after midnight and said I was going to bed. I knew they'd be working on the play for hours.

I lay awake thinking about everything. I would be losing my friends too. Mel, I'd be losing Mel and that was the worst. She'd been such a light in my life, full of strength and energy and wit, such amusing droll company, such fun always. I was worried about her too - she had that benign tumour at the base of her skull she'd told me about. She and Werner seemed to live separate lives. Her daughter was a teenager full of angst, and her son was already 12. And Gabby, what would Pas and Gabby do without each other?

I thought about the mountain too, Table Mountain, towering over our daily lives, beautiful, challenging, ever changing. Like a great mother presence, silent and brooding. Her presence was beginning to oppress me, to make me feel trapped, like I would never escape from her. Yet, it was so difficult, to give up the life we'd made, the friends, the social network; give it all up and go back to cold, wet, dark England; give up the outdoor lifestyle! Pascale hardly ever wore shoes, we all lived in shorts and T shirts; give up the open-door social network, where you could turn up at anyone's house unannounced and help yourself to a drink from their fridge, plonk down on their sofa or in their garden and join in whatever they were doing. All that would go. I fell asleep in the end, but spent a restless night, tossing and turning, thinking about it all…

Events were pushing us in a direction, events over which we seemed to have less and less control. There were still several things yet to happen that would combine to give us the final push.

Dave as the Devil in Fall & Redemption of Man.

Chapter 35: Squatter camps

It was such a cold wet winter that last one we spent in Cape Town. Sometimes it rained all day, although there were a few warm sunny days in between, we were wearing light jumpers or jackets. Now at least I had a purpose, a focus for my attention – I was teaching crafts at Brooksfield, three mornings a week, instead of sitting at home staring at the four walls focusing on my emotional distress. One Sunday night, when Dave was not performing, I asked him for ideas.

'What will I do with them tomorrow?'

'Er, masks – you could get them to make masks. Masks are very powerful, when you put them on it takes away inhibitions, you can do things, say things that you wouldn't do normally.'

'Great idea, they could cut out the shapes then colour them – and it's something to take home to the parents.' [This was important as parents wanted to see that their fees were being used constructively].

'Or you could cut out faces from magazines and mount them on card, make holes where the eyes are.'

'Yes, yes.' I was hunting in a box in the corner. 'Let's see what I've got... Mel gave me some old mags – 'She' and' Vogue'...' I was turning the pages, 'Yes lots of faces. I'll need scissors, glue, and string.'

The kids at Brooksfield were aged 3-6, so we only had small plastic blunt-ended scissors, but we had large bottles of paste, paint and I could buy some string on the way in.

Next day was sorted and now I could relax. Pas was asleep in bed and Dave wanted to do some writing. It would be nice to have a relaxed evening together.

There was a quiet knock on the door. I opened it to find Tommy, the hunchback standing there grinning at me.

'Hey Tommy, come in,' I sighed to myself. 'Can I get you something to eat?' He nodded and I had some stew left in the pot, so gave him a plate and a hunk of bread.

Dave said 'Wanna beer Tommy?' He was sipping from his own beer bottle.

'No thanks Dave.'

I knew Tommy didn't drink alcohol, so I poured a glass of juice and put it next to him. Dave was smoking a joint which he passed to Tommy, which he puffed reflectively.

'How goes it at Crossroads?' I asked. Crossroads squatter camp was a large sprawling illegal shanty town spread out over the Bush not too far from where we had lived in Philippi. Tommy had been living there for some time.

'Yew haven't heard?'

'Heard what?'

'The government's decided to flatten all the squatter camps verrry soon, in the next few days They're sending in the bulldozers and police.'

Dave and I glanced at each other.

'But Tommy, its winter, its cold and wet, the camps are full of women and children. Where will they all go?'

He shrugged.

'They'll take them somewhere won't they, put them in shelters?'

He laughed and shook his head at my naivety.

'Tommy, where will you go if they knock down Crossroads? What will you do?'

Tommy did not answer. He stared out the window frowning.

'You can stay here for a few nights until you've sorted something?'

'No, I'll go up North somewhere, don't worry, I can take care of myself.'

'Look Tommy, if there's something we can do?'

But Tommy was independent and determined. The regime was clamping down after the riots of last year and the Group Areas Act was being strictly enforced. We could get into trouble too if we broke the rules, the curfew.

Dave tried to lighten the atmosphere. He started telling Tommy a story about the CAPAB tour of the townships.

'We're in this township right, near a place called Oudtshorn, you heard of it? Yeah, anyway that's where all the ostrich farms are, round there. See that egg over there.'

He pointed to the huge ostrich egg that he'd brought back from Oudtshorn, blown himself, the one I'd painted with patterns and varnished.

Soo... we're in the township right, gonna do this Irish play in this kind of huge community shed thing? And there's a sort of makeshift stage at one end and loads of chairs. They're all full, the whole community is out, come to see the show. People are calling out to each other, drinking beers, talking, as we're going on with the play, and then halfway through there's a big commotion. We have to stop the show, some poor sod has keeled over, someone's calling for a doctor. Anyway he gets lifted out and we carry on with the show. Then, about 10 minutes later two dogs come down the middle aisle and right in front of the stage, they start rutting. People are shouting at them, throwing things at them, even some guy gets up and kicks them. But it seems like they're fucking locked together,' he laughed, 'or should I say locked together fucking. Anyway, some guys got them out in the end. That was a real show-stopper!'

'Did you finish the show, Dave?' Tommy was smiling.

'Yeah, somehow we got through it. Man that was some mad tour. Most of the time, to save money I slept in the back of the truck with the stagehands. You wanna try their homegrown grass - those guys. Phew! That stuff can blow your head off. I dunno how I got on stage some days. Me and those guys had a few wild nights. Some of those CAPAB actors *really* didn't like me staying with the stagehands at night. They couldn't get their heads round it. But I had a great time.'

After a few more stories, Tommy got up to go. He always turned up without warning and after he left, we might not see him for several months.

'Tommy look after yourself, yeah', said Dave.' I can't see how they're gonna knock down Crossroads, it's too big.'

'It's alright Dave. I'll see you soon.'

'Look Tommy, if anything happens ...come back here, remember what I said - you can sleep on the couch for a few nights if you need to...' I hugged him.

Two days later, everyone was talking about the squatter camps, it was front page news in the Cape Times.

There'd been a dawn raid and the police had turned up at Modderdam squatter camp with the army and bulldozers. The Cape Times had several pages of pictures of women with babies strapped to their backs, clutching a few belongings salvaged, before the bulldozers wrecked their little shacks, or huddled under plastic sheets to shelter from the wind and rain. The English-speaking liberals of the Cape were appalled, as I was. The churches were sending people with any form of transport out to the camp and bringing them back to shelter in their churches. People were asked to bring food and blankets to the churches. I put some tins and old clothes of Pas's in a cardboard box and drove it over to one of the churches mentioned in the article. It was chaotic there; people were all over the pews, children running about, noise and melee. I was directed to the vestry, which seemed to be full of white parishioners sorting heaps of clothes and blankets and tins of food.

I had lost the baby about six weeks before and was still weak and fragile, mentally and physically. I did not feel capable of doing much to help. However the whole situation compounded for me the difficulties of continuing to live in South Africa. This was not our country, if we stayed I couldn't keep on saying nothing, and that meant risking the attention of the secret police. After discussing it with Dave, I wrote a very strong letter to the Cape Times, comparing government action to the treatment of the Jews by the Nazis. I knew that if it was printed, I was drawing attention to us, but I was so incensed I didn't care. It must be time to get away from this country. It was never printed. Dave swears it was after that the clicks started on our phone, whenever we picked it up, you'd hear two clicks. Was our phone being tapped?

At first everyone thought the people sleeping in the churches would be safe from the army and the police as the churches were in white areas. The Cape Times gave it a lot of coverage for the first week or so, and then like all news, the fuss died down. There was a lot of stuff about the churches being legal havens and sacred and therefore somehow outside the law. Lawyers talked about how the government would have to take it to the courts....

Government made its move two weeks later. The 5 a.m. dawn raid by the police cleared the churches and they took all the people away in trucks and dumped them in the bush somewhere.

We were appalled, when we heard about it, frustrated, angry, but there was little anyone could do.

* * *

Chapter 36: Mel gets ill and goes away

The phone was ringing in the sitting room. I was in the bathroom brushing my teeth. It was Monday morning and I was getting ready to take Pas to school and teach my classes. I was worrying about a little boy called Jonathan in one of my classes. He'd been born with Cerebral Palsy and had very little physical motor coordination. Melissa had taken him on, because his mother wanted him to mix with ordinary kids in a normal school environment, rather than go to a special school. The problem was he needed a great deal of one-to-one attention, which then meant less for all the other kids. The previous day, I had given him a lot of my time, showing him how to hold a blunt-end scissors and cut out shapes on his own. It was difficult with his jerky uncoordinated hand movements, but I felt that he had made some progress and told his mother so. I was wondering if this progress could be sustained or whether he would have forgotten everything by today.

I heard Pas pick up the phone,

'Hello! Who dat? Huh? She in the toilet. What? Oh, okay.'

'Who is it Pas? Tell them I'm just coming...'

It was Mariette, one of the teachers at school. She was an early riser and always got there by eight a.m. She told me Mel was not there, the house was in a bit of an uproar. The night before, Mel had been rushed to Groote Schuur hospital with suspected meningitis. Lena had got the children up and Werner had gone to work. She wondered what to do about the school and the teachers and the other parents.

'I'm on my way,' I put the phone down. 'Pas! Shoes on quickly! We have to go.'

* * *

When someone has meningitis the last thing they want is visitors, so although I was itching to go visit her, I couldn't. Mel was in hospital for the rest of the week and so we all had to pull together to keep the school going without her guiding presence. I rang Werner in the evening every day for a bulletin on how she was. His answers were always brief and curt.

On Friday, he told me they were discharging her next day. I rang on Sunday and finally spoke to Melissa. She sounded exhausted. On Monday morning, I got to Brooksfield early and went up to see her in the house. She looked terrible, her hands were shaking as she took one of her long cigarettes out of the packet and could barely light it. She'd lost weight and she'd been slim already. Her skin was pale and clammy, whatever medication she was on, made her sound vague. She was in her dressing gown. She told me what had happened.

'I just thought it was a really bad migraine. ... I was in bed with the curtains drawn. ...I think I took some Doloxene to sleep it off.'

She paused and took a drag on her cigarette. Her hand was trembling.

'Lena came in with some water, I think...she says I was talking rubbish, delirious. She must have called Werner and then....the doctor came. He tried to sit me up, but I couldn't bend my neck. The pain was... unbelievable, my head felt like ... it was cracking open. An ambulance came and took me to Groote Schuur. They did a lumbar puncture...'

'Oh no!' I'd had one before my epidural to give birth to Pas.

'They put a needle in my spine, just here.' She pointed to a place at the base of her spine.

'What for?'

'It's a test they do to see if it's meningitis, it's the only way.'

'And was it?'

'Wull, they think it might have been viral meningitis. It's not as bad as the bacterial one, but the problem is there's no treatment, just painkillers and rest.'

'They can't give you antibiotics? Oh no. Is it better now? I mean the pain, the pain's gone yeh?'

'Yis, yis much better,' but her face looked strained when she said it. 'Oh I couldn't move my head for two days, I couldn't lift it off the pillow. Now I can walk about ... carefully.' She moved her head slowly from side to side, wincing slightly. 'I'm all right, hey? I just need a rest. I'm going away for a week to this cottage –it's the other side of Swellendam, about two hours away. Tilly's going to drive me and Helga's going to meet us there and stay for a couple of days. Then Dieter's coming down. Obviously, no one knows he's coming. Werner thinks Helga'll be there all week. I have to get away from him, to think.'

'You mean, think about you and Werner, whether you're going to stay together?'

She nodded, 'Something like that...'

I didn't know what to say. I was upset and shocked at how fragile she looked. Mel was the nearest thing to family that I had in South Africa - like my 'older' sister.

'I'm going to get dressed and put on some makeup. Then I'll come down to greet the parents as they arrive. I think it's important that they see me.'

Jesus, I thought, how on earth is she going to manage that?

'You go on down. I'll see you in the study in a little while.'

When she came down, she was dressed smartly and quite heavily made up.

'Wow! What a transformation!'

She smiled and made a face at me. 'The wonders of makeup, eh?'

'Are you sure you want to do this?'

'Yis I must. But come with me,' she smiled,

'... in case I keel over.'

We walked round the school, and she greeted the arriving parents who were bringing their kids into the three classrooms. Then I walked back with her to the house. I looked at her, her face was covered with a thin sweat and her breathing was shallow. The effort had cost her a great deal and now she was spent. I didn't want to leave her, but had to get back to my class. Just then Helga arrived, she took one look at Mel and our eyes met.

'Wie gehts darling? You look ... tired, but a week's rest away from zis place will improve you, Ja? Have you packed a bag yet, no? OK, we go upstairs, you sit on ze chair in your bedroom and tell me what you want to take, huh? Zen you say goodbye to the kids and we go. Ja?'

Mel was in no state to argue and Helga took her arm, to help her walk up the stairs. I gave Mel a short hug and went back to my class. I knew she was in safe hands.

When I came out of my class, three hours later, she was gone. I didn't hear from her for the rest of the week, but I heard from Tilly that Kathy had been there when they arrived and had brought supplies for the week. The cottage location was in a remote rural area, totally peaceful. I was glad that she was somewhere where no one would be bothering her and all she had to do was rest.

* * *

But it seemed that the universe had other ideas. Something catastrophic was about to be thrown at all of us.

Chapter 37: What happened to Werner?

How he took the turning that night none of us could
fathom. He knew the way home from a hundred, a thousand
journeys. He could have driven it blindfold, that route back
from the German club in Cape Town to his home in Rondebosch. It was like some ghastly crime fiction plot, except
there was no foul play. It was so strange, so odd that he took
a wrong turning. Who will ever know what was in his head
that night? Maybe he'd had more to drink at the club than he
usually did? It was dark and the rain was torrential, sheeting
down. He took that wrong left turn, the road before his own
and perhaps due to alcohol and a poor overall mental state,
after all his marriage was not going well, he did not see the
great cut or ditch there, designed to carry the rains away from
the suburbs. He was not expecting it to be there until too late,
didn't take evasive action in time and didn't lean hard on the
wheel with his left hand. Suddenly there he was, sailing
straight over a 12-foot wide ditch. Except he didn't, did he?
The car flipped upside down. Was it then that he fell out or
did he try and climb out? And under him, what was usually
a dry gulley was, because of two weeks solid heavy rain, a
raging torrent 8 feet deep. Did he fall conscious or uncon-
scious into the grey churning water before being dragged
along for miles?

* * *

The following morning, I woke and looked out the window.
Oh relief! The rain had stopped at last, the sky was blue. I
dressed myself and Pas for school. Melissa was still away,
although she was due back the following morning. I wanted
to get to school early, to make sure someone was there to
greet the parents bringing their children to school. In the
event, when I arrived, there were other teachers and a few
parents hanging around outside. I parked the car, lifted Pas
out and strolled towards them. Pas saw Gabby holding on
to Lena's hand in the doorway and the two of them went indoors with Lena following behind. Then I noticed Tilly and
Karl were there and they looked towards me as I approached. There was something not right about the atmosphere, about the way they looked at me. I stared at them
and then Tilly came towards me. Werner had not come
home last night, had not gone to work. No one knew where

he was. They knew he'd left the German club at around mid-night and the rain had been exceptionally heavy at the time. He had not arrived home, apparently.

We kept racking our brains for a reasonable explanation. We knew that Melissa was in the cottage and that Dieter was visiting her there. Tilly, me and Helga were the only ones that knew. I said softly,

'My God! He couldn't possibly have decided to drive to the cottage could he? Maybe he got up really early and left to go there?' Tilly looked at me.

'I don't zink so. He's not so ... unpredictable. Still ... I zink I hev the phone number at home, I think she scribbled it down for me somewhere. Perhaps I should ring her just in case.'

Helga and I went into the school, made sure that teachers were settled in the classes, that all the arriving children were ushered through. We needn't have worried – everyone, all the staff, knew what to do, they didn't need us to tell them. Then we went upstairs to the lounge and sat and smoked and waited for Tilly to return. Karl meanwhile, decided to drive back to the German club and see if they knew anything more. The phone rang in the hall and Lena answered it. I could hear her talking in Afrikaans, she was saying 'Ja, Ja,' and her voice sounded serious. Just then, Tilly walked back in the front door. Lena put the phone down and turned to Tilly and said something quietly in Afrikaans. Helga and I were standing at the top of the staircase looking down

'Mein Gott!' I heard her say softly.

'Was is das? Vat heppens?' Helga called down.

Tilly looked up at us and started walking up the long stair-case.

'It was the police. They found Werner's car. Over a gulley, two roads away.'

'But... ver's Werner? Vasn't he inside the car?'

'No, they don't know ver he is, but they say the gulley was full of water last night, deep water'.

'Oh! Oh no!' My hand flew to my mouth to stop a scream. 'Oh shit!' This was shocking news. I squashed down my first terrible thought that if something had happened to him, Melissa would be free. Wasn't that what she wanted? But she wouldn't have wanted any harm to come to Werner... no way.

'I rang Mel earlier,' Tilly was saying 'I told her zat Werner had not come home. She and Dieter were leaving immediately. They'll be here in a couple of hours.'

We all decided to carry on with our routines for the next hour or so. Tilly would come back in an hour, to be here when Melissa arrived. Myself and Helga would be back in a couple of hours anyway to pick up the kids.

When I returned, I went straight up to the lounge. A few people were gathered there, word had got around. We heard the front door opening and Tilly jumped up and rushed downstairs. I heard Mel's voice, it was calm and matter fact. She went into the kitchen to see Lena. I stood up uncertain and looked at my watch. It was time for the kids to come out of school, I had to go and pick up Pas from the classroom. I didn't want to be in the way. I saw Tilly in the hall. She said she would take Melissa out for a drink somewhere. I said I'd come back later. Then Mel came out of the kitchen. She smiled as if nothing had happened. I went up to her awkwardly. She smiled again.

'I'm fine, don't worry, he'll turn up, Werner always does.'

'But ...' I stammered, 'Are you sure...?' Her laugh peeled across the hall.

'Of course. Now, why don't you fetch Pas, go home and I'll talk to you later, you can ring me...'

'Ok.' I felt as I always did when Mel talked to me, like her little sister, worrying about nothing, being pushed away so the grown-ups could deal with things - an odd feeling for someone who was the oldest of four.

Except this time my psychic antennae knew. This time something was seriously wrong and somehow Mel was not seeing it, not recognising it at any level. Just then the front door opened and in swept Tilly, matter of fact, armed to the teeth with reassurance and calm patter.

'OK daahling! I'm taking you out. I have this vonderful hairdresser in town. I phoned him and he's going to do your hair, you'll look fabulous when he's finished with you. Kom, grab your jacket, let's go.'

I stood quite still in absolute astonishment, as Tilly swept her out in a kind of whoosh. She was gone. I was stunned. Why wasn't anybody accepting the enormity and the reality of what had happened. Werner could well be dead and yet everyone was acting like nothing had happened. It was totally bizarre. I could tell by Mel's eyes that she had hopped off the planet into Star Trek land. But why were the rest of them playing this charade – to protect her from the truth? And what about Gabby, she was so small and adored her Daddy.

I sighed and turned in to the annexe, walking towards Pas's class, puzzling it over in my head. Some of the other parents were walking with me and the kids started emerging. One of them – an Afrikaans woman called Kathy said quietly to me,

'Any news? I heard Werner didn't come home last night. Is he all right?' I looked at her wondering how much I could tell her.

'I don't know. I wish I did. He's still missing though. We're just hoping he's OK.'

Am I hoping that I thought? I didn't like him very much. And Mel had not been happy with him for a long while. Then I remembered that yesterday evening, when I went to fetch Pas, who'd spent the afternoon with Gabs and Lena, I'd bumped into Werner in the hall. We'd made awkward conversation for a minute of the 'Hi how are you' variety. In fact, I was beginning to think about how to edge away and get out. But there was something about the way he was talking to me, something compelling and intense. He had never before made any attempt to have a conversation with me, had seemed to ignore me totally. So I paused and looked at him, a little puzzled.

He was awkward, his eyes looking over my shoulder, everywhere but at my face.

'I vaz zinking maybe, perhaps... er ...'

'Yes?' I prompted watching his face for some sign of what he was going to come out with.

'I vaz zinking about maybe getting Melissa a small gift....'

Wow, I thought, that'll be a first. She had told me that he had never given her anything, not on her birthday or Christmas or anything. Not one gift. Ever. What had brought this on? I looked at him speculatively. Was he beginning to suss out the affair?

He was on a roll now. 'I vondered what I should get her? Vat do you zink?'

My God! Now he was asking for my opinion. Whatever next? I wanted to help him, but my mind went blank with surprise at the question. I knew they didn't have much money, Mel seemed always to be struggling to pay the bills....the costs of running a school and three kids – two in private schools, I supposed.

'Erm, how about some flowers? Mel loves flowers.'

He looked puzzled, as if such a thought, that she might like flowers had never before crossed his mind.

'Ver? Ver can I get some... flowers...tonight!?'

Oh fucking hell, I thought. Tonight, he wants them tonight. Jesus. What is going on?

'Um... er, well, they sometimes have them in that garage down the road. You know, that one past Claremont.'

I was looking at his face closely, curiously. For the first time I was seeing him, really seeing him as a human being. He wanted to do something for Mel at last. I felt a huge sadness for him, because it was too late. I knew he'd already lost her. He'd made little effort for so long.

I sighed and returned to the present. Werner had turned towards the door, walking purposefully. 'Er, bye Werner ... hope you find them...' He glanced over his shoulder at me and then opened the door and was gone.

Would I see him again?

Kathy's daughter was tugging at her mother's skirt for attention.

'Mama, Mama!' showing her the results of today's art work in class, lots of squiggles and swirls in bright primary colours on a sheet of paper. Kathy had turned her attention from me and I saw Pas running out of the class with her own sheet of paper. I moved towards her quickly, wanting to get away from further questions from Kathy.

'Well, bye Kathy, see you tomorrow'.

I took Pas home for the afternoon, Dave took the car. I rang later. Helga and Karl were with Mel and they were all drinking wine. There was no news, Mel was still sure he was going to turn up.

The next day I took Pas to school. I was teaching for several hours, four groups that day. I saw Mel briefly before I went to my class room. She looked pale and was smoking heavily. We looked at each other, but there was nothing to say. Plainly there was no news. After my teaching was over, Pas went in to the kitchen with Gabby and Lena. I went up to the lounge where Mel was sitting with Helga and Karl. Wine was on the table, there was desultory conversation, an air of waiting.

The situation, with Werner being missing, went on for three days. Melissa was not eating. We were all back and forth an hour here or there taking it in shifts to check on her, to keep her company. I made her a poached egg on toast, in one of those shifts and tried to coax her to eat it. It lay on its limp toast on the plate on the table, untouched for several hours. Melissa just drank tea or wine and jumped every time the phone rang. She chain-smoked and so did I.

On the third day, when I arrived there was still no news. Werner had not turned up nor been found. How long was this going to go on? Lena let me in and I found Helga and Tanya chatting in the hall downstairs in hushed voices.

'What are we going to do if....'

'Who knows, dahlink? Maybe today ... No it's no good. Karl went to the site yesterday before dark. You know vat he said? He said it's impossible. No one could have lived through that. The car's bedly smeshed up.'

Just then Karl arrived and confirmed what Tanya had reported.

'Ja, it's true. If you saw ze car... It's a bluddy right-off', he said in his thick German lilt. 'No one could have survived in that.'

'Has anyone told Mel?' I looked at the three of them, eyebrows raised. There was silence. Everyone shifted and looked uncomfortable. I felt impatient with them all then, impatient with this charade, no one telling Mel, letting her carry on the fantasy. For how long?

'Well ...' I paused. 'Shall I tell her, someone should?' I looked at them again, hoping for a reprieve, that one of them would say, 'No I'll tell her.' They were supposedly her closest friends, they were all older than me. But no one did. So I turned and walked across the hall, up the long wide staircase slowly.

At the top, the spacious room opened out, with lots of light from big windows. She was sitting on one of the two voluminous brown leather sofas. I looked at her sitting there wearing her pink slacks and a white frilly blouse. Her big brown eyes were made up and she had bright pink lipstick on her wide mouth. She looked at me smiling and I felt again like a girl-child in the presence of a mature woman. She puffed at a cigarette and then spoke

'Well here we are - still waiting aren't we my dear?'

And I knew I had to do it now, quickly. For three days she had held onto the belief, the false hope that he was still alive. She seemed still to be convinced that he was wandering around with amnesia and that any minute he was going to walk in the door, his memory restored. Or there would be a phone call from someone, a hospital perhaps, they had found him that he'd had a knock on the head, only now was he returning to consciousness and asking for her.

'Mel! We have to talk, I have to tell you something.'

It felt like I was part of some fake melodrama, this whole thing wasn't real. I was an actor saying lines in a play. Her eyes fixed on mine and I held her gaze, she knew that the fantasy was about to end and she looked cornered, like a wild animal.

'Mel, Karl went to see the car,' I paused. 'It's a write off. He said no one could have survived the state it's in.'

A small cry came from her lips and she jumped to her feet, looking around wildly for an escape route. Then she turned and ran towards her bedroom, ran in and shut the door. I stood there not knowing what to do. Should I leave her or should I follow? Then I thought ' *I can't leave her, what if she harms herself*?' and I went to the door, turned the handle and went in. At first I couldn't see her; I looked around the room and said her name softly

'Mel, Mel, where are you?'

A small moan drew me to the wardrobe, she was in the wardrobe. I looked in and saw her, folded up, with her arms wrapped around his clothes, her face buried in them.

'Leave me,' her voice was hoarse. 'I need to be on my own.'

I turned and walked quickly from the room.

* * *

Werner's body was found later that day. It had been washed up several miles down the gulley. The next days and weeks passed in a blur, the funeral took place about a week later.

* * *

We continued in our preparations for leaving South Africa. Werner's death was the final push. All that had happened to us in South Africa seemed to culminate in the disaster of his death. After that, somehow we had to come to terms with the shock of it all, I felt we'd finally lost heart for being there. Looking back now, I can see that I'd had some kind of emotional breakdown and the only way to continue living my life was to somehow shut it all down. I wanted to support Mel too, who was going through her own dark days. We met up, talked, laughed sometimes and our lives carried on as if everything was as normal. But it wasn't, it would never be again.

The only remedy for me was to get back home, to London, to see my family, to start afresh. We had thought we could live there and somehow avoid the worst strictures of apartheid. In retrospect, it was not until we got to Kenya, where we stopped off for two weeks on the way back to UK that we began to really see the full effects that living with apartheid had had on us – over time we'd got used to life being like that. Suddenly we were in a black African country, where everyone mingled together freely in restaurants, in hotels, everywhere and the relief was intense.

Our days were counting down now to the day of departure. Dave's last night in Veronica's Room (playing a cold psychopathic killer), was coming up. The reviews had come and gone '*David Janes as Larry only comes into his own in the final moments tapping his watch with maniacal menace, rather reminiscent of Anthony Perkins in 'Psycho'*', one had said.

DRAMATIC CHILL IN IRA LEVIN THRILLER

By Diana Wemyss

AT THE BAXTER STUDIO: Veronica's Room is being presented by Off-Centre, Directed by Jo Dunstan.

Veronica's room is most-ly shrouded. Preserved as it was when she left it something in 1935, a macabre shrine for the ghoulish games of some very unhinged players.

As in the first act when the dustcovers are slowly removed from the props so the twisted psyche of the characters is peeled back with creeping horror.

Susan, an ingenuous college girl, and her boy-friend of a few days are invited home by an Irish couple to see the photograph and the room of a girl whom they say died of TB and who closely resembled Susan.

The couple persuade Susan to impersonate Veronica, the dead girl in order to reassure Veronica's sister Cassie who is dying of cancer. But it transpires that their motives are a lot more sinister. Susan is to be sacrificed in a cathartic vengeance . . . or is it?

One needs to be a bit obtuse. To divulge the plot entirely would take the goosefish feeling from

Ira Levin

the play. And goosey you do feel from the moment the woman takes a key from around her neck and slips it quietly into the door of Veronica's room — while the innocent Susan prattles on in the bathroom off stage.

Ethwyn Grant's woman was really very good. As the centre on which the play hinges she is required to put across a pretty unbelievable, twisted character with actions that could have easily degenerated into the melodramatic.

The others in the cast also did well. Philip Boucher is evil wrapped in joviality, Pippa Dyer is the bubbly student, duped and then awfully enlightened. David Janes as Larry only comes into his own in the final moments tapping his watch with maniacal menace rather reminiscent of Anthony Perkins in Psycho.

The Baxter Studio takes a little getting used to. Theatre in the round is all very well but one doesn't really want everything jammed up under your nose as is the case if you sit in front. It is to the credit of the actors that they never seemed restricted by the nearness of the audience which could have become a physical hazard.

'a Levin's sensational new thriller "Veronica's oom" opens at the Baxter Theatre tonight for a hree-week season. Here are David Jane, Pippa Dyer and Phillip Baucher in a scene from the play.

BAXTER

BAXTER THEATRE CONCERT HALL-STUDIO UCT. MAIN ROAD, ROSEBANK

THEATRE Tonight at 20h30 MURDER AMONG FRIENDS

STUDIO Opens Tonight 20h15 VERONICA'S ROOM A Thriller by Ira Levin, author of Rosemary's Baby (R2.50), matinees 1h11

He was also in a long running drama series for Springbok Radio and he had been told that the writers were going to make him the murderer. He had to tell them he was leaving - they had to think again and write him out.

Thomas and all the little girls who came to play had to be told too. Thomas by now had been bringing his little brother too. He took the news stoically enough.

'Yew goin bek to Inglan eh? It's far away, yeh? When'll yew come bek? Uts cold in Inglan... will ut be snowing?' (How prophetic he was).

I wanted to give him something, something that would keep him going and set him up a little, for after we'd gone. I took him down to Mowbray one day, to a small Building Society. I explained to him that I was putting some money for him, into an account and it was for him and his brother. I explained to him about saving for something he wanted. The concept of bank accounts and savings was completely alien to him, but I put the small savings book in his hand, on the day we left the Mowbray cottage and hugged him close.

The removal of Cape Coloured peoples from the area was about to be resumed we'd heard, so he and his parents probably wouldn't be there much longer anyway. I wondered afterwards if he kept it, lost it, got all the money out (about 30 Rand – about £15) straightaway or what ... but I wanted him to think about having something for himself, perhaps making some money one day and putting it in a bank, to know how it worked.

Pas hated having her picture taken

Pas was four now and it was easier to explain things to her. Actually she was four going on forty sometimes, she could understand people in a way that often surprised me, better than some adults could. She was excited that we were going to Mel's house for a week, so she and Gabby would be together. The idea of flying on an aeroplane was exciting too. She could not understand the enormity of it all though, the changes that were to come.

Chapter 38: This Is Tomorrow Calling....

The day dawned. The day of the party, our final party, our farewell to all the friends made, in our two and a half year stay in South Africa. It was several months since Werner's funeral. Dave's run in 'Veronica's Room', had been a great success. There'd been terrific reviews.

We knew we had to go, we'd talked and talked it through after Crossroads and the funeral.

'I can't keep quiet any more Dave, I just can't. If we stay I'll do something, say something...'

'I know darling, I keep having to bite my tongue.' I knew what he meant – Dave could be caustically satirical at times, if something or someone annoyed him.

'And I've had some great parts....it's just ...' his tone was wistful, '... if we stayed, I had work lined up for another year, it's a shame.'

'Yes, you're just beginning to be well known. You said someone asked for your autograph again the other day, when you came out of the Baxter?'

'Oh, Ja dahling, all the time – such a trial... my public you know!'

We smiled, but sadly, we knew we had to go, Dave had achieved his main goals, he'd had some great lead parts and as an actor he had grown enormously. He could never have had the opportunities, the experience and the parts he'd had in South Africa had we stayed in London. We'd not intended to stay, it had been a stepping stone to perhaps other parts of Africa, maybe Kenya, but it hadn't panned out that way. There had been great work for an English actor here and he'd found plenty with mixed-race casts with the most innovative theatre companies in Cape Town. It had not been difficult, as in England, to develop connections with the small network of actors and directors.

For me in particular, Cape Town had been [geographically at least] the ideal place to live – the climate warm and temperate, long summers, short winters, good rainfall making the landscape often as green as England, beautiful beaches and scenery. The city life and the sea were in close proximity.

But political and personal factors had quickly darkened the dream. What could the future hold, with the canker of apartheid growing and spreading and choking every facet of life here? The riots, the censorship and the recent brutal clampdowns of the regime - the squatter camp evictions were a large part of our decision to go - this was not our land, our country, we were not South African. If we stayed I knew I couldn't keep quiet any longer. My letter to the Cape Times comparing the government tactics over the squatter camps to the Nazis had risked drawing the attention of the secret police already. I had a child to consider and if I protested too loud, I'd be taken away from her. I didn't want to risk that.

We didn't want our child growing up in this environment, going to segregated schools to learn the Afrikaaner version of history, where the emphasis was on the NGK (Dutch Reform Church) version of the bible which justified their right to rule the 'non-whites'.

I was homesick for the fair-minded British way of life, in spite of its flaws, for being able to mix freely with whomever I chose, without that choice being determined by race. I was homesick also for my family. Having been this far away, for so long I'd developed an idealised picture of them all. After all that had happened in recent months, I wanted the comfort and support I felt sure they'd give.

I'm pausing here for a moment to reflect on the great difference between my expectations and the actual reality of what happened on our return. I'd put the dysfunctionality of my family into a box at the back of my mind – or was it their inability to cope with my mental state, all we'd lived through, on our return? But that's another story.

In fact Mel and our other friends had become our family. I was reluctant to leave her and them behind, after all we'd faced together. Mel had become like a sister to me then. After Werner's death, she had ended (or put on hold?) her close liaison with Dieter and had withdrawn, as I had done after losing the baby, from everyone but close friends and family. She would go back to Dieter one day, but that would require time and distance. Maybe that relationship would be fractured forever. Meanwhile she was immensely kind and supportive in our last days in Cape Town.

Returning to the day of the party - of course the sky was blue and as the sun rose the day was getting hotter. It was the beginning of summer. The Sou'Westers – the great winds that blew across Cape Town in the October spring, were dying down. One of Table Mountain's peaks was visible, as always, from the street where we lived and would soon leave.

The party was to be in the large back garden of Mel's house and Brooksfield School. We moved out of our cottage in Harefield village and Mel organised us to stay with her for a week and then our last two weeks, before flying back to London, would be spent with Dieter in his big house in Table View - from the beach nearby you could see the distinctive outline of Table Mountain in the distance.

We organised a pavement sale at knock-down prices, of all our household goods. The local mixed-race population swooped on the cooker, fridge and bed, even the old settle went. There was nothing left but our suitcases of summer clothes and we'd be returning to the UK in winter (a severe one as it later turned out).

Dave was organising the braai, it was going to be the normal fare for any South African barbecue. There'd be half a sheep cut into chops, pork chops, big rounds of fat boereworst sausage, large chicken pieces. If people wanted steak as well, they knew to bring their own. Mel had organised Lena to help me prepare bowls of salad and potato salads, cheeses and long loaves.

The actual braai itself was (as usual) an old oil drum cut in half lengthways, on a criss-cross stand – the charcoal covered the bottom ready to be lit. All day we were preparing - Steve and Pete were helping with crates of bottled lager, buckets of ice and wine. Big jugs would be filled with alcoholic fruit punches. We knew how to throw a party.

Another important consideration was the sound system, the music and the dancing. The big storeroom at the bottom of the garden had been cleared. Both Dave and I had always loved to dance – he whirled and twirled and strutted like Mick Jagger and I liked to get down and boogie too. We'd take a dance floor by storm and soon everyone would be joining in. Our teenage years had been in the 60s, in the era of the

Beatles, the Rolling Stones, Hendrix, Motown, and Soul. We'd danced and partied our way through the birth and rise to rock star legend of most of them. Hendrix was dead (2 weeks after the 1970 Isle of Wight festival, where we'd seen his last show) and the Beatles were now mainstream mega stars.

I had prepared some tapes with all my favourite dance numbers. I knew they'd make the party go – The Stones, Hot Chocolate, The Bee Gees, The Eagles, Fleetwood Mac, 10cc, and my new album by Bryan Ferry and Roxy Music, 'In Your Mind', with my favourite track 'This is Tomorrow Calling', which was sure to get people on the dance floor - a very exciting and unusual sound building to a massive crescendo.

We'd been inviting people for weeks.

'How many is it now Dave?' I asked on the morning of the party. He was carrying crates of bottled beers into the old storeroom and was putting as many as would fit into two big plastic bins, where bags of ice had been emptied into the bottom.

'Where'd you want these?' Steve was carrying two big crates of glasses.

'On that long table over there.' I indicated the back wall.

'God I don't know, everyone, but everyone has said they're coming. Must be over a hundred by now... I hope there's going to be enough booze.' Dave was looking round frowning.

'We told everyone to bring meat for the braai and a bottle,' I reminded him ...and don't get too drunk.' As usual he just grinned at me.

'I'll be too busy running the bar.'

'And dancing with me.'

'Hey baby,' he was putting his arms round me, 'We'll take that dance floor by storm, won't we?' I pushed him away.

'Gerroff, stop mucking about, DON'T get drunk.' Then I relented a bit and smiled,

'Yeh we will, we'll show them! Can't wait for a good dance, it's been so long. Now tell me again, who's coming?'

'Let's see,' he was counting on his fingers, 'Mel, Steve's bringing two friends and Lily, Patsy and Nigel, Dieter, Jane and Herman – are they coming?. Di's in Jo'burg still so she can't come, all the CAPAB actors – and the stagehands – did I tell you about how I slept in the truck with those guys on tour, man the joints they rolled!'

'Yes!' I was impatient. 'Who else?'

'Er, the casts of all those shows from St Georges and Jo Dunstan – oh actually I think she said she can't come, one of the few...oh yeh, the cast from Veronica's Room, about 20 Brooksfield parents, Patsy, Robert, ...'

'Have we left anyone out?'

'You invited Tommy from Crossroads?'

'Yes, yes but I think he may have gone away.'

'Of course Peter and Elisha – it's great he's got a new girl-friend isn't it? Everyone... most people said they're coming. The black and coloured guys may not be able to stay long as they have to get back to the townships.'

'The Group Areas Act strikes again...' I was doing my verbal impression of a 'Rock Spider' – the name the English-speaking South Africans gave (behind their backs) to the extreme Afrikaaners.

Soon we'll be away from the 'Group Areas Act,' I thought to myself. I can't wait. But I'll miss all my friends so much, I sighed. I was still getting over the shock of losing the baby and Werner's tragic death. I'd lost weight and was now very slim. I'd been to a homeopathic practitioner, who had given me pills to 'rebalance', make me stronger. I was emotionally fragile from everything that had happened and we were throwing ourselves into another huge life change.

Pink Floyd's album, 'Another Brick In The Wall' was playing, when the first guests started to arrive, the coals of the braai were glowing red hot by then and soon the metal, five-foot grid over them was covered with chops and boereworst, spitting and sending curls of smoke upwards. The smell of meat roasting permeated the air around and in a short while people got into the serious business of eating and drinking, plates piled up with different meats - or cheeses, bean chilli and salads for our vegetarian friends.

I went into the main house around 8 pm, Pas and Gabby were in the kitchen with Lena. I passed Noelle on the way, Mel's teenage daughter,

'Have you seen mah mother?' She asked.

'I think she's in the garden, talking to Tilly.' Noelle was 15 now, at that difficult teenage stage, absorbed in her own little world and often tongue-tied. She too was dealing with Werner's loss, he had been the only father she remembered. She swept past me without a glance. I went into the kitchen and found Lena giving the girls toast and cheese.

'Come on Pas,' I was wobbling slightly on my wedge platforms. 'Time for bed now.'

'No Mummy, got finish me san'widge.' She was nibbling at a corner, making it last. Gabby was giggling and the two little heads were whispering together, but Lena fixed Gabby with a look -

'Yew too ay? Bed naw!'

I took Pas's hand feeling sad suddenly for her - her close bond with Gabby, was soon to end and she too had to start again, a new life and new friends to make. No more outdoor lifestyle. Pas rarely wore shoes and then only flip-flops. The soles of her little feet were like leather and she could run around barefoot anywhere.

I was itching to return to the party, but I knew the ritual had to be followed or she would not sleep - getting her in to bed, no story tonight there wasn't time. I sang to her as I often did. I knew the lyrics and tune of every Beatle song, but this was her favourite for dropping off to sleep:

When I wake up early in the morning, lift my head,

I'm still yawning.

When I'm in the middle of a dream, stay in bed,

float up stream...

Please don't wake me...'

Soon her eyes were closing and I crept out of the room, impatient to get back to the party. I'd have to check on her every hour, but she usually slept soundly once she was off. I checked my make-up in the bathroom mirror on the way out.

I was wearing dark blue high-waisted bell-bottoms and a fitted white shirt. My hair had been cut the week before by our mad gay hairdresser friend Alex, into a short bob with a wing of hair falling across one eye. Yep, I looked fine! Tonight I was going to forget all the dramas and troubles of the last few months.

I could hear 'You Make Me Feel Like Dancing' playing loud as I stepped back into the garden. I strode into the dancing room and kicked off my shoes. Time to boogie. Dave saw me crossing the room – he was already dancing with Pam and she was laughing at something he was saying. I walked over and let the music take hold of me and of course we took centre stage, whirling, stepping, jumping.

Sometime later, I took a breather and sat next to Steve. Dave went back out to oversee the braai and have a beer. Steve started talking about our leaving.

'I don't want you to go, you know that don't you?'

'I know Steve, I'm going to miss you and all our friends'

'No you don't understand,' he was saying, 'I want *you* to stay, I've never told you before, about how I feel about you...' I looked at him closely, he was looking down at his hands.

'I don't want you to leave...' there were tears in his eyes.

Bloody hell, I thought to myself. Maybe that was why Lily had tried to ban him from coming to see me. He was a very special friend, but I hadn't realised his feelings were that strong.

Hotel California came on and I grabbed his hand and pulled him onto the dance floor.

'Come on Steve, I have to dance to this,' and as the closing bars of the song were playing, I zoomed off into the garden. There was Dieter, big, solid, calm, man-mountain Dieter, who I'd had a secret crush on for a long time. Earlier that evening, Alex, my hairdresser friend, had given me his own silver chunky ID bracelet as a leaving memento. I sat down on the bench next to Dieter, fiddling with the bracelet, thinking about what Steve had said. Dieter was a man of few words. He didn't look at me, but there was always a strong electric charge between us.

'Wie gehts?' I said to break the silence. He glanced at my wrist and the ID bracelet.

'Was is dis?'

I explained that Alex had given it to me. His face went dark and suddenly he grabbed my wrist and pulled the bracelet off with his big meat-loaf hands, snapping it and then threw it across the garden. I looked at him in shock. Shit! I thought, looking round to see where Dave was. He was busy turning over some chops on the braai and talking to some of the actresses. They were all laughing.

'What did you do that for?' I was rubbing my wrist.

'I don't vant you wearing somezing from another men,' his expression was glowering, his face red.

I was getting up to retrieve the bracelet, saying 'don't be ridiculous', but he growled,

'Leave it!' The power of his dark mood frightened me, he was being so possessive. I had to get away - I stood and walked off and went to find Mel. She and Dieter were still good friends but, after Werner's death some months before there had been a distance, their friendship had cooled. This was all getting too much for me.

Then I heard the opening bars of 'This is Tomorrow Calling' and I was drawn irresistibly back to the dance floor. I was whirling and turning and letting the music flow through me, moving to the beat, the building crescendo of sound and Bryan Ferry's voice, blotting out the pain and the dramas. None of it was going to get to me tonight.

At 7 a.m. the next morning, two thirds of the guests had gone. I had fallen asleep on the couch in the living room for a few hours and then I'd woken up and wandered out into the garden. Dave was by the braai again and he was putting more lamb chops and chicken on the braai, blowing the coals back to life and the meat was sizzling.

'Breakfast?' he said slightly slurring and puffy eyed. A few others were beginning to wander over, getting up from dozing on chairs about the garden.

'Anyone want a beer?' He was looking round, '... hair of the dog?' He fished around in the melted, ice bin, pulling out a bottle triumphantly and fizzing off the cap.

'Urrgh!' My stomach turned over at the thought of any more alcohol. 'Not me...' The Party had worn off and I felt utterly miserable to be leaving all my friends behind, leaving Mel and Di and Peter and Steve and Dieter and so many others. And leaving Table Mountain and the lovely Cape Town climate. But we had to go and it would be nice to see my family again. That thought cheered me.

* * *

Hours later we were in Dieter's big Germanic living room with the huge Bavarian copper chimney in the centre-well, above the unlit fire-pit. Sheep and goat-skin rugs were scattered about on the stone floor. I lay out, dozing on a big leather couch, Pas was running in and out to the swimming pool in the garden with her large rubber ring. My head was throbbing. Dave seemed to be outside having another beer with Dieter, I could hear their voices. It was all over now - the party, the farewells. Dave wandered in to see how I was. He was grinning all over his face.

'That was one helluva party, wasn't it?'

'One, we'll always remember.'

* * *

Two weeks later we were flying to Kenya for a week's holiday in Mombasa. From there it was a fourteen hour flight back to the UK and one of the coldest winters for twenty years.

THE END

Dave and Pas on the beach near Dieter's place in Table View

End notes

Chapter 7

Portuguese man-o-war jellyfish: Stings usually cause severe pain to humans, leaving whip-like, red welts on the skin that normally last 2 or 3 days after the initial sting, though the pain should subside after about an hour. However, the venom can travel to the lymph nodes and may cause, depending on the amount of venom, a more intense pain. A sting may lead to an allergic reaction. There can also be serious effects, including fever, shock, and interference with heart and lung function. Stings may also cause death, although this is extremely rare/ Wikipedia 2011

Chapter 8

Afrikaaner poet - Breyten Breytenbach –'Once freed from Polsmoor prison, Breytenbach wrote a more direct account of his incarceration, The True Confessions of an Albino Terrorist (1986). In his best-known work, the author describes being ensnared by his captors and subjected to years of psychological and physical deprivation and gives his vision of South Africa's future prospects. This disturbing book, with its detailed depiction of a horrifying penal system, was critically acclaimed as an important contribution to South African prison literature. http://www.answers.com/topic/breyten-breytenbach

The Group Areas Act, enacted in 1950, came into effect in the 1960s onwards and resulted in the forced removal of many non-white communities along the Liesbeek and Black Rivers....... With the implementation of the Group Areas Act in the 1960s, communities situated in close proximity to the Liesbeek and Black Rivers in the areas of Black River, Mowbray, Rondebosch, Claremont and Protea Village were forcibly removed to areas on the Cape Flats and deprived of a valuable resource of recreation and livelihood. Mowbray was proclaimed a white group area in 1961.

Ref:http://209.85.229.132/search?q=cache:JkRAqI7FCi UJ:rivers.thamesfestival.org/files/6922+Mowbray+-+Group+Areas+Act&cd=1&hl=en&ct=clnk&gl=uk   [Accessed 25/7/09] River of Life River Liesbeek

Chapter 19

'Lovers(and Losers)', a stage play in two parts by **John Willard**, written in 1922 and later made into a movie – several times.

Chapter 22

Transkei was absorbed back into South Africa in 1994, restoring its peoples to citizenship

Chapter 23

Hector Pietersen, the child whose sister was running alongside a young man; carrying his body went to front pages all over the world

Outside South Africa, the BBC reported: 16 June 1976: Soweto protest turns violent

'At least 12 people are reported to have been killed in a series of violent clashes between black demonstrators and police in several South African townships

Angry youths threw stones and beer bottles at police, as a protest against the compulsory use of Afrikaans as the main teaching language in black schools, turned violent. The violence spread from one end of the city to the other. The Times newspaper called it, the worst outbreak of racial violence seen in South Africa since the Sharpeville massacre 16 years ago. There are known to be at least two black children among the dead and two white men. The final number of dead may be much higher. Ambulance drivers say they were unable to get through the crowds to reach the injured.'

[In fact it is now known that 20,000 schoolchildren took part in the Soweto riots and the death toll was eventually c.360, most killed by the brutal open-fire tactics of the police]

SWAPO

The South West African Border War, commonly referred to as the Angolan Bush War in South Africa and also known as the Namibian War of Independence, refers to the conflict that took place from 1966 to 1989 in South-West Africa (now Namibia) Wikipedia 24/7/2010.

'bantu' the term used by the government and the police to refer to any black person. The term came from indigenous nomadic tribes that moved south from Central Africa about

5000 years previously. The Zulus were among their descendants. The term became discredited due to its association with the apartheid government

Chapter 24

Steve Biko who lived in Grahamstown at that time was made subject to a banning order soon after the start of the unrest on June 16th 1976, ordering him not to travel or have meetings with other activists. He continued to ignore the ban until his death in custody in September 1977. We heard nothing about him until it was reported (a small article in the Cape Times) that he'd 'jumped' from a tenth floor window at the police centre. I didn't find out who he was or his importance in the struggle until after we'd left South Africa.

Hummingbird - In fact it must have been a **sunbird** according to my friend Di. She says there are no hummingbirds in South Africa. They look quite similar though

Chapter 35

The Modderdam squatter camp was destroyed by two bulldozers during one week in August 1977, and as residents watched their homes being razed they chanted freedom songs and hymns, charged policemen and threw furniture onto the road. Some even set fire to their own shacks before the authorities could reach them...

'The government moved against the other large squatter camps of Modderdam and Univale in 1977, but was unable to touch Crossroads directly.

>>>
>>>

In the 70s and beyond, the term **Cape Coloured** was widely used for people descended from all the mixed peoples of the earlier part of the 20th century, Dutch, tribal Africans – i.e. Zulus, Xhosas, Tswanas and more, English, German, Spanish, Indian, Malay. They called themselves that in conversation, in government, in writing, continuing to do so up until relatively recently. This is changing apparently. Educated peoples from mixed origins no longer accept this term. As in the UK, this group of people now use terms like 'mixed race' or 'mixed heritage' to describe their ethnic origins.

Author

Anna Meryt has been writing all her life.

She has had many poems published in anthologies, including The West In Her Eye, and Her Mind's Eye (ed. Rachel Lever, 1996). Highgate Poet's 2014 anthology is the most recent.

She has been a performance poet for many years and is a member of Highgate Poets, a very active poetry group in North London. In 2011 she won first prize in the Lupus International poetry competition for her poem Bulawayo – about her birth place. Her first poetry pamphlet was published in 2013 – Heartbroke and the second - Dolly Mix in 2014.

This is her first book – a memoir set in South Africa in the 1970s, where she lived for a few years with her husband and small daughter. She has started her next memoir, set in Indonesia and London.

Have a look at her blog: http://www.ameryt.com/

Leave comments there too if you like – a couple of lines would be really good. Or leave comments on Amazon (scroll down from the listing). Thank you.

Made in the USA
Columbia, SC
06 July 2020

13408537R00183